THE JOURNAL OF
BRIGHAM

THE JOURNAL OF BRIGHAM

BRIGHAM YOUNG'S OWN STORY IN HIS OWN WORDS

COMPILED BY LELAND R. NELSON

Council Press
Provo, Utah

"Your journals will be sought after as history and as scripture. This is the way the New Testament came, what we have of it, though much of the matter there was written by the Apostles from their memory of what had been done, because they were not prompt in keeping daily journals."

Joseph Smith
Young Women's Journal, Vol. 2, page 466

"The view of (Brigham) Young portrayed by nineteenth-century correspondents and hack writers . . . is, in most instances, vastly different from the image one discerns from his own personal writings."

Dean C. Jessee*

*See The Writings of Brigham Young by Dean C. Jessee
Western Historical Quarterly, 1973, Volume 4, pp. 273-294

Introduction

Although many books have been written *about* Brigham Young, here at last is his own story in his own words, a compilation of his first-person writings from his manuscript history.

This volume destroys once and for all the popular, but false image of Brigham Young as a tough, unspiritual colonizer who had no business calling himself a prophet of God. A very different man is found in his journal writings—a simple man who liked to work with his hands, a humble man constantly seeking guidance from his God, a strong man ready to wrestle or fight in defense of his friends, an intelligent man who could debate effectively with professors and lawyers, an affectionate man with many friends, and a loyal man who could be depended upon by his God and his people.

The writings covering the early years, 1801 to 1844, were taken primarily from hand-written diaries and were edited under President Young's direction to correct spelling and grammar, and were first published serially in the Millennial Star beginning in 1867. After he became leader of the Church in 1844, he began to lean more heavily on scribes for the keeping of his journal. His writings dated August 8, 1844 to February 28, 1846 are published in the Documentary History of the Church, volume 7. And his writings with dates from March 1, 1846 to July 31, 1847 are available on microfilm at the Brigham Young University Library and at the Utah Historical Society in Salt Lake City. All of the original documents are in the archives of the LDS Church Historical Department in Salt Lake City. The microfilmed writings have been copied in their entirety in a volume titled *Manuscript History of Brigham Young 1846-1847*, by Eldon J. Watson, available at some libraries.

This volume is a compilation of the first person writings in Brigham Young's manuscript history. There has been no attempt to edit or re-write. However, many of the repetitive or uneventful writings have been eliminated in order to fit Brigham Young's own story, in his own words, into a single volume.

Contents

Foreword

When I first announced to the people in my office that I was compiling the Journal of Brigham, I received an unexpected response from a young woman who tried to talk me out of the project because in her opinion Brigham Young lacked humility and compassion.

As I engaged in background research looking at some of the Brigham Young biographies on bookstore shelves, I began to understand why she felt as she did. And I discovered that many other individuals (both in and out of the LDS Church) felt as she did.

Probably the best selling Brigham young biography in recent times is *Lion of the Lord* by Stanley Hirshon, published by Alfred A. Knopf in 1969. I had browsed through this interesting book before, but as I began to read the introduction as a researcher with a purpose, I could hardly believe what I read.

I had always supposed Doctor Hirshon's book to be a scholarly endeavor. After all, he is a well-published history professor at Queens College in New York. The John Simon Guggenheim Memorial Foundation subsidized Dr. Hirshon's efforts for an entire year while he did research on Brigham Young, and the American Philosophical Society gave Doctor Hirshon money to write the book. Surely with that kind of high-brow money behind it, the book ought to be a legitimate scholarly contribution to the understanding of Brigham Young.

However, this is *not* the case. Doctor Hirshon says in his preface, ". . . those who have previously studied Young have scoured the wrong places. The key to understanding him is not in the Rocky Mountains but in the Midwest and along the Atlantic Coast, not in secret materials but in the rich holdings of Yale University, of the New York Public Library, and of the National Archives . . . as the footnotes to this book attest, the amount of material in these journals, most of which I was fortunate enough to use in bound volumes in the New Jersey Historical Society. . ."

Hirshon's *Lion of the Lord* is a well-researched summary of east coast newspaper articles written by hack writers and non-mormon journalists seeking to sensationalize the plight of a pecular people and its leader Brigham Young. To lead people to presume that a book conceived from such sources could give an accurate picture of what Brigham Young was really like is a cruel joke.

I don't profess to be a scholar, but it didn't take me more than half an hour to find out that the seems of LDS Church historical department in Salt Lake City are literally bursting with historical information on Brigham Young. There is a 47,735-page manuscript history, 21 volumes of letter books totaling 15,000 pages, three personal diaries (over 400 pages) written in Brigham Young's own hand, nine office journals, and seventeen boxes of loose papers. A total of over 100 boxes of Brigham Young historical documents, and Hirshon says the Rocky Mountains is the wrong place to study Brigham Young.

I shouldn't be too harsh on Hirshon, however. The Church isn't in the habit of allowing writers and historians to snoop around in its sacred historical records. It made no exception for Hirshon, and left him in somewhat of an awkward position. He had a fat grant from the Guggenheim Foundation to study Brigham Young, but he couldn't get into the hull of the battleship where the records of Brigham Young were kept, he had no alternative but to go to the New Jersey Historical Society. He could have given the money back to Guggenheim, but with foundation money so hard to get in the first place, no scholar with any salt ever thinks about giving back grant money.

I wonder if the Guggenheim Foundation would give me $10,000 to write a biography on Joseph Stalin if I agreed to do the research in the Provo City Library. Actually, there's a lot of material on Stalin floating around the Provo area—the John Birch Society and the Freeman Institute are very aggressive in Utah. Other than my lack of scholarly credentials, such a grant wouldn't be very different than the grant given Hirshon to research Brigham Young in east-coast newspaper files.

It is no wonder that Hirshon presented Brigham Young, as did the authors of his source material, as a hard-nosed union boss with above average organizational ability. "He may not have been the towering giant his church likes to depict, but he was an unusual man nonetheless," concluded Hirshon.

As I read this material I began to understand why the young lady mentioned above, and others, in and out of the church, have an unrealistic opinion of Brigham Young. I quickly came to the conclusion that there was a definite need to publish the Journal of Brigham.

The next problem was to get access to Brigham Young's first person manuscript history which was put together from his personal diaries, dictations to more than 20 scribes and other documents. The task turned out to be much easier than I at first supposed. I didn't even need special permission to get into any "secret files." Everything I needed was readily available right here in Provo at the Brigham Young University library.

I might add here that Brigham Young's personal diaries were edited to correct spelling and grammar as the diaries were incorporated into the manuscript history. Brigham said in a speech to the saints that he and Heber C. Kimball, "never went to school until we got into Mormonism . . . we never had the opportunity of letters in our youth, but we had the privelege of picking up brush, chopping down trees, rolling logs, and working amongst the roots, and of getting our shins, feet and toes bruised . . . I learned to make bread, wash dishes, milk the cows and make butter . . . those are about all the advantages I gained in my youth." (Journal of Discourses, Volume 5, p 97.)

Brigham's diary entry for November 26, 1839, while crossing Lake Erie is as follows:

"We had anexelent time on the lakae, the wind arose about one o'clock in the morning, I went up on deck and I felt impres in spirit to pray to the Father in name of Jesus for a forgiveness of all my sins and then I fet to command the winds to sees and let ous goe safe on our Jorney. the winds abated and glory & ouner & prase be to that God that rules all things."

When the original diary entries, such as this one, were prepared for publication in the Millennial Star and the official manuscript history they were edited under Brigham Young's direction to reflect correct grammar and spelling, as do the passages published in this volume.

I found the first portion of Brigham's first-person history, covering the period from his birth in 1801 to the death of Joseph Smith in 1844 had already been published serially in the *Millennial Star* beginning May 9, 1863. The second period, August 1844 to February

1846, was published in the *Documenary History of the Church*, volume 7.

The third period, February 1846 to July 1847 was available on microfilm reproductions of a typed copy of the original in Church headquarters. The microfilm material was in an inconvenient format for duplicating, and some of the edges were out of focus, making reading difficult. Fortunately, this portion of Brigham Young's history had already been copied and published in a type-written volume by Elden J. Watson of Salt Lake City in 1970, and using this volume as a constant reference I was able to quickly and accurately glean out the first person writings for the Journal of Brigham.

At this point I made the decision to end the Journal of Brigham with the arrival of the saints in the Salt Lake Valley. After arriving in the valley, President Young became less involved in the writing of his history. In fact, the format was changed from first to third person and became less useful and interesting for one seeking insight into the personality and character of Brigham Young.

The next task before me was to reduce a huge pile of Brigham Young's first-person writings into a single, manageable volume. I did not edit or re-write a single sentence. I merely eliminated repetitive or uneventful passages with my red felt marker as I carefully read each page. I went through the material three times before I was satisfied that the writings in the *Journal of Brigham* represented the essence, the most meaningful of Brigham Young's first-person writings as found in his manuscript history.

The more I read, the more grateful I became that I had undertaken the project. As illustrated in the above diary entry, I discovered a spiritual man who in the middle of the night prayed from the deck of a storm-tossed ship for a forgiveness of his sins while crossing Lake Erie on a missionary journey. When he felt the spirit come upon him he commanded the waters to be still, and they obeyed.

I discovered a missionary with a sense of humor. While sharing a bed with George Albert Smith on a mission to the eastern states, the bed bugs were so numerous and aggressive that the two missionaries were forced to flee the bed and spend the night crouched in the corner over a lone candle, seeking revenge on every bug they could catch by roasting it over the candle (see page 62).

I discovered an expert debater who sold a college professor on the advantages of polygamy while traveling together on a river boat from St. Louis to Cincinnati (see pages 57-58).

I discovered a compassionate man who—at the risk of his own life and freedom—lingered on in Nauvoo, long after he should have gone so he could perform temple ordinances for his people. Brigham's wagon was loaded and ready to go west, and he had already given the order for the others to leave, but when he discovered throngs of people still gathered around the temple, refusing to leave because they wanted their endowments, he abandoned his wagon and performed temple ordinances night and day so those wanting the blessings of the temple could have them (see page 128).

These and many more fascinating writings are contained in the *Journal of Brigham*. Anyone who will read this volume will discover a strong and colorful prophet who loved and obeyed his God with all his might.

Leland R. Nelson

FAMILY BACKGROUND

My grandfather, Joseph Young, was a physician and surgeon in the French and Indian war. He was killed by the falling of a pole from a fence in 1769.

My father, John Young, was born March 7, 1763, in Hopkinton, Middlesex County, Massachusetts. He was very circumspect, exemplary and religious, and was, from an early period of his life, a member of the Methodist Church.

At the age of sixteen he enlisted in the American Revolutionary war, and served under General Washington. He was in three campaigns in his own native State and in New Jersey. In the year 1785 he married Nabby Howe, daughter of Phinehas and Susannah, whose maiden name was Goddard. In January, 1801, he moved from Hopkinton to Whitingham, Windham County, Vermont, where he remained for three years, opening new farms.

He moved from Vermont to Sherburn, Chenango County, New York, in 1804, where he followed farming, clearing new land, and enduring many privations and hardships with his family, incidental to new settlements.

My mother bore to my father five sons and six daughters.

In 1813 my father removed to Cayuga Co., New York, and continued farming and making improvements.

My mother died June 11, 1815.

In 1817 my father removed to Tyrone, Steuben Co., in which year he married widow Hannah Brown, who bore to him one son, Edward, born in Wayne, Steuben Co., New York, July 30, 1823.

In 1827 my father removed to Mendon, Monroe Co., where he continued farming.

In 1831 he heard the Gospel preached by Elders Eleazer Miller and Elial Strong; and in the month of April, 1832, he went with his sons, Joseph and Phinehas H., to Columbia, Pennsylvania, to investigate the principles of the Church of Jesus Christ of Latter-day Saints, and to see the Saints, and their method of administration, where he was baptised on the 5th of April, by Elder Ezra Landon.

He removed to Kirtland with his family, in the fall of 1833; and in 1834 he was ordained a Patriarch by President Joseph Smith, and blessed his family. He

1

was the first ordained to that office in the Church.

September 19th, 1838, in company with his daughter, Fanny, and his grandson, Evan M. Greene, and family, he left Kirtland for Missouri. On arriving at Fayette, in that State, he found himself in the midst of General Clark's command of militia, amounting to about one thousand men, who left that night for Far West. The next day he proceeded to Old Chariton, and found the General had left a guard at the ferry, so he had to return to Illinois. They were frequently met by companies said to be militia, who declared that if they knew they were Mormons they would kill them. When they returned to Columbia General Gaines was there raising a company to go to the assistance of General Clark to exterminate the Mormons, and Evan M. Greene made application to General Gaines for a pass to go out of the State with the company, representing that his grandfather was a revolutionary soldier. The General replied, that if he would change his wagon, which was a very good eastern wagon, for a Virginia wagon, or would go on horseback, they could go without molestation, otherwise he could give him no pass that would benefit them. Thus they were compelled to change their wagon, and could get nothing but an old Virginia dearborn, and getting into this they travelled without even being hailed by the companies they met, which were not a few. He went to Morgan County, Illinois; from thence he went to Quincy in 1839, on a visit to his children, where he died on the 12th day of October.

1801-1836

I was born in Whitingham, Windham county, Vermont, June 1, 1801. At an early age I labored with my father, assisting him to clear off new land and cultivate his farm, passing through many hardships and privations incident to settling a new country.

My parents were devoted to the Methodist religion, and their precepts of morality were sustained by their good examples. I was labored with diligently by the priests to attach myself to some church in my early life. I was taught by my parents to live a strictly moral life, still it was not until my twenty-second year that I became serious and religiously inclined. Soon after this I attached myself to the Methodist church.

October 8th, 1824, I married a young woman by the name of Miriam Works, daughter of Asa and Jerusha Works, in Aurelius, Cayuga county, New York, where I resided eighteen years, following the occupation of carpenter, joiner, painter and glazier. In the spring of 1829 I removed to Mendon, Monroe county, where my father resided. The next spring I first saw the Book of Mormon, which brother Samuel H. Smith brought and left with my brother Phinehas H. Young.

In the fall of 1831, Elders Alpheus Gifford, Elial Strong and others came to Mendon to preach the Everlasting Gospel, as revealed to Joseph Smith, the Prophet, which I heard and believed.

In January, 1832, my brother Phinehas and I accompanied Heber C. Kimball, who took his horses and sleigh and went to Columbia, Pennsylvania, where there was a Branch of the Church. We travelled through snow and ice, crossing rivers until we were almost discouraged; still our faith was to learn more of the principles of Mormonism.

We arrived at the place where there was a small Branch of the Church; we conversed with them, attended their meetings and heard them preach, and after staying about one week we returned home, being still more convinced of the truth of the work, and anxious to learn its principles and to learn more of Joseph Smith's mission. The members of the Branch in Pennsylvania were the first in the Church who received the gift of tongues.

Immediately after my return home from Pennsylvania I took my horse and sleigh and started to Canada after my brother Joseph, taking my brother-in-law, John P. Greene, who was then on his way to his circuit, preaching the Methodist doctrine. We rode together as far as Sackett's Harbor. After finding my brother Joseph, and explaining to him what I had learned of the Gospel in its purity, his heart rejoiced, and he returned home with me, where we arrived in March.

April 14th, 1832, I was baptized by Eleazer Miller, who confirmed me at the water's edge. We returned home, about two miles, the weather being cold and snowy; and before my clothes were dry on my back he laid his hands on me and ordained me an Elder, at which I marvelled. According to the words of the Savior, I felt a humble, child-like spirit, witnessing unto me that my sins were forgiven.

About three weeks afterwards my wife was also baptized. This was in the town of Mendon, in Monroe county. I tarried during the summer preaching the Gospel in the regions round about, baptizing and raising up churches.

September 8th, 1832, my wife died of consumption, leaving me two little girls, Elizabeth, born Sept. 26th, 1825, in Port Byron, Cayuga county, N.Y. and Vilate, born June 1st, 1830, in Mendon, Monroe county, N.Y. In her expiring moments she clapped her hands and praised the Lord, and called upon brother Kimball and all around to praise the Lord. After my wife's death I made my home at bro. Kimball's.

A few weeks after my baptism I was at brother Kimball's house one morning, and while family prayer was being offered up, brother Alpheus Gifford commenced speaking in tongues. Soon the Spirit came on me, and I spoke in tongues, and we thought only of the day of Pentecost, when the Apostles were clothed upon with cloven tongues of fire.

In September, 1832, brother Heber C. Kimball took his horse and wagon, brother Joseph Young and myself accompanying him, and started for Kirtland to see the Prophet Joseph. We visited many friends on the way, and some Branches of the Church. We exhorted them and prayed with them, and I spoke in tongues. Some pronounced it genuine and from the Lord, and others pronounced it of the Devil.

We proceeded to Kirtland and stopped at John P. Greene's, who had just arrived there with his family. We rested a few minutes, took some refreshment, and started to see the Prophet. We went to his father's house and learned that he was in the woods, chopping. We immediately repaired to the woods, where we found the Prophet, and two or three of his brothers, chopping and hauling wood. Here my joy was full at the privilege of shaking the hand of the Prophet of God, and received the sure testimony, by the Spirit of prophecy, that he was all that any man could believe him to be, as a true Prophet. He was happy to see us, and bid us welcome. We soon returned to his house, he accompanying us.

In the evening a few of the brethren came in, and we conversed together upon the things of the kingdom. He called upon me to pray; in my prayer I spoke in tongues. As soon as we arose from our knees the brethren flocked around him, and asked his opinion concerning the gift of tongues that was upon me. He told them it was the pure Adamic language. Some said to him they expected he would

4

condemn the gift brother Brigham had, but he said, "No, it is of God, and the time will come when brother Brigham Young will preside over this Church." The latter part of this conversation was in my absence.

We tarried about one week in Kirtland, held meetings nearly every night, and the blessings of the Lord were extensively upon us. I baptized one man while in Kirtland, by the name of Gibson Smith, the father of Newel K. Whitney's wife, who had just come from Connecticut to learn the things that were being revealed. Being convinced of the truth of the work, he requested me to go into the waters with him.

We returned home in October, and made preparations for leaving our friends and families. In company with my brother Joseph, I started for Kingston, Upper Canada, on foot, in the month of December, the most of the way through snow and mud from one to two feet deep.

In crossing from Gravelly Point to Kingston, on the ice which had frozen the night previous, the ice was very thin and bent under our feet, so that in places the water was half shoe deep, and we had to separate from each other, the ice not being capable of holding us. We travelled about six miles on the ice, arrived in Kingston, and found a friend who was going that evening near the place where we were first to call. We commenced preaching and bearing our testimony to the people. Proceeding to West Loboro, we remained about one month preaching the gospel there and in the regions round about. We baptized about 45 souls, and organized the West Loboro and other Branches.

In the month of February, 1833, we started for home, crossing from Kingston on the ice, just before it broke up. I tarried in Mendon, making my home at brother Kimball's, and preaching in the neighboring country.

April 1st, 1833, I started on foot for Canada again, arrived at Lyon's-town, where my brother Joseph and I had preached. I remained preaching, and baptized thirteen and organized a Branch of the Church, among whom was a young man, Jonathan Hampton, whom I ordained a Priest and took with me.

I went to Theresa, Indian River Falls, near Ogdensburgh, where I found brother David W. Patten preaching the Gospel to his friends in that neighborhood; tarried four or five days; preached five discourses and baptized seven persons, among whom were brother Patten's mother, brothers and sisters, Warren Parrish and wife.

I then went to Ogdensburgh, took steamboat to Kingston, and proceeded to Earnestown, where I tarried a few days at brother James Lake's, and then visited the Branches at West Loboro and neighborhood, preaching and baptizing as we journeyed.

About the 1st of July I gathered up the families of brother Lake and son and started for Kirtland, accompanied by brothers Daniel and Abraham Wood, and proceeded to Kirtland, where, after tarrying some time enjoying the society of the Prophet and assisting to locate brother Lake and family, I returned to Mendon in company with father Bosley of Avon.

In the month of September, in conformity to the counsel of the Prophet, I made preparations to gather up to Kirtland, and engaged a passage for myself and two children with brother Kimball, and sent my effects by canal and lake to Fairport. We arrived in Kirtland in safety, travelling by land, where I tarried all winter, and had the privilege of listening to the teachings of the Prophet and enjoying the society of the Saints, working hard at my former trade.

In the fall of 1833, many of the brethren had gathered to Kirtland, and not finding suitable employment, and having some difficulty in getting their pay after they had labored, several went off to Willoughby, Painesville and Cleaveland. I told them I had gathered to Kirtland because I was so directed by the Prophet of God, and I was not going away to Willoughby, Painesville, Cleaveland, nor any where else to build up the Gentiles, but I was going to stay here and seek the things that pertained to the kingdom of God by listening to the teachings of his servants, and I should work for my brethren and trust in God and them that I would be paid. I labored for brother Cahoon and finished his house, and although he did not know he could pay me when I commenced, before I finished he had me paid in full. I then went to work for father John Smith and others, who paid me, and sustained myself in Kirtland, and when the brethren who had gone out to work for the Gentiles returned, I had means, though some of them were scant.

In February, 1834, I married Mary Ann Angel, who took charge of my children, kept my house, and labored faithfully for the interest of my family and the kingdom. While the Prophet Joseph was gathering up the Elders of Israel to go up to Missouri and assist the brethren that had been driven from Jackson county, I was preaching and laboring for the support of my family. My brother Joseph Young arrived, and I requested him to go with me to Missouri. He hesitated; but while walking together a few days afterwards we met the Prophet, who said to him, "Brother Joseph, I want you to go with us up to Missouri." I informed the Prophet that my brother was doubtful as to his duty about going, to which the Prophet replied, "Brother Brigham and brother Joseph, if you will go with me in the camp to Missouri and keep my counsel, I promise you, in the name of the Almighty, that I will lead you there and back again, and not a hair of your heads shall be harmed," at which my brother Joseph presented his hand to the Prophet, as well as myself, to confirm the convenant. The brethren continued to come in from various parts of the country to Kirtland, and on the 5th of May we started for New Portage, the place appointed for organization.

May 7, brother Joseph Smith and the remainder of the brethren having arrived, we began to organize, and on the 8th, the organization being completed, we started on our journey. We arrived at brother Burgett's, Rush Creek, Clay county, Missouri, on the 23rd of June, and passed through the scenes of cholera and death, as related in the history of Joseph Smith. We remained one week attending to the sick and burying the dead. About seventy of the brethren were attacked with the cholera, and eighteen died.

President Joseph Smith called the members of the camp of Zion together, and told them if they would humble themselves before the Lord, and covenant that they would from that time forth obey his counsel, that the plague should be stopped from that very hour, and there would not be another case in camp, whereupon the brethren with uplifted hands covenanted that they would from that very hour hearken to his counsel and obey his word, and the plague was stayed according to the words of the Lord through his servant.

July 4th, my brother Joseph and myself, in company with several of the brethren, started for home, and walked all the way, arriving in Kirtland in August, having performed a journey of about 2000 miles on foot, in a little over three months, averaging forty miles per day while travelling.

In the fall of 1834, Denis Lake instituted a lawsuit before Justices Dowen and Hanson, against brother Joseph Smith, charging him $30 a month for going up in Zion's camp to Missouri, alleging that Joseph had promised him a lot of land. I was called up by the attorney for the prosecution, General Paine, and questioned. I was asked if I went up to Missouri with the said camp? I answered I did. I was asked what tools I took with me. I replied, a good gun and bayonet, plenty of ammunition, a dirk, an ax, a saw, a chisel, spade, hoe, and other necessary tools. I was asked what I meant to do with my gun and ammunition. I replied, I meant to defend my property, myself and my brethren from thieves and robbers. I was asked how much I understood a lot of land to mean. I told them, in the burying yard it generally meant six feet. Joseph's attorney, Mr. Bissell, hearing me answer these and similar questions so readily and definitely, punched the prosecuting attorney on the shoulder and asked him if he had any more questions to ask *that witness*. He said no.

Mr. Collins being examined, testified that Joseph had promised all who would go up in camp should return, and that many had gone up, and when they returned some were dead and some were alive. Joseph's attorney, taking advantage of the witness' words, remarked that the witness had testified that they all returned, and that was all Mr. Collins said Joseph had promised.

Thirty witnesses were summoned to attend this trial (three of whom were sectarian priests,) for the purpose of impeaching the testimony of Joseph Smith, at which they made a signal failure.

I mention such cases, wherein I took a part, in my history, realizing that there are but few of the vexatious proceedings of the world and the apostates, against Joseph, noticed in his history.

I tarried in Kirtland during the fall and winter, quarrying rock, working on the Temple and finishing off the printing-office and school-room.

February 14th, 1835, brother Joseph Smith called a council of Elders, at which the Quorum of the Twelve Apostles were selected in the following order—viz., Lyman E. Johnson, Brigham Young, Heber C. Kimball, Orson Hyde, Luke Johnson, David W. Patten, William E. McLellin, John F. Boyington, William Smith, Orson Pratt, Thomas B. Marsh and Parley P. Pratt. After the organization of the Twelve and the first Seventy, we held councils frequently, in which we received much instruction from the Prophet pertaining to the duties of our calling.

May 2—While the Elders were assembled in council, the Prophet Joseph called upon me to go and preach the Gospel and open the door of salvation to the aborigines, or the seed of Joseph, upon this continent, and Elders Amos Orton and John P. Greene were appointed to accompany me. Brother Joseph said, "This will open the door to all the seed of Joseph."

I started in company with the Twelve of the 4th of May, at 2 o'clock, a.m., and arrived at Fairport at 6 o'clock, where we went on board of a steamboat which was just starting out, and arrived at Dunkirk about 4 o'clock, p.m.

I remained at Dunkirk preaching for a few days. I visited Julius Moreton (a relative of mine), and preached the Gospel to him; but he was not inclined to receive its principles. He was a man considerably advanced in years—had never made a profession of religion, but was very much of a gentleman. To avoid calling on me to ask a blessing at table, he asked the blessing himself, probably for the first time in his life.

We proceeded to Westfield, where with our brethren of the Twelve, we attended a Conference. After the Conference was over, the Quorum of the Twelve proceeded eastward, two going together preaching the Gospel and meeting together to hold Conferences in the different Branches, according to previous appointment.

At Lyonstown, N.Y., brothers O. Hyde, William Smith and myself returned to Kirtland, as witnesses for President Joseph Smith in a case before the county court. As soon as we were liberated, we again started and joined the Twelve in holding Conferences, preaching and baptizing, regulating and organizing the Churches through the eastern country. We returned to Kirtland September 25th.

I remained at home during the fall and winter, occasionally going out and preaching to the neighboring branches. In the course of the winter there was a Hebrew school started, which I attended until February 22, 1836, when I was called upon by the Prophet to superintend the painting and finishing of the Temple, upon which I labored until March 27, when the Temple was so far finished as to be dedicated to the Lord by the Prophet, with the assembled Quorums of the Church and as many members as could possibly be accommodated. On this occasion the power of God was displayed, as recorded in the history of Joseph Smith.

I attended the solemn assembly, and, with my brethren of the Twelve, received my washings and anointings, and was privileged to listen to the teachings and administrations of the Prophet of God. We also attended to the washing of feet, which ordinance was administered to me by the Prophet Joseph.

In the spring of 1836, in company with my brother Joseph, I started for the Eastern States, visited our relatives, and preached the Gospel to them, many of whom believed our testimony and were baptized. We travelled through New York, Vermont and Massachusetts.

I left my brother Joseph in Boston, and with brother Lyman E. Johnson went to Salem, where we met the Prophet Joseph and the brethren who were with him. August 6, Joseph received a revelation concerning that city.

After tarrying with the Prophet a few days I returned to Boston, where I took steamer for Portland, Maine. Started about 5 p.m., and about 10 o'clock there came up a storm, and the vessel being old and shattered, she could not withstand the storm; and after tossing about in the waters a few hours we put into Port Ann, and spent a very pleasant day picking whortleberries and going over the grounds upon which the inhabitants were drying the codfish. Many acres were covered with the flakes upon which the codfish were spread, this being the principal employment of the people.

Next evening I proceeded to Portland, arriving there about daylight the following morning, and continued my journey to Newry, Oxford Co., where I met Elder Lyman E. Johnson, and we held a Conference on the 12th, 13th and 14th of August, at which I was called to preside.

I returned to Boston, where I found my bro. Joseph, who had been doing a good work. We baptized 17 in Boston.

We started for Kirtland, stopped at Providence, R.I., tarried a short time and preached to the Saints and others who came to hear us; then proceeded on our journey through Rhode Island, Connecticut, the west part of Massachusetts and New York, and preached by the way, arriving at Kirtland the latter part of September, where I remained through the fall and winter, laboring with my hands to sustain my family, and preaching to the Saints.

At this time the spirit of speculation, disaffection and apostacy imbibed by many of the Twelve, and which ran through all the Quorums of the Church, prevailed so extensively that it was difficult for any to see clearly the path to pursue.

On a certain occasion several of the Twelve, the witnesses to the Book of Mormon, and others of the Authorities of the Church, held a council in the upper room of the Temple. The question before them was to ascertain how the Prophet Joseph could be deposed, and David Whitmer appointed President of the Church. Father John Smith, brother Heber C. Kimball and others were present, who were opposed to such measures. I rose up, and in a plain and forcible manner told them that Joseph was a Prophet, and I knew it, and that they might rail and slander him as much as they pleased, they could not destroy the appointment of the Prophet of God, they could only destroy their own authority, cut the thread that bound them to the Prophet and to God, and sink themselves to hell. Many were highly enraged at my decided opposition to their measures, and Jacob Bump (an old pugilist) was so exasperated that he could not be still. Some of the brethren near him put their hands on him, and requested him to be quiet; but he writhed and twisted his arms and body saying, "How can I keep my hands off that man?" I told him if he thought it would give him any relief he might lay them on. This meeting was broken up without the apostates being able to unite on any decided measures of opposition. This was a crisis when earth and hell seemed leagued to overthrow the Prophet and Church of God. The knees of many of the strongest men in the Church faltered.

During this siege of darkness I stood close by Joseph, and, with all the wisdom and power God bestowed upon me, put forth my utmost energies to sustain the servant of God and unite the Quorums of the Church.

Ascertaining that a plot was laid to waylay Joseph for the purpose of taking his life, on his return from Monroe, Michigan, to Kirtland, I procured a horse and buggy, and took brother William Smith along to meet Joseph. We met him returning in the stage coach. Joseph requested William to take his seat in the stage, and he rode with me in the buggy. We arrived in Kirtland in safety.

A man named Hawley, while plowing his field in the State of New York, had an impression rest down on his mind, with great weight, that he must go to Kirtland and tell Joseph Smith that the Lord had rejected him as a Prophet. He accordingly started right off, with his bare feet, and, on arriving in Kirtland, told Joseph that the Lord had rejected him for allowing John Noah, a Prophet of God, to be cut off from the Church, and for allowing the women to wear caps and the men to wear cushions on their coat sleeves. He was called up before the Bishop's court and disfellowshipped.

He went through the streets of Kirtland one morning, after midnight, and cried, "Woe! woe! unto the inhabitants of this place." I put my pants and shoes on, took my cow-hide, went out, and laying hold of him, jerked him round, and assured him that if he did not stop his noise and let the people enjoy their sleep without interruption, I would cow-hide him on the spot, for we had the Lord's Prophet right here, and we did not want the Devil's prophet yelling round the streets. The nuisance was forthwith abated.

In October my cousins Levi and Willard Richards arrived in Kirtland. Willard, having read the Book of Mormon, came to inquire further concerning the work of God. I invited him to make his home at my house, which he did, and investigated thoroughly the principles and doctrines set forth by the Prophet and Elders of the Church. Dec. 31st, he requested baptism at my hands, which ordinance I administered to him in presence of Elder Heber C. Kimball and others, who had spent the afternoon in cutting the ice to prepare for the ceremony.

1837-1838

March 13th, 1837, I started in company with Dr. Willard Richards for the Eastern States, on a special mission appointed us by the Prophet Joseph. We travelled by stage coach through Ohio and Pennsylvania to Buffalo, New York. Riding day and night over very rough roads, we became very weary, and tarried a short time to rest ourselves, then took stage coach again, and travelled as far as Canandaigua, where we stopped two nights and one day. While here I visited Martin Harris.

Proceeding on our journey, we rode day and night till we arrived in Albany. Visited Troy, where we transacted considerable business. I purchased from a gentleman there a fine tavern establishment, which was situated in Auburn, directly across the street from the gate of the Penitentiary, which property I still own.

We travelled day and night until we arrived at West Stockbridge, Berkshire Co., Mass., at the Dr.'s old homestead, which he had left the year before. We stayed with Father Richards and family a short time, then proceeded to New Haven, and from thence to New York City, where we stopped a day or two and took steamboat for Boston by way of Providence, visiting the brethren in Lynn and Salem, also many of the friends and brethren in the country; transacted much business, and returned to Berkshire county.

On my return, near Utica, I left the canal and visited my friends in Madison county. Here I found my cousin Hepzibah Richards, who accompanied us by canal as far as Buffalo, where I left my cousins Phinehas and Hepzibah and a few other friends whom I had gathered up by the way. The ice being still on the lake, steamboats were laid up, but I proceeded by stage to Kirtland, and arrived the latter part of May. As soon as the lake was open my friends came on to Kirtland.

June 1st, there were a few missionaries appointed for England—Heber C. Kimball and Orson Hyde, of the Twelve. Brother Kimball was very anxious I should go, but brother Joseph told him that he should keep me at home with him. Brother Willard arrived a day or two before the mission started, and was appointed to accompany them. I accompanied the mission as far as Fairport, and saw them safe on board a steamboat for Buffalo.

July 25th, I baptized my cousin Albert P. Rockwood, to whom my brother Joseph and I had first introduced the latter-day work in July, 1836. I called on him in March last, in company with brother Willard, on business transactions. He came to Kirtland a few days ago, and having searched into the Work, and being satisfied that Joseph was a Prophet, he requested baptism at my hands.

I started from Kirtland on a mission to the east, accompanying the Prophet Joseph, his brother Hyrum, David W. Patten, Sidney Rigdon and Thomas B. Marsh, on their way to Canada. When we arrived at Painesville, the Prophet was arrested by an officer for some pretended debt. Joseph immediately entered into trial before the court, which found no cause of action. After his release he was again arrested and brought before the court, when he was again dismissed. He was arrested the third time, and on examination was held over to trial. Brother Anson Call, who had lately joined the Church, stepped forward and proffered to become his bail.

The sheriff, who was personally acquainted with brother Call, took him to one side and advised him strongly against being bail for the Prophet, asserting the Prophet would be sure to abscond, and he would lose his farm; but brother Call willingly became his bail. On being released he was arrested a fourth time, for a debt of a few dollars, which was paid forthwith, and the fifth time he was arrested, which cause was soon disposed of, and he concluded to return to Kirtland for the night. As he got into his buggy, an officer also jumped in, and catching the lines with one hand, put his other hand on Joseph's shoulder and said, "Mr. Smith, you are my prisoner."

Joseph inquired what was the cause of action. The officer informed him that a gentleman, a few months previous, had left a stove with him, for the price of which he was sued. Brother Joseph replied, "I never wished to purchase the stove, but the gentleman insisted on putting it up in my house, saying it would bring him custom." Joseph left his watch and other property in security, and we returned home to Kirtland.

Next day we started again, and travelled by land as far as Ashtabula, shunning Painesville and other places where we suspected our enemies were laying in wait to annoy Joseph. We tarried in Ashtabula through the day, wandering over the bluffs, through the woods and on the beach of the lake, bathing ourselves in her beautiful waters, until evening, when a steamboat arrived from the west. We went on board and took passage for Buffalo. I gave the Prophet my valise for a pillow, and I took his boots for mine, and we all laid down on the deck of the vessel for the night.

We arrived in Buffalo early the next morning. Joseph and the brethren proceeded to Canada. I took the cars for Lockport, with brother A. P. Rockwood, and from thence we took a line-boat for Utica.

August 18—Took steamer, *Daniel Webster*, at Buffalo, for Fairport. When out about three quarters of a mile from the end of the pier, a lady fell from the stern of the vessel. The engines were immediately stopped, and the yawl lowered, into which the first mate, Mr. Clark, and two hands jumped, and returned in search of her. When the mate saw her she was about ten feet under water. He dropped his oar and dived into the water like a fish. He was gone about one minute, and brought her up, his left hand clasping the back of her neck and holding her at arm's length from him. The two hands took her from the mate into the yawl, and returned to the vessel. She was soon able to speak, and quite recovered in the course of the afternoon and evening. Her name was Jane Groves. The passengers on board, in a few minutes, made up a purse of $60 to the mate for saving her life. I learned from the lady herself the cause of her falling into the water. She had left her family and friends in the city of Buffalo, and had got on the taffrail to take a farewell look at the city, and on coming down she slipped into the water. Here I learned something I did not know before, that the motion of the water caused by the paddles will keep a person from sinking. I arrived in Kirtland August 19th.

September 3—This day was appointed for the Saints to meet in Conference to reorganize the Church. Owing to the disaffection existing in the hearts of many, I went to the brethren whose votes could be relied on, early in the morning, and had them occupy the stand and prominent seats. At 9, a.m., the services commenced; Joseph and his first counsellor were received, his second counsellor, F. G. Williams, was laid over, not being present. The members of the Quorum of the Twelve in good standing and the authorities, generally, were sustained. We were also enabled to disfellowship those of the Twelve and others seeking to bring disunion and destruction upon the Church. The apostates and disaffected, not being united, were compelled to endure the chagrin of witnessing the accomplishment of the will of God and his Prophet.

On the morning of December 22nd, I left Kirtland in consequence of the fury of the mob and the spirit that prevailed in the apostates, who had threatened to destroy me because I would proclaim, publicly and privately, that I knew, by the power of the Holy Ghost, that Joseph Smith was a Prophet of the Most High God, and had not transgressed and fallen as apostates declared.

On reaching Dublin, Indiana, I found my brother Lorenzo and Isac Decker, and a number of other families who had stopped for the winter. Meanwhile the Prophet Joseph, brothers Sidney Rigdon and George W. Robinson came along. They had fled from Kirtland because of the mobocratic spirit prevailing in the bosoms of the apostates.

Here the Prophet made inquiry concerning a job at cutting cord-wood and sawing logs, after which he came to me and said, "Brother Brigham, I am destitute of means to pursue my journey, and as you are one of the Twelve Apostles who hold the keys of the kingdom in all the world, I believe I shall throw myself upon you, and look to you for counsel in this case." At first I could hardly believe Joseph was in earnest, but on his assuring me he was, I said, "If you will take my counsel, it will be that you rest yourself and be assured, brother Joseph, you shall have plenty of money to pursue your journey."

There was a brother named Tomlinson living in the place, who had previously asked my counsel about selling his tavern-stand. I told him if he would do right and obey counsel, he should have an opportunity to sell soon, and the first offer he would get would be the best. A few days afterwards brother

Tomlinson informed me he had an offer for his place. I asked him what offer he had; he replied he was offered $500 in money, a team, and $250 in store goods. I told him that was the hand of the Lord, to deliver President Joseph Smith from his present necessity.

My promise to Joseph was soon verified. Brother Tomlinson sold his property and gave the Prophet three hundred dollars, which enabled him comfortably to proceed on his journey.

The day Joseph and company started, Isaac Seeley and wife arrived. The house was pretty well littered up. I sat writing to my wife, but I welcomed them to the use of the house and what was left in it. Brother Samuel H. Smith came along, who tarried with me until my brother Lorenzo returned from Cincinnati, and brother Decker from Michigan, whose families had gone forward with Joseph. We prepared to follow, and started on, overtaking the Prophet four miles west of Jacksonville, Illinois, where there was a Branch of the Church.

After stopping a few days and resting, we proceeded to Quincy, where we found the river frozen over, though it had been broken up. Joseph and I went down to the river and examined the ice. We soon learned that by going through the flat boat which lay the end to the shore, and placing a few planks from the outer end on the ice, we could reach the heavy ice which had floated down the river a few days previous, sufficient to bear up our teams. We hauled our wagons through the boat and on to the ice by hand, then led our horses on to the solid ice, and drove across the river by attaching a rope to the wagon and to the team, so that they would be some distance apart. The last horse which was led on to the ice was Joseph's favorite, Charlie. He broke the ice at every step for several rods.

After leaving the boat we struck out in a long string, and passed over in safety. Two or three hours afterwards brother Decker and family, and D. S. Miles, crossed on our track, but it was with great difficulty and risk that they got across, many times having to separate from each other and get on to a solid cake, the ice was so near breaking up.

We travelled from the river about six miles and camped for the night: next morning proceeded on our journey. When we arrived at Salt River we found that the ice had broken up so that we could not cross. The ferryboat was sunk, and we tarried a day or two at this place.

Brother Joseph said to me one morning, "Let us go and examine the ice on the pond." We found the old ice had sunk, and had not left the pond when the river was broken up, and there had another foot of ice frozen over; and by plunging our wagons 2½ or 3 feet into the water, we could gain the solid ice on the pond; at the other shore we found the same.

We got our wagons and horses across the ice, then took a canoe which lay in the pond, and placed one end of it on the shore and the other on the solid ice, and walked through the canoe on to the ice, and pulled the canoe across the ice to the other shore.

In this way we crossed the families and landed directly in the woods, on a very steep sideling hill. We managed to get our wagons along the cleft of the bank; six or eight men held them up, and thus we worked our way on to the road.

14

We proceeded on our journey to Huntsville, where we met some of the brethren from Far West. Brother John P. Barnard had come from Far West with a carriage, into which he put Joseph's family, and we proceeded on our journey.

One day while crossing a large prairie, six or eight miles from any house, we crossed a small stream. The ground was frozen deep on each side, and we sprung one of the axletrees of brother Barnard's carriage. Brother Barnard said we could not travel with it any farther. Brother Joseph looked at it and said, "I can spring that iron axletree back, so that we can go on our journey." Brother Barnard replied, "I am a blacksmith, and used to work in all kinds of iron, and that axletree is bent so far round that to undertake to straighten it would only break it." Brother Joseph answered, "I'll try it." He got a pry, and we sprung it back to its place, and it did not trouble us any more till we arrived at Far West, March 14, 1837. Brother Barnard, seeing this done, concluded that he would never say again that a thing could not be done when a Prophet said it could.

I purchased a small improvement on Mill Creek, located my family and proceeded to fence in a farm. I bought several pieces of land and obtained deeds for them.

My wife was taken very sick, so that her life was despaired of for a long time. In the course of the fall and fore part of the winter, she recovered her health so that she could journey with me to Illinois.

As soon as the Missourians had laid by their corn, as they call it, they commenced to stir up the old mob spirit, riding from neighborhood to neighborhood making inflammatory speeches, stirring up one another against us. Priests seemed to take the lead in this matter, as related in the history. I had no communication, correspondence or deal with the Missourians, consequently they did not personally know me, which gave me a good opportunity to learn their acts and feelings unsuspected. I knew men in the course of the fall to gather up their flocks and herds, and take their families into their wagons, and then burn up their houses and leave for other parts. I afterwards saw their names attached to affidavits, stating that Mormons had driven them from their homes and burned their houses. This was quite effectual in raising prejudice against us.

At the time that the exterminating army of Governor Boggs, commanded by Generals Lucas and Clark, came in sight of Far West, I observed their approach, and thought that it might be the militia of the State which had come to the relief of the citizens; but to my great surprise I found that they were come to strengthen the hands of the mobs that were around us, and which immediately joined the army.

Some of these mobs were painted like Indians, and "Gillum," their leader, was also painted in a similar manner, and styled himself the "Delaware Chief," and afterwards he and the rest of the mob claimed and obtained pay as militia, from the State, for all the time they were engaged as a mob, as will be seen by reference to the acts of the Missouri Legislature.

Many Saints were wounded and murdered by the army, and several women were ravished to death. I saw brothers Joseph Smith, Sidney Rigdon, Parley P. Pratt, Lyman Wight and George W. Robinson, delivered up by Colonel Hinkle

15

to General Lucas, but expected they would have returned to the city that evening, or the next morning, according to agreement, and the pledge of the sacred honor of the officers that they should be allowed to do so, but they did not return at all.

The next morning General Lucas demanded and took away the arms of the militia of Caldwell County, (which arms have never been returned,) assuring them that they should be protected; but so soon as they obtained possession of the arms, they commenced their ravages by plundering the citizens of their bedding, clothing, money, wearing apparel, and everything of value they could lay their hands upon, and also attempting to violate the chastity of the women in sight of their husbands and friends, under the pretence of hunting for prisoners and arms. The soldiers shot down our oxen, cows, hogs and fowls, at our own doors, taking part away and leaving the rest to rot in the streets. The soldiers also turned their horses into our fields of corn.

At this time General Clark delivered his noted speech. I copy a portion of it as follows:—

"Gentlemen,—You whose names are not attached to this list of names, will now have the privilege of going to your fields and of providing corn, wood, &c. for your families. Those that are now taken will go from this to prison, be tried, and receive the due demerit of their crimes; but you (except such as charges may hereafter be preferred against,) are at liberty as soon as the troops are removed that now guard the place, which I shall cause to be done immediately.

It now devolves upon you to fulfil the treaty that you have entered into, the leading items of which I shall now lay before you. The first requires that your leading men be given up to be tried according to law; this you have complied with. The second is, that you deliver up your arms; this has also been attended to. The third stipulation is, that you sign over your properties to defray the expenses that have been incurred on your account; this you have also done. Another article yet remains for you to comply with, and that is, that you leave the State forthwith. And whatever may be your feelings concerning this, or whatever your innocence is, it is nothing to me. General Lucas (whose military rank is equal with mine,) has made this treaty with you; I approve of it. I should have done the same had I been here, and am therefore determined to see it executed.

The character of this State has suffered almost beyond redemption, from the character, conduct and influence that you have exerted; and we deem it an act of justice to restore her character by every proper means.

The order of the Governor to me was, that you should be exterminated, and not allowed to remain in the State. And had not your leaders been given up, and the terms of the treaty complied with before this time, your families would have been destroyed and your houses in ashes.

There is a discretionary power vested in my hands, which, considering your circumstances, I shall exercise for a season. You are indebted to me for this clemency. I do not say that you shall go now, but you must not think of staying here another season, or of putting in crops; for the moment you do this, the citizens will be upon you; and if I am called here again in case of non-compliance

16

with the treaty made, do not think that I shall act as I have done now. You need not expect any mercy, but *extermination*, for I am determined the Governor's order shall be executed.

As for your leaders, do not think, do not imagine for a moment, do not let it enter into your minds that they will be delivered and restored to you again, for their fate is fixed, the die cast, their doom is sealed.

I am sorry, gentlemen, to see so many apparently intelligent men found in the situation that you are; and oh! if I could invoke that great Spirit of the unknown God to rest upon and deliver you from the awful chain of superstition, and liberate you from those fetters of fanaticism with which you are bound—that you no longer do homage to a man.

I would advise you to scatter abroad, and never again organize yourselves with Bishops, Priests, &c., lest you excite the jealousies of the people and subject yourselves to the same calamities that have now come upon you.

You have always been the aggressors—you have brought upon yourselves these difficulties by being disaffected, and not being subject to rule; and my advice is, that you become as other citizens, lest by a recurrence of these events you bring upon yourselves irretrievable ruin."

I was present when that speech was delivered, and when fifty-seven of our brethren were betrayed into the hands of our enemies as prisoners, which was done at the instigation of our open and avowed enemies, such as William E. McLellan and others, aided by the treachery of Col. Hinkle.

In addition to the above speech, General Clark said that we must not be seen as many as five together. "If you are," said he, "the citizens will be upon you and destroy you; but you should flee immediately out of the State. There is no alternative for you but to flee, you need not expect any redress; there is none for you."

With respect to the treaty mentioned by General Clark, I have to say that there never was any treaty proposed or entered into *on the part of the Mormons*, or any one called a Mormon, except by Colonel Hinkle. And with respect to the trial of Joseph and the brethren at Richmond, I did not consider that tribunal a legal court, but an inquisition, for the following reasons:—Joseph Smith was not allowed any evidence whatever on his part, for the conduct of the court, as well as the Judge's own words, affirmed that there was no law for Mormons in the State of Missouri; and I know that when Joseph left the State of Missouri, he did not flee from justice, for the plain reason that the officers and the people manifested by their works and their words that was neither law nor justice for the people called Mormons.

The brethren were compelled to give away their property by executing a deed of trust at the point of the bayonet. Judge Cameron and others stood and saw the brethren signing away their property, and then they would run and kick up their heels, and said they were glad of it; "we have nothing to trouble us now." Judge Cameron also said, "God damn them, see how well they feel now." General Clark also said he had authority to make what treaties he pleased, and the Governor would sanction them.

17

Although there was so much opposition and persecution carried on against the Saints in Missouri, I never knew a Latter-day Saint break a law while I was there; and if the records of Clay, Caldwell or Daviess Counties were searched, they could not find one record of crime against one of our brethren, or even in Jackson County, so far as I know.

When the State Legislature convened, they appropriated $2,000 to the citizens of Daviess and Caldwell Counties, the Mormons of Caldwell not excepted. Judge Cameron, Mr. McHenry and others attended to the distribution. This same committee would drive in the brethren's hogs (many of which were identified,) and shoot them down in the streets, and without further bleeding, and half dressing, they were cut up and distributed by McHenry to the poor, at a charge of four or five cents per pound which, together with a few pieces of refuse goods, such as calicoes, at double and treble price, soon consumed the appropriation.

1839

Thursday, February 14—I left Missouri with my family, leaving my landed property and nearly all my household goods, and went to Illinois, to a little town called Atlas, Pike county, where I tarried a few weeks; then moved to Quincy.

Sunday, March 17—I held a meeting with the brethren of the Twelve and the members of the Church in Quincy, Illinois. A letter was read to the people from the committee in behalf of the Saints at Far West, requesting teams and money to be sent back to remove fifty families of the Saints, who were left destitute of the means to move with, from there to Quincy. Though the brethren were poor and stripped of almost everything, yet they manifested a spirit of willingness to do their utmost, offering to sell their hats, coats and shoes to accomplish the object. We broke bread and partook of the sacrament. At the close of the meeting $50 was collected in money, and several teams were subscribed to go and bring the brethren. Among the subscribers was widow Warren Smith, whose husband and son had their brains blown out and another son shot to pieces at the massacre at Haun's Mill. She sent her only team on this charitable mission.

Monday, March 18—I met in council with several of the Twelve Apostles, and advised them all to locate their families in Quincy for the time being, that we might be together in council. A letter was read, from Dr. Isaac Galland, concerning the half breed tract of land in Lee county, Iowa. I advised the brethren to purchase land there, for we probably would move northward. Elder Wilford Woodruff was presented and sustained to be one of the Twelve. Elder George A. Smith having been appointed by the Prophet as one of the Twelve, in place of Thomas B. Marsh, who had fallen, was also presented and sustained.

We met in council in Quincy relative to our Quorum going up to Far West and fulfilling the following:—(*Doctrine & Covenants Section 118*).

Many of the Authorities considered, in our present persecuted and scattered condition, the Lord would not require the Twelve to fulfil his words to the letter, and, under our present circumstances, he would take the will for the deed; but I felt differently and so did those of the Quorum who were with me. I asked them, individually, what their feelings were upon the subject. They all

19

expressed their desires to fulfil the revelation. I told them the Lord God had spoken, and it was our duty to obey and leave the event in his hands and he would protect us. . . .

Thursday, April 18—I left Quincy in company with Orson Pratt, Wilford Woodruff, John Taylor, George A. Smith and Alpheus Cutler for Far West, to fulfil the revelation. Brother Orson Pratt and myself rode with brother Woodruff in his carriage, and John Taylor and George A. Smith rode with Father Cutler; we travelled 24 miles to the ferry opposite Marion City, crossed the river and camped at the bluffs.

Friday, April 19—We rode 34 miles and spent the night at the town of Clinton.

Saturday, April 20—We rode 30 miles and camped.

Sunday, April 21—We passed through Huntsville, crossing a nine mile prairie; the roads were full of the Saints, who were fleeing from Missouri to Illinois, having been driven from their houses and lands by the exterminating order of Governor Boggs, and that, too, against all the laws of the State and the Constitution of the United States.

We met brother John E. Page and his family on a sideling hill, with his load turned bottom-side upwards: among other things, he had upset a barrel of soft soap, and he was elbow-deep in the soap, scooping it up with his hands. I told him I wanted him to go to Far West with us. He replied, he did not see that he could, as he had his family to take to Quincy. I told him his family would get along well enough, and I desired him to go up with us. He asked how much time I would give him to get ready. I answered, five minutes. We assisted in loading his wagon; he drove down the hill and camped, and returned with us. We travelled 30 miles and camped for the night.

Monday, April 22—We passed through Keetsville, rode 30 miles and camped.

Tuesday, April 23—We rode 36 miles, and camped for the night on a creek near a grove six miles east of Tenney's Grove. Elder Maginn went out to buy corn, and as he tarried all night we felt afraid lest he might have fallen into the hands of the mob.

Wednesday, April 24—We remained at the grove, where Elders Elias Smith, Theodore Turley and Hyrum Clark, (of the committee who were left to attend to the removal of the poor,) who had been driven from Far West, met us; they informed us that on the 16th, the mob came into Far West and tantalized the committee on the subject of the revelation, saying that was one of Joe Smith's revelations which could not be fulfilled, as the Twelve and the Saints were scattered to the four winds; and threatened them severely if they were found in Far West next day. They turned round, and on the 25th accompanied us to Father Timothy B. Clark's, near Far West.

Early on the morning of the 26th of April, we held our Conference, cut off 31 persons from the Church and proceeded to the building spot of the Lord's House, where Elder Cutler, the master workman of the house, then re-commenced laying the foundation, agreeably to revelation, by rolling up a large stone near the south-east corner.

The Twelve then offered up vocal prayer in the following order:—Brigham Young, Heber C. Kimball, Orson Pratt, John E. Page, John Taylor, Wilford Woodruff and George A. Smith; after which we sung "Adam-ondi-Ahman."

As the Saints were passing away from the meeting, brother Turley said to Page and Woodruff, "Stop a bit, while I bid Isaac Russell good-bye;" and knocking at his door, called brother Russell. His wife answered, "Come in—it is brother Turley." Russell replied, "It is not; he left here two weeks ago," and appeared quite alarmed; but on finding it was Turley, asked him to sit down; but he replied, "I cannot; I shall lose my company." "Who is your company?" inquired Russell. "The Twelve." *The Twelve?*" "Yes; don't you know that this the twenty-sixth, and the day the Twelve were to take leave of their friends on the foundation of the Lord's House, to go to the islands of the sea? The revelation is now fulfilled, and I am going with them." Russell was speechless, and Turley bid him farewell.

Thus was this revelation fulfilled, concerning which our enemies said, if all the other revelations of Joseph Smith were fulfilled that one should not, as it had day and date to it.

We rode 32 miles and camped at the Grove for the night. We learned that a mob had collected in different places, and on their arrival in Far West they found out we had been there and transacted our business.

We had entered into a covenant to see the poor Saints all moved out of Missouri to Illinois, that they might be delivered out of the hands of such vile persecutors, and we spared no pains to accomplish this object until the Lord gave us the desires of our hearts. We had the last company of the poor with us that could be removed. Brothers P. P. Pratt and Morris Phelps were in prison, and we had to leave them for a season. We sent a wagon after brother Yokum, who had been so dreadfully mutilated in the Haun's Mill massacre that he could not be moved.

Saturday, April 27—We started early this morning from the Grove; the company consisted of seven of the Twelve, several of the committee left at Far West to close up business, and a few families of the Saints. We continued our journey to the Mississippi River, and on the 2nd of May we crossed on the steam ferry-boat to Quincy, Illinois.

Friday, May 3—In company with my brethren of the Twelve. I rode out to Mr. Cleveland's to visit brothers Joseph and Hyrum Smith, it being the first time we had seen them since their release from prison, where they had been confined about six months, and were under sentence of death. They had escaped from prison, and were en route for Quincy, while we were going up to Far West.

It was one of the most joyful scenes of my life to once more strike hands with the Prophets and behold them free from the hands of their enemies; Joseph conversed with us like a man who had just escaped from a thousand oppressions and was now free in the midst of his children.

Thursday, May 16—I left the committee room in Quincy, Ill., and started for Commerce, in company with brother Woodruff. We crossed Bear Creek, and while rising a steep hill my near horse balked, allowing the wagon to back and it came near running off a deep dugway. I caught the hind wheel against my shoulder, and held the wagon and load by main strength until brother Woodruff came to my assistance and blocked my wagon, after which we ascended the hill in safety. Travelled 15 miles and camped.

We arrived in Commerce on the 18th, and called upon brother Joseph and his family. Brother Joseph had commenced laying out the city plot.

On the 21st., I crossed the Mississippi, and took an excursion into the country, in company with brothers Joseph, Hyrum, Sidney, Wilford, George A., and several other brethren. We rode over a beautiful country of prairie and timber; brother Joseph's horse ran away with him about a quarter of a mile before he held him up. Joseph B. Nobles prepared a dinner for us. We re-crossed the river about 4 p.m. In the evening, while brother Nobles was plowing a piece of ground which he had obtained from Mr. Kilburn for a garden, a man named Campbell, accompanied by a mob, came up to brother Nobles, armed with clubs, and taking his horse by the bit, ordered him off from the ground; brother Nobles left the ground for the sake of maintaining peace.

Thursday, May 23—I crossed the Mississippi with my family, and took up my residence in a room in the old military barracks, in company with brother Woodruff and his family.

Friday, May 24—I walked out with five others of the Twelve to the prairie, visited many mounds and the grave of a Lamanite chief.

Saturday, May 25—I crossed the river with several of the Twelve to Commerce, and spent the day in council with Joseph.

Sunday, May 26—Crossed the river and attended meeting at the house of the Prophet: Elders O. Pratt and J. Taylor preached.

There was much of the spirit of mobocracy made manifest at Montrose by some outlaws who remained there; some cut down the barns belonging to the military station, lest the Saints might have the use of them.

Saturday, June 1—A Conference was held in Quincy; President Joseph Smith presided. He informed the Seventies it was not the will of God that they should appoint, or have committees to take care of their poor, but that Bishops were the authorities that God had specially appointed for that purpose; which counsel was immediately responded to.

Tuesday, July 2—Brothers Joseph, Hyrum and others came over the river to Montrose, and went out on the prairie and looked out the site for a city for the Saints, which was called Zarahemla. We dined at brother Woodruff's; after dinner the Presidency, Twelve, and a few others met at my house; President Hyrum Smith opened the meeting by prayer. Elders W. Woodruff, G. A. Smith, and T. Turley were blessed. Brother Hyrum Smith gave the Twelve some good advice; brother Joseph taught many important and glorious principles calculated to benefit and bless them on their mission, unfolding keys of knowledge whereby to detect Satan and preserve us in the favor of God.

Thursday, July 4—President Joseph Smith had taken the sick into his house and door-yard until his house was like an hospital, and he had attended upon them until he was taken sick himself and confined to his bed several days.

Monday, July 22—Joseph arose from his bed of sickness, and the power of God rested upon him. He commenced in his own house and door-yard, commanding the sick, in the name of Jesus Christ, to arise and be made whole, and they were healed according to his word. He then continued to travel from house to house and from tent to tent upon the bank of the river, healing the sick as he went, until he arrived at the upper stone-house, where he crossed the river in a boat, accompanied by several of the Quorum of the Twelve, and landed in Montrose.

He walked into the cabin where I was lying sick, and commanded me, in the name of Jesus Christ, to arise and be made whole. I arose and was healed, and followed him and the brethren of the Twelve into the house of Elijah Fordham, who was supposed to be dying, by his family and friends. Joseph stepped to his bedside, took him by the hand and commanded him, in the name of Jesus Christ, to arise and be made whole. His voice was as the voice of God. Brother Fordham instantly leaped from his bed, called for his clothing and followed us into the street.

We then went into the house of Joseph B. Nobles, who also lay very sick, and he was healed in the same manner; and when, by the power of God granted unto him, Joseph had healed all the sick, he re-crossed the river and returned to his home. This was a day never to be forgotten.

During my further stay in Montrose, I attended meetings and administered to the sick when I was well myself.

Saturday, September 14—I started from Montrose on my mission to England. My health was so poor I was unable to go thirty rods to the river without assistance.

After I had crossed the river I got Israel Barlow to carry me on his horse, behind him, to Heber C. Kimball's, where I remained sick till the 18th. I left my wife sick, with a babe only ten days old, and all my children sick and unable to wait upon each other.

Tuesday, September 17—My wife crossed the river and got a boy with a wagon to bring her up about a mile to brother Kimball's to see me.

I remained until the 18th at brother Kimball's, when we started, leaving his family also sick.

Brother Charles Hubbard sent his boy across the prairie fourteen miles to a shanty on the railroad, where brother O. M. Duel lived. Sister Duel helped the boy to get our trunks out of the wagon. We went into the house, feeling very much fatigued. She made us a cup of tea which very much revived us. We tarried there one night.

In the morning brother Duel took us in his wagon, and carried us as far as Lima, about twelve miles. When brother Duel left us, he gave each of us a dollar to help us on our journey. A brother then took us into a wagon and carried us to Father Mikesell's near Quincy.

We tarried in Quincy a few days, and began to recover, and preached a few times. We procured a meeting house close to the Congregationalists and we began at different hours from them; but taking a notion to disturb us, they rang their bell furiously after we had commenced our meeting. Elder Page was preaching, and he preached so loud as to drown the bell, and thus brought out hundreds who otherwise would not have come to meeting. We received some little assistance from the brethren.

Lyman Wight took us into a one-horse wagon, and carried us to brother C. C. Rich's, at Burton, where we stayed over night.

Next morning brother Rich carried us to brother Wilbur's. We tarried over night, and brother Wilbur took us in a buggy and carried us to Father James Allred's, in Pittsfield, where we remained all night; and Father Allred carried us to the neighborhood where brother Harlow Redfield lived, where we preached at a small Branch of the Church. Next day the brethren carried us on to Scott county to Brother Decker's, near Winchester.

Tuesday, October 1—Went to Lorenzo D. Young's, where we tarried and recruited.

Friday, October 4—Brother Lorenzo carried us to Jacksonville. We staid over night. A sister in the Church hired a man and buggy to carry us to Springfield where we were kindly received by the brethren. Here I was sick and confined to my bed for a few days. Brother Libeus T. Coon, who was then practising medicine, waited upon and nursed me.

On the 11th, resumed my journey in company with brothers H. C. Kimball, Geo. A. Smith, Theodore Turley and brother Kimball's father-in-law, Mr. Murray. The brethren had exchanged horses at Springfield, and with a little assistance from the brethren there, we obtained a two-horse wagon. The sisters fitted me up a bed in the wagon to ride on, as I was unable to sit up.

We travelled eight miles, and put up with Father Draper for the night. When we went into the house, brother Geo. A. Smith dropped on to the hearth a bottle containing some tonic bitters, which the brethren had prepared for us because of our sickness. At this Father Draper was very much astonished, and said, "You are a pretty set of Apostles, to be carrying a bottle of whiskey with you." We explained to him what it was; this appeased his righteous soul, so that he consented to have us stay over the night.

Next morning we pursued our journey and arrived at Terre Haute on the 17th. Brother Kimball and myself put up at Dr. Modisett's, who belonged to the Church. The other brethren put up at Milton Stowe's, who lived in one of the doctor's houses.

In the evening the doctor called in to see them, brother Stowe being very poor, and the brethren quite ill in health. The doctor expressed great sympathy for them when he returned to his house—relating over the poverty of brother Stowe and the brethren's ill health, he shed many tears, but he did not have quite sympathy enough to buy them a chicken or given them a shilling, though he was worth some four or five hundred thousand dollars.

In the course of the evening brother Kimball became very ill. The doctor said he could give him something that would help him, but the old man was so drunk he did not know what he did do, and he gave brother Kimball a table spoonful of morphine. His wife saw him pour it out, but dare not say a word, but believed it would kill brother Kimball. A few minutes after he took it, he staightened up in his chair, and said he felt very strange, and thought he would lie down; and on his making a motion to go to bed, he fell his length upon the floor. I sprang to him, rolled him over on his back, and put a pillow under his head, and began to inquire what the doctor had given him. I learned he had given him morphine. Brother Kimball soon came to, and spoke faintly and said, "Don't be scared, for I shan't die." We got him on the bed, and I nursed him through the night. I changed his under clothing five times, and washed him previous to changing his clothes. I found him covered with sweat, at first like thin honey. This gradually wore out towards morning, and he sweat naturally. He was scarcely able to speak, so as to be understood, through the night.

The next day brothers Geo. A. Smith, Theodore Turley, Reuben Hedlock and Mr. Murray, started with the wagon and three horses for Kirtland, Ohio—the horses had pretty well given out. We gave them what money we had, except five dollars, and told them to take good care of the team and make all possible speed; if they did not, we would be in Kirtland before them.

We tarried in Terre Haute until the 22nd, when brother A. W. Babbitt and Dr. Knight came to Terre Haute to see us. Next day Dr. James Modisett sent his son and carriage, and took us twenty miles. We went from thence to Pleasant Garden with brother Babbitt, and put up with brother Jonathan Crosby, cabinet-maker. Found a few brethren who were well and in good spirits.

We remained there a few days preaching to the few brethren and others who wished to hear. We learned that brother Babbitt had been preaching through the country with good success, and had baptized five.

We tarried till Saturday, the 26th, when brother Babbit took us in his buggy and carried us twelve miles, to the house of a brother Scott, where we tarried over night. The family were very glad to see us.

Next morning brother Scott sent his little son John, and carried us fifteen miles to Belleville. Travelled several miles in the rain. We put up at an inn for the remainder of the day and night. I was quite ill, and brother Kimball sat up with the landlord and his lady, quite late, preaching to them.

Next morning the landlord rose up early and talked to the citizens about the travellers who had put up with him the night before, and what he had heard them say concerning the Gospel. The neighbors flocked in, had many inquiries to make, and were very anxious we should tarry and preach in the place. The stage came along about 10 o'clock, and we went on our way for Kirtland.

While in Pleasant Garden we obtained some money, so that with the five dollars we previously had, amounted to $13.50. When we got into the stage, we did not expect to be able to ride but a short distance. We rode as far as Indianapolis, paid our passages, and found we had sufficient means to take our passages for Richmond, Ia.

When we arrived at this place we found we had means to take us to Dayton, to which place we proceeded and tarried over night, waiting for another line of stages. We expected to stop here and preach until we got means to pursue our journey. I went to my trunk to get money to pay my bill, and found that we had sufficient to pay our passages to Columbus, to which place we took passage in the stage and tarried over night.

When I paid my bill I found I had sufficient to pay our passages to Wooster. We tarried till the after-part of the day, and then took passage for Wooster. When we arrived there I went to my trunk again to get money to pay our bill, and found sufficient to pay our passages to Cleveland.

When we got to a little town called Strongsville, towards evening, within about 20 miles of Cleveland, I had a strong impression to stop at a tavern when I first came into the town, but the stage did not stop there, so we went on. We arrived at Cleveland about 11 o'clock, and took lodgings and remained till next morning.

Sunday, November 3—Brother Kimball and I attended the Episcopalian church in the forenoon. While we were walking down the street to the hotel, we met Mr. Murray, and learned that the brethren who left us in Terre Haute had just arrived in Cleveland. Mr. Murray was as much astonished to see brother Kimball alive as though he had seen one risen from the dead. We walked down the street with him a short distance and met the brethren, from whom I learned they had stopped at the tavern in Strongsville, where I wished to stop the night before. They had met with brother John Taylor at Dayton, where he was left a few weeks before at a tavern, very sick, by Father Coltrin, who proceeded to Kirtland. Brothers Taylor and Hedlock got into the stage with us early in the afternoon, and rode as far as Willoughby. We proceeded to Kirtland, and arrived that evening, where we found a good many friends and brethren who were glad to see us. I had a York shilling left; and on looking over our expenses I found we had paid out over $87.00 out of the $13.50 we had at Pleasant Garden, which is all the money we had to pay our passages, to my certain knowledge, to start on. We had travelled over 400 miles by stage, for which we paid from 8 to 10 cents a mile, and had eaten three meals a day, for each of which we were charged fifty cents, also fifty cents for our lodgings.

In company with my brother, John Young, I visited brother and sister Kent, my brother-in-law and sister, and found them well and in good faith. There was some division of sentiment among the brethren in Kirtland, many of whom lacked the energy to move to Missouri last season, and some lacked the disposition. Some of the brethren thought that our sickness was owing to some great wickedness we had been guilty of.

Sunday, November 10—Brother Taylor preached in the forenoon, in the Temple, and brother Kimball in the afternoon.

We spent our time in Kirtland in visiting the brethren and recruiting our health.

Sunday, November 17—I preached in the forenoon, brother Taylor in the afternoon. In the evening I anointed brother Taylor in the house of the Lord. He had previously washed himself in pure water with castile soap; then we all went to the Temple. Brother Kimball opened the meeting by prayer; I then anointed brother Taylor with pure sweet oil, and pronounced such blessings as the Spirit gave utterance. Brother Taylor then arose and prayed for himself. Brother Turley, one of the Seventies, was anointed by D. S. Miles, one of the Presidents of the Seventies, which was sealed by loud shouts of hosannah; then their feet were washed and the meeting closed.

A Council was held with brothers Kellog, Moreton, and the leading brethren in Kirtland. It was proposed that some of the Elders should remain there and preach a few weeks. Brother John Moreton said that they had had very many talented preachers, and he considered that men of ordinary talents could do no good in that place.

We disposed of our wagon, horse and harness, and picked up what money we could gather, which was insufficient to convey us to New York. There was not a healthy man among us, and some more fitted for a hospital than a journey.

Monday, November 18—I went to Newbury, to brother R. Potters'; returned to Kirtland.

Friday, November 22—Elders Kimball, Taylor, G. A. Smith, Hedlock, Turley and myself, proceeded to Fairport. The lake was so rough that no boat came into port until the 26th, when we went on board the steamboat *Columbus*, at one o'clock, and arrived in Buffalo next morning. We had an excellent time on the lake. The wind rose about one o'clock in the morning. I went upon deck and felt impressed in spirit to pray to the Father, in the name of Jesus, for a forgiveness of all my sins, and then I felt to command the winds to cease, and let us go safe on our journey. The winds abated, and I felt to give the glory and honor and praise to that God who rules all things.

The boat stopped at Erie, Pa. She had no freight and but few passengers, and coming out of the harbor she ran against the pier, which was covered with an immense body of ice. She struck it with such force that she ran right up on the ice out of the water, and remained a short time, and then slid backwards into the water without damage.

Wednesday, November 27—We took passages on the stage, but found our Ohio money would not pass current, and we had to go to a broker's and exchange for Buffalo money by paying a heavy discount.

On arriving at Batavia, we put up at the Genesee House, dedicated our room to the Lord, and had a prayer meeting, asking the Lord to open up our way.

Elder Hedlock left our company here, to visit some Branches of the Church.

We took the cars for Rochester. Elder Kimball left us at Byron to visit his friends. Arriving at Rochester, we took the stage and rode all night, and arrived at Auburn at ten a.m. Here, being short of means, Elders Taylor and Turley proceeded to New York, and brother George A. and I concluded to stop and preach until the Lord should open the way.

We visited my cousin George Brigham, who listened very attentively to our teachings. He took us to a hotel, where we slept in a damp room and took additional cold.

We walked to Moravia, and found brother Isaac C. Haight and a small Branch of the Church, which had recently been built up in that neighborhood. I preached several times. Brother George A.'s lungs were so bad he could not preach.

Friday, December 6—Brother Haight took his team, and we rode with him to brother Joseph Murdock's, in Hamilton, Madison county, where we arrived on the 7th, in the evening. Brother George A. was confined to his room sick, and received a thorough series of Thompsonian nursing. I found the Saints in confusion; they had the gift of tongues among them, and the interpretation, and they were so ignorant of the nature of these gifts that they supposed that everything which was spoken in tongues was immediate revelation from God; a false spirit had therefore crept in, and division was the result. I taught them that when they spoke in tongues the language might be from the Lord, but with that tongue they spoke the things which were in their hearts, whether they were good or evil; the gift of tongues was given for a blessing to the Saints, but not to govern them, nor to control the Elders, or dictate the affairs of the Church. God had placed in the Church different gifts; among which were Apostles, Prophets, helps and governments, and wisdom was profitable to direct. Before leaving, the Saints came to an understanding on these matters. The brethren were very kind to us: brother Benager Moon gave me satinette to make me an overcoat; sister Lucetta Murdock made it for me; this was a great blessing to me, as I had worn a quilt, with a comforter run through it, in lieu of an overcoat, all the way from Nauvoo, which had not much of a ministerial appearance. Held meetings on Tuesday and Thursday evenings.

Friday, December 20—Went to Eaton, and visited cousins Fitch and Salmon Brigham, and on Saturday to Hamilton, and called on Phinehas Brigham. While at cousin Phinehas Brigham's, he had many inquiries to make about the Prophet. I preached the Gospel to him so plainly that he could not make any reply, but had to acknowledge that what I taught was Scriptural and reasonable, and he could not gainsay it; but being a very staunch Baptist and a deacon too, he regretted very much his son was not there, who was educated for a Baptist priest. He thought if his son was there he might be able to enlighten my mind and point out my errors, although he was not able to do it himself.

We had not conversed an hour before his son, the priest, came in, to whom he introduced me, and then sat down with a great deal of composure, believing the son would be able to rebut the doctrine I had advanced. The son, with all the solemnity and air of a priest, commenced to ask questions. I answered them, and, in return, asked him a few questions, giving him the liberty to rebut any statement I had made by bringing Scripture testimony, as I had read my doctrine from the Bible; but he could not give me any light, neither could he answer the questions I asked him, and he was too much of a gentleman—young and inexperienced—to commence a tirade of abuse, as older priests generally did on the character of Joseph Smith and the Book of Mormon, consequently he sat mute as a stock.

I continued my visit with the family for a short time, and when I was about to leave I told them that Baptistism, Methodism, Presbyterianism, Quakerism, Shakerism, and every other ism I had studied and learned, for I desired to know the truth, and found I could put all their doctrines, when simmered down to truth, into a snuffbox of the smallest class, put it into my vest pocket and go on my way; but, when I found "Mormonism," I found that it was higher than I could reach with my researches, deeper than I was capable of comprehending, and calculated to expand the mind and lead mankind from truth to truth, from light to light, from grace to grace, and exalt him in the celestial kingdom, to become associated with the Gods and the angels. I bade them good night, and went over the hill to Hamilton, and staid at brother Murdock's.

Sunday, December 29—Elder Blakeslee preached. Brother George A., who had been confined to brother Murdock's house during the last three weeks, was now so far recovered as to be able to proceed; and on the first day of January, 1840, brother James Gifford took us in his sleigh to Waterville, where we stayed over night with brother Sykes. This evening brother Blakeslee read us several chapters of a work which he had written for publication; and as he earnestly solicited my opinion on the subject, I pointed out to him so many palpable errors in principle and doctrine, that I convinced him his work would have to undergo a thorough revision before it could be published to the world as the doctrines of the Church of Jesus Christ of Latter-day Saints.

1840

Tuesday, January 7—Elder Smith and I took stage for West Stockbridge, starting at daybreak; the weather cold and the snow very deep. Elder Smith's health still very poor, and though only thirty-two years of age, his eyesight was so impaired by disease that I had to wait on him while travelling, and select his food and put it on the plate, as he could not tell one dish from another. While I was settling our bill, I heard some gentlemen conversing, who said, "Do you know that old gentleman who came in the stage?" He was answered "No." "Do you know that young man that waits on him?" "No."

We arrived at West Stockbridge, and I proceeded to Richmond and sent a team for brother George A. I preached on Wednesday evening amid considerable opposition, and brother George A. on Thursday evening. While we were opening the meeting, three sons of sectarian deacons threw a quantity of sulphur on the stove, which was very hot; it produced such heavy fumes that some left the house, others raised the windows and opened the doors. It was with great difficulty we could proceed with the meeting. After the stench had a little abated, Brother George A. said it was the first time he had ever been permitted to visit the State of Massachusetts. He had heard much from his childhood of the refined morals, high state of Christianity and perfect order that reigned predominant in this State, and of the great missionary exertions made to civilize, moralize and Christianize almost every portion of the world. He said he had travelled in the west, north and south; met in congregations with the savages of the forest, and he had never seen so mean a breach of good order and decency before in his life. His first impression was that some sectarian preacher, a wholesale dealer in fire and brimstone, in making an exposition of his creed, had got so near hell that he had been unable to take all the brimstone away with him. At least, he considered himself in no danger of catching the itch in Massachusetts, for the smell of brimstone indicated it was thoroughly cured.

Friday, January 17—Edwin Pearson took his horse and cutter, and brought us to Canaan, Litchfield county, Connecticut. In some places the snow was fifteen feet deep. We stayed at Gibson Smith's, and visited the Saints on Canaan

31

Mountain, and preached at brother Francis Benedict's.

Sunday, January 19—We preached at Sheffield Mills. We visited the scattered Saints in this vicinity, and on Sunday, the 26th, I preached a lengthy discourse at the house of brother French.

Monday, January 27—Brother French carried us in a sleigh to New Haven. We put up at Lewis' Tavern, where we anxiously waited for a steamboat. We visited the New Haven Museum.

Thursday, January 30—We took steamboat and started, but on getting out a few miles a portentious cloud in the east caused the captain to return, and we went back to the hotel.

Next day we took steamboat and went within eighteen miles of New York. When we came into the channel of East River, we found it frozen over. The captain ran his boat as far into the ice as he could, but the ice was so thick he had to land us at Frog's Point, where we hired a Paddy's dirt-cart to carry our luggage a mile, when, with other passengers, we hired a market-wagon to carry us to Harlem, paying all our money on our arrival there. It was late in the evening, and all the stages had left for New York but one, which had only two horses; sixteen of us got on to it, and we arrived in New York by 10 p.m. When we landed I observed Captain Stone, the commander of the steamer, come out of the coach, and asked him if he would have the goodness to pay this gentleman's fare and mine (pointing to brother George A.) He replied, "With pleasure." I thanked him. He said it was all right, and, shaking hands with us both, bade us God speed. We left our trunks in the baggage-room of the North American House, and soon found brother P. P. Pratt and family, who lived at No. 58, Mott-street. We were heartily received by the family, and returned thanks to God for having preserved us and brought us in safety so far on our mission to the nations of the earth.

Saturday, February 1—Spent the day at brother Pratt's; my health was feeble.

Sunday, February 2—Attended three meetings at the Columbian Hall, Grand-street. Elder George A. Smith and myself preached.

I attended a meeting in some part of the city every evening during the week, and on Sunday, 9th, preached three times in the hall. I again attended meetings every night during the week, and was constantly conversing with people and teaching them the principles of the Gospel. Passing from Brooklyn to New York, I jumped on to the ferry-boat with my left arm extended, meaning to catch hold of the stanchion, but I fell on a large iron ring on the deck, which put my shoulder out of joint. I asked brother Hedlock to roll me over on my back, which he did; I directed brothers Kimball and Hedlock to lay hold of my body, and brother Pratt to take hold of my hand and pull, putting his foot against my side, while I guided the bone with my right hand back to its place. The brethren wound my handkerchief round my shoulder and helped me up. When I came to a fire I fainted, and was not able to dress myself for several days.

Sunday, February 23—I attended meeting. Elder P. P. Pratt preached.

I visited Long Island and preached in the counties of King and Suffolk, at

Hempstead, Rockaway, Brooklyn and other places. At the last meeting I held, I told the people I was on a mission to England with my brethren; I had never asked for a dime in all my preaching, but we had not sufficient means to proceed, and if any one wished to contribute to help us, I would thankfully receive it. After meeting, $19.50 was put in my hands. We baptized nine, and returned to New York.

Wednesday, March 4—Attended a Conference with the Church in New York. Elders Kimball, Parley P. and Orson Pratt and Geo. A. Smith were present. Much instruction was given to the Saints, and a number of Elders were ordained.

On Sunday I taught the Saints to ask the Elders, when they came to stay with them, if they wished water to wash their feet. In the evening we went to brother Addison Everett's; sister Everett asked us if we would have some water to wash our feet; having no fire, she brought us a bucket of ice and water, and we washed our feet, the cold, however, was alleviated by our exceeding good humor.

We engaged our passages for Liverpool on board the *Patrick Henry*, a packet ship of the Black Ball Line, Captain Delino, and paid $18 each for a steerage passage, furnished our own provisions and bedding and paid the cook $1 each for cooking. Brother H. C. Kimball and myself occupied a lower berth, brothers Parley and Orson Pratt the one over us, brothers George A. Smith and R. Hedlock an upper berth at their feet; two Englishmen occupied the berth below. The brethren in New York furnished us with an ample supply of provisions by donation; the sisters made us ticks and filled them with straw for beds and filled some bags with straw for pillows.

Monday, March 9—A large number of Saints came down to the wharf to bid us farewell. When we got into the small boat to go out to the ship, the brethren sand, "The gallant ship is under weigh;" we joined them as long as we could hear. When we got on board, the vessel weighed anchor; the steam-tug took us out to Sandyhook. Brother L. R. Foster, the presiding Elder of the New York Branch, came out to the Hook and returned with the tug. We set sail, and by sunset lost sight of our native shore. I was sick nearly all the way and confined to my berth. For eight days we had a fair wind, from the eighth to the tenth day a very heavy gale, from the eleventh to the thirteenth day part of our bulwarks were washed away and the water ran down the hatches in large quantities.

Monday, April 6—We landed in Liverpool; I got into a boat with Elders Kimball and P. P. Pratt, and when I landed on the shore I gave a loud shout of hosannah. We procured a room at No. 8, Union-street. The ship failing to get into the dock with the tide, I sent a boat for brothers O. Pratt, Geo. A Smith and R. Hedlock.

We held a meeting, partook of the sacrament and returned thanks to God for his protection and care exercised over us while on the waters, and asking that our way might be opened before us to accomplish our missions successfully.

Tuesday, April 7—We found Elders John Taylor and John Moon, with about thirty Saints who had just received the Work in that place.

Wednesday, April 8—Went to Preston by railroad, and found a multitude of Saints who rejoiced at our arrival and made us welcome.

Thursday, April 9—Brother Willard Richards came to Preston; I was so emaciated from my long journey and sickness that he did not know me. He gave us an account of the condition of the Churches in the British Isles. I wrote for brother Woodruff to come to Preston and attend Conference with us.

Sunday, April 12—I met with several of the Twelve in the Cock-pit, Preston, and bore testimony to a crowded assembly of the truth of the Gospel.

Tuesday, April 14—I met in Council with six of the Twelve in Preston, viz., Heber C. Kimball, P. P. Pratt, Orson Pratt, Wilford Woodruff, John Taylor and George A. Smith, this being the first council held by a majority of the Quorum of the Twelve in a foreign nation. Elder Willard Richards was ordained to the office of an Apostle, and received into the Quorum of the Twelve by unanimous vote, agreeable to a revelation given to Joseph Smith in Far West, July 8, 1838. I was chosen standing President of the Twelve by unanimous vote.

Wednesday and Thursday, April 15 and 16—Attended a general Conference of the Church of Jesus Christ of Latter-day Saints, held in the Temperance Hall, Preston, Lancashire, England. Elder Heber C. Kimball was chosen to preside, and Elder William Clayton, clerk. There were represented 1,671 members, 34 Elders, 52 Priests, 38 Teachers and 8 Deacons.

During this Conference we resolved to publish a monthly periodical in pamphlet form, to be edited by Elder P. P. Pratt, also to publish a selection of hymns, and that Elders P. P. Pratt, John Taylor and I select said hymns.

Friday, April 17—I met with the Quorum of the Twelve at mother Moon's. She presented a bottle of wine for us to bless and partake of, which she had kept for forty years, and she said there was something providential in its preservation, for when she was married she designed to use it, but forgot until the event was over, and when her first child was married it was also forgotten, and so it had passed over several events until she now had the privilege of presenting it to the Quorum of the Twelve Apostles. We spent the day in conversing and counselling with each other pertaining to the things of the kingdom of God.

Tuesday, April 21—We took coach to Dudley, and had a plain view of the old Dudley Castle, the age of which is not known; it is partly in ruins. We rode to Worcester, and spent several hours in the city, visited the noted ancient Cathedral, which is 400 feet in length, and contains many fine specimens of sculpture of ancient bishops, lords and princes, some of which, historians say, have been there for 700 or 800 years, and are reported to be as fine specimens of statuary as can be found in Europe. Nearly every portion of this majestic edifice is carved out of solid marble; the pulpit is carved out of one block. It also contains a small chapel hewn out of solid marble. The Church of England holds service in this Cathedral twice each day in the year; we remained during the afternoon service, at the close of which we rode to Ledbury.

On the road we passed through the town of Malvern, at the base of Malvern Hills, the most beautiful range of hills in England, being among the highest and affording the most splendid prospect of the surrounding country for 30 miles.

Surrounding one of the highest hills, which is called the Herefordshire Beacon, are many large intrenchments one above another, supposed to have been made by the ancient Britons for a retreat in time of war. These hills have been a famed place of resort for the kings, queens, princes, lords and nobleman, and also the poets of England during the summer season. We had a view of Eastner Castle as we passed along. We spent the night at Mr. Francis Pullen's, having travelled 51 miles.

Monday, July 6—I attended a general Conference of the Church in Britain, in the Carpenter's Hall. Elders H. C. Kimball, P. P. Pratt, W. Woodruff, J. Taylor, W. Richards and Geo. A. Smith, were present. Elder P. P. Pratt, President; William Clayton, Clerk

There were represented 41 Branches, comprising 2,513 members, 56 Elders, 126 Priests, 61 Teachers and 13 Deacons. Increase the last three months, 842 members, 22 Elders, 74 Priests, 23 Teachers and 5 Deacons. The Apostles present, and 20 Elders, volunteered to devote their time exclusively to the work of the ministry.

Tuesday, July 7—I attended a general Council of the Church officers in the Councilroom of the *Star* office, Manchester, at which the missionaries were assigned their fields of labor. I addressed the meeting at length, upon the duties and calling of the servants of God.

Sunday, July 12—I preached in the hall in the morning, and brother Woodruff in the evening. We confirmed four. Soon after our Conference brother P. P. Pratt started for America, to bring his family to England, and I took charge of the *Millennial Star*, and edited the same, assisted by brother W. Richards. I was much confined to the office for several months, proofreading the Hymn Book, conducting and issuing the *Millennial Star*, Hymn Book and Book of Mormon, giving counsel to the Elders throughout the European Mission, preaching, baptizing and confirming.

Friday, August 21—I visited the Church at Preston; remained three days, and preached.

Sunday, August 23—Ten were confirmed in the hall, Manchester, and on Sunday, 30th, twenty were confirmed.

Saturday, September 5—I went from Manchester to Liverpool, accompanied by brother W. Richards, and in the evening organized a company of Saints to sail for the land of Zion. Elder Theodore Turley was appointed to preside, with six Counsellors.

Sunday, September 6—I preached in Liverpool.

Tuesday, September 8—The *North America* sailed with 200 souls. Brother Richards and I accompanied the Saints about fifteen or twenty miles; left them in good spirits, and returned to Manchester on the 10th.

Brother John Benbow, who had furnished two hundred and fifty pounds sterling towards printing the Hymn Book and Book of Mormon, relinquished all claim to said money, except such assistance as his friends, who might wish to emigrate to America the next season, might need, leaving the remainder at the disposal of Willard Richards, Wilford Woodruff and myself, who borrowed said monies for the benefit of the Church of Jesus Christ of Latter-day Saints forever; also the avails of the Gadfield Elm Chapel, when sold, which money we paid out in emigrating brethren to Nauvoo.

Wednesday, September 16—Removed to No. 1, Chapman Street.

Wednesday, October 7—I sat in Council with the Twelve and several other officers. In the evening attended a discussion between Elder Alfred Cordon and Mr. John Berry, who attempted to prove the Book of Mormon false, and baptism by immersion not essential to salvation. Elder Cordon replied, proving the Book of Mormon true, and baptism by immersion a Gospel ordinance and essential to salvation. There were about 1,500 people present.

Thursday, October 29—Elder Kimball and I went to Southport, accompanied by Elders Peter Melling, James Whitehead, Robert McBride and wife, and sister Alice Highton. The Patriarch blessed us, and prophecied that there were those present who should not sleep in the grave until they should see the Son of Man come in his glory—namely, brother Kimball and myself.

Sunday, November 1—We went and heard the Rev. Mr. Beckwell preach. In the afternoon Elder Kimball preached to a very attentive congregation, and I preached in the evening, congregation attentive.

Monday, November 2—Returned to Liverpool and proceeded to Manchester, where we found brothers Levi Richards, Lorenzo Snow, J. Blakeslee and James Burnham, who had just arrived from America on a mission.

Sunday, November 8—I had organized the Priesthood in Manchester to meet every Sabbath morning, and distribute themselves throughout the different parts of the city to preach in the streets. In this way they occupied about forty preaching stations, at each one of which the congregation were notified of our regular meetings in the Carpenter's Hall. This so annoyed the sectarians, particularly the Methodists, that they made complaints to the mayor, who issued an order to have all street preachers arrested. I went to the Priesthood meeting in the morning, and felt impressed to tell the brethren to go home. The police, who had been instructed to arrest all street preachers that morning, took up about twenty, who all proved to be Methodists. When the magistrate learned they were not "Mormons," they were dismissed.

I baptized John Taylor, of Manchester, who had been an infidel.

Tuesday, November 10—Went to Pendleton.

Sunday, November 15—I went to Duckinfield with Elder Charles Miller, and preached in the forenoon. In the interval heard a gentleman and his daughter play beautifully on a double harp. Met with the Church in the afternoon; then went to Stockport and preached in the evening, and returned to Manchester.

Saturday, November 28—Elder Kimball and I left for Gret's Green, near West Bromwich; we called on the Saints. We met a man staggering, and on inquiring the reason, he informed us that he had not tasted bread for two days. Elder Kimball gave him sixpence.

Sunday, November 29—I preached at Gret's Green in the morning. We staid over the afternoon meeting and then walked to Birmingham, where we heard Elder Snow preach. Brother Kimball and I followed him.

Monday, November 30—We took the cars for London, where we arrived at 6 p.m., and found brother Woodruff well and in good spirits.

Tuesday, December 1—I preached in Barrett's Academy, London; Elder Kimball followed me.

Wednesday, December 2—Elders Kimball, Woodruff and myself called on a few friends.

Thursday, December 3—We visited the Tower of London, the Horse Armory, the Jewel Room and the Thames Tunnel. I preached in the evening in Barrett's Academy.

Friday, December 4—With brother Woodruff I visited Buckingham Palace and Westminster Abbey.

Saturday, December 5—I walked out with brother Woodruff to try and find the Book of Mormon, having heard that it was published and for sale by some unknown person, but could not learn anything about it.

Sunday, December 6—With Elder Kimball and Robert Williams I attended service at St. Paul's Cathedral this morning. Met with the Saints at Barrett's Academy at 3 p.m.; brother Kimball preached; about fifty present. In the evening I preached, and was followed by brothers Kimball and Woodruff. We had a very interesting meeting; one person applied for baptism. Several of the Aitkenites were present; they wished us to call upon them—thought they would be baptized; one of them purchased a hymn-book. Afterwards the Saints met at Father Connor's, and partook of the sacrament.

Monday, December 7—Elders Kimball, Woodruff and I accompanied Dr. Copeland to the College of Surgeons, and went through every department of it. We also visited the National Gallery. Brother Kimball baptized one.

Wednesday, December 9—We visited St. Paul's Cathedral, and went through each apartment from the crypt to the ball, which is about 400 feet high. We crossed London Bridge and the Iron Bridge over the Thames, and also visited the British Museum.

Thursday, December 10—We walked over Blackfriar's Bridge and called at Zion's Chapel, to attend a sacrament meeting of the Aitkenites, but they refused us admittance, fearing lest we should break up their society. In the evening, Elder Woodruff preached, and brother Kimball and I bore a plain and forcible testimony.

Friday, December 11—I started for Cheltenham, where I remained over Sabbath, and preached twice to a very attentive congregation.

Monday, December 14—I attended the Gadfield Elm Conference; had a pleasant time.

Thursday, December 17—Spent the day at Father Kington's, and had a good visit with the Saints in the evening at brother Pitt's.

Friday, December 18—Visiting and counselling the Saints.

Sunday, December 20—I preached in the morning at Froom's Hill, and in the afternoon and evening at Stanley Hill. Staid at brother Oakey's, and had a good time with the Saints.

Monday, December 21—Attended Conference at Stanley Hill. I find fathers and mothers, sisters and brothers, wherever I go.

Friday, December 25—I attended a Conference at Hanley, Staffordshire Potteries, with Elder Geo. A. Smith. There was represented an increase of 6 Elders, 26 Priests, 10 Teachers, 9 Deacons, and 356 members since last July Conference. We had a good time, and gave the Saints much instruction. We ordained 6 Elders, 4 Teachers and 3 Deacons. Staid with brother Geo. A., at Samuel Johnson's.

1841

Friday, January 1—I attended a Conference in Liverpool, Elders P. P. Pratt and John Taylor were present. The Work of God was reported to be progressing favorably in the regions round about, and also in Wales and Ireland.

Brother Willard Richards and I wrote a lengthy article on Election and Reprobation for the *Millennial Star*.

Monday, January 18—Brother Willard and I commenced reading the Book of Mormon, and preparing an index to the English edition.

Wednesday, January 20—I preached in the hall in the evening.

Thursday, January 21—We completed the index, which was immediately put in type, and finished the printing of the first English edition of 5,000 copies. I preached at brother Green's.

Sunday, January 24—I preached in the Music Hall twice, on Election and Reprobation.

Saturday, February 6—Elders Richards, Taylor and I met at brother Richard Harrison's, and organized the company of Saints emigrating on the ship *Sheffield*, Capt. Porter, Elder Hyrum Clark, President.

Sunday, February 7—Spent the day in Liverpool. The *Sheffield* sailed with 235 Saints.

Thursday, February 11—I met in counsel with Elders Richards and Taylor, and set apart the Presidency over the ship *Echo*, Daniel Browett, President.

I was engaged in writing letters to the Twelve and Presiding Elders throughout the kingdom in relation to emigration. I wrote to Elder Geo. A. Smith in relation to the Twelve returning home, and as to emigration; also informing him that the Book of Mormon was bound, and for sale at 5s. per copy, retail.

Thursday, February 25—Attended a blessing-meeting at brother Domville's; Patriarch Melling officiated.

Thursday, March 11—Elder Kimball and I went to Liverpool, where we met Elder Richards and Taylor, and appointed Thomas Smith and William Moss to take charge of the Saints about to sail on the ship *Alesto*. In the evening attended a blessing-meeting.

Friday, March 12—Attending to the brethren about to sail for America, and in the evening attended a blessing-meeting at brother Mitchell's.

Monday, March 15—Attended a blessing-meeting at brother Domville's.

Wednesday, March 17—The *Alesto* sailed with 54 Saints. With brother R. Hedlock I visited the Saints in Harden; he preached in the evening. Staid all night with brother Joseph Ellis.

Saturday, March 20—Went to Overton, and on Sabbath, 21st, preached in the morning, and in the evening at brother Price's. Had a large congregation.

Monday, March 22—I preached; congregation attentive.

Tuesday, March 23—I walked fifteen miles to Chester, and from thence by rail to Liverpool.

Thursday, Friday and Saturday, March 25, 26 and 27—Brother Richards and myself were detained at the Liverpool Post-office, as witnesses in the case of "The Queen *v.* Joseph Holloway," for not delivering letters in due session. We were also engaged packing and sending off Books of Mormon to pay those who had loaned us money to carry forward the printing and binding.

Sunday, April 4—I attended meeting at the Carpenter's Hall, in company with the Quorum of the Twelve; there were nine of us present, who individually bore testimony to the Bible, the Book of Mormon, and to Joseph Smith being a Prophet of the Most High God. I staid with brother Walker at Salford.

Monday, April 5—The Quorum of the Twelve met, and resolved that the 17th day of April be appointed for the Apostles who are going to America to set sail from Liverpool. It was also resolved that the Twelve do business at the Conference as a Quorum, and call upon the Church as a Conference to sanction the same.

Wednesday, April 7—Attended council with the Twelve. We blessed Elder O. Hyde, who was on his mission to Jerusalem.

Tuesday, April 13—I walked through Manchester, it being the fair, with Elders Woodruff and Smith. We saw a great variety of curiosities: a man nearly eight feet high, weighing 450 lbs., and a pig 1,200 lbs., a living skeleton, a great variety of wild beasts, an elephant, said to be the largest in Europe; lions, leopards and tigers, all in one cage, with their keeper in the midst of them, playing with them; he would make them all lie down and then lie on the top of them.

Wednesday, April 14—We wrote an epistle to the Churches, which was signed by nine of the Twelve.

Thursday, April 15—Elders O. Pratt, W. Richards, George A. Smith, Levi Richards and myself, having bid the Saints in Manchester good-bye, went to Liverpool, and arrived in time to attend a tea-party at the Music-hall, where 200 Saints were seated at table together. I addressed the meeting a short time, and was followed by several of the Twelve. At the close of the party the Twelve met a few moments, and agreed to sail on Tuesday.

Sunday, April 18—We met with the Saints in Liverpool, and the Twelve occupied the day in preaching and bearing testimony to the people.

Monday, April 19—We spent the day in getting our baggage on board, intending to draw out into the river, but the wind being unfavorable, we remained on shore.

Tuesday, April 20—Elders H. C. Kimball, O. Pratt, W. Woodruff, J. Taylor, Geo. A. Smith, W. Richards and family, myself and a company of 130 Saints, went on board the ship *Rochester*, Captain Woodhouse, at Liverpool, for New York. We gave the parting hand to Elders O. Hyde and P. P. Pratt, and a multitude of Saints who stood upon the dock to see us start. We drew out into the river Mersey, and cast anchor in sight of Liverpool, where we spent the day and night.

It was with a heart full of thanksgiving and gratitude to God, my heavenly Father, that I reflected upon his dealings with me and my brethren of the Twelve during the past year of my life, which was spent in England. It truly seemed a miracle to look upon the contrast between our landing and departing from Liverpool. We landed in the spring of 1840, as strangers in a strange land and penniless, but through the mercy of God we have gained many friends, established Churches in almost every noted town and city in the kingdom of Great Britain, baptized between seven and eight thousand, printed 5,000 Books of Mormon, 3,000 Hymn Books, 2,500 volumes of the *Millennial Star*, and 50,000 tracts, and emigrated to Zion 1,000 souls, established a permanent shipping agency, which will be a great blessing to the Saints, and have left sown in the hearts of many thousands the seeds of eternal truth, which will bring forth fruit to the honor and glory of God, and yet we have lacked nothing to eat, drink or wear: in all these things I aknowledge the hand of God.

Wednesday, April 21—The wind is favorable; busily engaged nailing down and lashing our luggage to prepare for sea. The anchor weighed and sails spread at 12 m. We had a good breeze through the day, but nearly all the passengers were sea-sick and vomited at a dreadful rate. The Twelve and the Saints occupied the second cabin, other passengers occupied the steerage. The fare was £3 15s.

The *Rochester* was a fast sailing ship, about 900 tons burthen, and passed all the ships that went out of port with us, among which was the *Oxford*, of the Black Ball Line.

Thursday, April 22—Many arose quite weak through vomiting and sickness. Pleasant morning; nearly out of sight of land; ten sail in sight. Elders Kimball and Woodruff assisted me in getting the sick passengers out of their berths to take the air. Elder Geo. A. Smith was quite sick with a severe cough.

Friday, April 23—Cloudy and some rain; contrary winds.

Saturday, April 24—Commenced at midnight to blow a gale; head wind; blew away our fore-topsail; all very sea-sick.

Sunday, April 25—Sea mountains high; head wind; ship rocking and pitching; nearly all sea-sick.

Monday, April 26—We partook of a little food this morning, but were weak and feeble. We still have head winds and rough sea, though the sun shines. We met and prayed for the sick and they began to amend.

Tuesday, April 27—Still high wind, the sick somewhat better; the Twelve are generally well.

1841

Wednesday, April 28—Strong head winds, which increased to a tempest. The sails were close reefed, the tempest raging furiously, sea running mountains high. We shipped heavy seas, and, while in the midst of this scenery, the cry of help was heard in our cabin; we rushed to the scene and found the ropes giving way and breaking which held about 40 tons of luggage, piled up between decks, consisting of heavy trunks, chests and barrels, which, if once liberated from their confinement, would with one surge be hurled with great force into the berths of men, women and children, and would have endangered the lives of all.

On seeing the foundation of this mass giving way, Elders Richards, Woodruff, Pratt and others sprang to the place of danger and braced themselves against the baggage and held it for a few moments until we partially secured it, when the captain sent several sailors with ropes, who made the same fast and secure. When this was done, I repaired to the aft quarter deck with brothers Kimball, Richards, Woodruff and Smith and gazed upon the grandeur of the raging tempest and the movements of the ship for a short time. We all went below, except Elders Woodruff and Richards, who remained until a heavy sea broke over the quarter deck, which thoroughly drenched brother Woodruff; brother Richards was partially saved by throwing himself under the bulwarks; they then thought it best to leave, and followed our example by coming below. We did not sleep much during the night, for boxes, barrels and tins were tumbling from one end of the cabin to the other, and in the steerage 15 berths were thrown down, nine at one surge, all the men, women, and children thrown together in a pile; but no lives were lost nor bones broken.

Thursday, April 29—The gale has ceased; sea rough; sun shines pleasantly; a fair wind for the first time since the day of sailing. We are sailing ten knots an hour; nearly all had a good night's rest; I was very sick and distressed in my head and stomach.

Friday, April 30—Fine breeze; sailing ten knots an hour; fears entertained that the ship was on fire, as smoke arose, but it was found to come from the cook's galley. Brother Woodruff, in the morning, was requested to carry the dishes to the cook for washing; he got his hands full of dishes of various kinds, and, as he stepped to the door of the galley, the ship gave a dreadful lurch and rocked until her studding sails reached the water; this unexpected heave plunged brother Woodruff head foremost about ten feet, the whole width of the galley. The cook, in trying to save him, fell on the top of him. As this was his first introduction to the galley since he had been at sea, he begged the cook's pardon for such an abrupt entrance and withdrew, leaving the cook with three smashed fingers to pick up his dishes at leisure, they being scattered from one end of the galley to the other. When the cook saw me, he beseeched me very earnestly, whoever I sent to the galley, for mercy's sake never to send Mr. Woodruff again, as he came nigh getting killed by him.

Saturday, May 1—Fine beautiful morning; the passengers have got over the sea sickness and all seem cheerful. Fair light breeze; water smooth; nineteen pieces of canvas spread; sailing twelve knots an hour.

Sunday, May 2—Strong favorable wind; cloudy; sailing twelve knots an hour. We saw a fin-back whale rise out of the water several times about twenty rods from the ship.

Monday, May 3—Morning calm; strong, fair breeze in evening; sailing twelve knots an hour.

Tuesday, May 4—Clear, serene morning; water almost perfectly smooth; scarcely air enough to move a sail. The captain took the names, ages and occupations of each person on board, to make correct entry when he arrives in port.

Wednesday, May 5—Warm, pleasant morning; almost a dead calm; sounded, but did not find bottom. We saw a large shoal of porpoises to the north of us. Elder Peter Maughan lost a child, six weeks old, this morning. His wife died a short time before he set sail. The body of this child was committed to the watery grave by sewing it up in canvas and tying a stone to it, sinking it in the sea on the Banks of Newfoundland, lat. 42° 25', long. 50° 10'. Evening chilly and foggy.

Thursday, May 6—Slight breeze; sailing eight knots an hour. All the Saints on board are well, except sister Richards, who is still feeble. We enjoy ourselves well, singing and praying with the Saints morning and evening.

Friday, May 7—Head winds and very foggy. A storm arose in the evening from the south-west. The sails were close reefed, the heavens gathered blackness, and the sea piled up into mountains. In the midst of this a fight ensued between the cook and the Irish, which was stopped by the first mate. We had the roughest night we had experienced on the voyage; the spars and other things were afloat on the main deck.

Saturday, May 8—Fair weather, but strong head winds; sea rough, shipping heavy seas.

Sunday, May 9—Strong, fair wind; sailing twelve knots an hour; the coldest day on the voyage.

Monday, May 10—Fine, pleasant morning, but calm.

Tuesday, May 11—Strong west head winds; sailing nine knots an hour. We passed a full-rigged ship standing the same way we were. We have passed every ship we came in sight of since we left Liverpool.

Wednesday, May 12—Head winds; fair weather, but cool. Capt. Woodhouse proclaims land in sight, which we soon saw with the naked eye. It proved to be Cape Sable, Nova Scotia.

Thursday, May 13—Dead calm, sea smooth, cloudy, head wind in the evening.

Friday, May 14—Dead calm to-day. .

Saturday, May 15—Pleasant morning, light breeze, sea smooth; saw a shoal of mackerel.

Sunday, May 16—A light breeze; sailing four knots an hour. We sounded and found bottom at twenty fathoms on Nantucket shoals.

Monday, May 17—Strong head winds; we came in view of Long Island, 3 p.m., took a pilot on board at 4, who informed us that they had not heard from the *Oxford*, nor any ship which left Liverpool at the time we did, nor for several days before; he also informed us that no word had been heard of the steam-ship *President*; all expected she was lost.

Tuesday, May 18—Strong north-west wind; sailing nine knots an hour. We heard of the death of General Harrison, President of the United States.

Wednesday, May 19—While passing through Sandy Hook we ran into a fishing smack, came near sinking her with all on board. We had a head wind and could not run into the dock; cast anchor at 11 a.m. at the quarantine ground. A steamer came down to get the latest Liverpool news. An editor, who came on board, paid the steamer $45 to bring him out to the ship to get the latest news.

Thursday, May 20—Warm, pleasant weather. We commenced early in the morning to get our luggage on deck. There was a fight between the carpenter and second mate, which was ended by the first mate striking the carpenter with a junk bottle, and, as he went to strike the second blow, I caught his arm and prevented him.

Two quarantine lighters came alongside the *Rochester* and took all the passengers and baggage to the Custom House, where we had to unload all the baggage, which was inspected by the officers, after which we reloaded on board the lighters, which took us to New York city.

When we arrived at the docks, we found them covered with horses and drays and a great crowd of draymen and pickpockets, who stood ready to leap on board and devour all our baggage, and, because we were unwilling to be robbed and felt disposed to do our own business without being forced to measures by draymen, they cursed and swore at a dreadful rate, and acted more like savages than civilized men; but, after much difficulty, we got our goods out of the lighters and loaded on drays, and had to keep constant guard over them to keep them from being stolen. Many attempts were made to steal our baggage. I collared some of the thieves, and threatened to throw them overboard if they would not let it alone. I was under the necessity of striking their fingers to keep them from carrying off the trunks they laid hold of.

We were until ten o'clock at night getting from the docks to an inn. We were all very much fatigued, for we had been constantly handling boxes, chests, barrels and trunks from sunrise till ten p.m., without eating or drinking. We took supper about midnight, and laid down to rest at the Battery Pavillion.

Friday, May 21—Brother Kimball, O. Pratt and myself took lodgings at the house of Elder Adams.

Sunday, May 23—The Twelve met in council in the morning. Elders Kimball, Pratt, Woodruff and myself gave an account of our mission to England to the Saints in the Columbian Hall, Grand Street.

Sunday, May 30—Forenoon, attended meeting. Elder Woodruff preached. Afternoon, held a Conference meeting. Evening, Elder Kimball addressed the people.

Monday, May 31—I visited the Saints on Long Island.

Tuesday, June 1—I returned to New York, and on the 4th, in company with Elders Kimball and Taylor, I left for Nauvoo, by way of Philadelphia.

Monday, June 7—Arrived in Pittsburgh.

Saturday, June 12—We started on board the *Cicero*. The water being very low, we ran on a sand-bar twelve miles below, and there remained all day and night. We went ashore and spent the time agreeably, having a good company with us.

Sunday, June 13—Remained all day on the sand-bar. I went ashore. We got off the bar about half-past seven in the evening.

Monday, June 14—Spent the time agreeably.

Tuesday, June 15—Proceeded down the river till about eleven a.m., when the boat stopped till about half-past twelve p.m. when we started. The condensed steam being let off, scalded a woman, her daughter, and a child by the name of Thomas. We laid up seven miles above Wheeling.

Wednesday, June 16—We started very early and, after proceeding about three miles, we ran on a sand bar; got off about 4 p.m., and soon arrived at Wheeling, where we staid all night. Capt. Thos. O'Connor was very kind to us.

Thursday, June 17—Proceeded on our way finely and arrived at Cincinnati on Sunday morning, the 20th. We went ashore and found several brethren. We went on board the Mermaid for St. Louis, and arrived in Louisville on the 22nd, at 6 p.m., where we remained all night and started at noon on the 23rd, and arrived at the mouth of the Ohio on Saturday the 26th.

Thursday, July 1—We arrived in Nauvoo, and were cordially welcomed by the Prophet Joseph, our families and the Saints.

Thursday, September 2—I was elected a member of the City Council, in place of Don Carlos Smith, deceased.

On my return from England I found my family living in a small unfinished log-cabin, situated on a low, wet lot, so swampy that when the first attempt was made to plow it the oxen mired; but after the city was drained it became a very valuable garden spot.

Although I had to spend the principal part of my time, at the call of brother Joseph, in the service of the Church, the portion of time left me I spent in draining, fencing and cultivating my lot, building a temporary shed for my cow, chinking and otherwise finishing my house; and as the ground was too damp to admit of a cellar underground, I built one with two brick walls about four or six inches apart, arched over with brick. Frost never penetrated it, although in summer articles would mildew in it.

Saturday, October 2—I attended Conference; much valuable instruction was given by the President, Joseph Smith. I addressed the Conference with regard to the appointment of suitable missionaries, and in regard to the importance of teaching abroad the first principles of the Gospel, and letting alone those principles they did not understand; also on the propriety of many of the Elders remaining at home, and working on the Lord's House, and the necessity of more liberal consecrations and more energetic efforts to forward the work of building the Temple and Nauvoo House. The congregation was immense, and the greatest unanimity prevailed.

Wednesday, October 6—I was very sick. Elders Kimball, Richards and Woodruff laid hands upon me, and I recovered.

Sunday, October 10—Met with the Twelve for the purpose of holding a council, but spent most of the day in visiting the sick.

Tuesday, October 12—Brothers Richards, Taylor and myself wrote a long epistle to the brethren scattered abroad on the continent of America, which was signed by eight of the Twelve, and published in the *Times and Seasons*.

Saturday, October 23—With Elders Richards and Taylor I attended a Conference at Lima; 424 members were represented, including 54 officers. We taught the brethren on the necessity of finishing and completing the House of the Lord in preference to anything else. The brethren unanimously voted to devote one-tenth of their time and property to the building of the Temple at Nauvoo, under the superintendence of President Isaac Morley and his counsellors.

Sunday, October 24—We continued our Conference and preached to the brethren.

Friday, October 29—Met in council with the Twelve.

Saturday, October 30—I met with the Presidency and Twelve at Hyrum's office. Joseph spoke on a variety of subjects—the gathering of nations, the building up of the kingdom of God, and the traditions and wickedness of this generation.

November 1 and 6—Attended City Council.

Sunday, November 7—Brother Joseph and several of the Twelve called on me. We went to meeting, when Joseph spoke on temperance, virtue, charity and truth. After the meeting I met with the Twelve and High Priests' Quorum. The word of wisdom was brought up; I expressed my views upon the subject, and said I considered it wisdom to use all things put into our hands according to the best judgment God would give us: wisdom was justified of her children.

Monday, November 8—I attended the dedication of the baptismal font in the Lord's House. President Smith called upon me to offer the dedicatory prayer. This is the first font erected and dedicated for the baptism for the dead in this dispensation.

Sunday, November 21—Brothers Hyrum Smith and John Taylor preached. At 4 p.m., brothers Kimball, Taylor and I baptized about forty persons in the font, for the dead; brothers Richards, Woodruff and George A. Smith confirming. These were the first baptisms for the dead in the font.

Sunday, November 28—Brother Joseph and the Twelve spent the day in council at my house.

Tuesday, November 30—Met in council with Joseph and the Twelve at my house, in relation to the *Times and Seasons*.

Wednesday, December 1—The Twelve met in council, and wrote an Epistle against rogues, thieves and scoundrels which was published.

On the 4th and 5th, attended a Conference at Ramus, and discontinued the organization of the Church at Ramus as a stake.

Wednesday, December 8—Returned from Ramus with the Twelve who attended Conference. We brought about a thousand dollars' worth of property for the Temple, which had been donated by the Saints at Ramus, consisting of horses, wagons, provisions, clothing, &c.

Sunday, December 19—The Twelve met in council at my house this morning. In the evening we met at Joseph's house, when Elder Kimball preached; he was followed by brother Joseph and myself.

Saturday, December 25—I partook of a Christmas supper with the Twelve at bro. Hiram Kimball's.

Sunday, December 26—I attended meeting at Joseph's house with several of the Twelve. Brothers Hyrum and Joseph Smith and I preached.

Monday, December 27—I met with the Twelve at brother Joseph's. He conversed with us in a familiar manner on a variety of subjects, and explained to us the Urim and Thummim which he found with the plates, called in the Book of Mormon the Interpreters. He said that every man who lived on the earth was entitled to a seer stone, and should have one, but they are kept from them in consequence of their wickedness, and most of those who do find one make an evil use of it; he showed us his seer stone.

1842

Saturday, January 1—I spent the day in company with the quorum of the Twelve, with our families, at brother Sylvester B. Stoddard's. He had prepared a feast for us, and we felt thankful to the Lord for this privilege of meeting, with our families, at the home of the Saints. In the evening I attended the City Council, which continued till midnight.

Sunday, January 2—I attended meeting at brother Joseph's house.

Thursday, January 6—I attended Conference at Zarahemla with brother Hyrum and several of the Twelve. The stake was discontinued, by order of brother Joseph, and a branch organized. John Smith was appointed president.

Monday, January 10—I visited at brother Taylor's; several of the Twelve and others were present, with their families. We had a pleasant time conversing on the things of the kingdom.

Wednesday, January 12—Met in council with the Twelve, and suspended Benjamin Winchester for disobedience to the First Presidency.

Monday, January 17—I met in council with the Twelve at Joseph's office. We consulted in relation to the printing and publishing, the council being unanimously opposed to E. Robinson's publishing the Book of Mormon, and other standard works of the Church, without being counseled so to do by the First Presidency.

Friday, January 28—The Lord having revealed, through Joseph, that the Twelve should take in hand the editorial department of the *Times and Seasons*, I bought the printing establishment, for and in behalf of the Church, from brother Ebenezer Robinson, at a very exorbitant price. The reason I paid such a price was, because the Prophet directed the Twelve to pay him whatever he asked. One item of his bill was $800, for the privilege of publishing the *Times and Seasons*, or good will of the office.

Saturday, January 29—Spent the day in council with the Prophet Joseph and Elders Kimball and Richards; we received excellent teachings.

Sunday, January 30—I attended meetings at Joseph's house. He preached in the morning and in the evening, concerning the different spirits, their operations, designs, &c.

Monday, February 21—I wrote a letter calling upon the churches to forward their Tithings and donations to the Trustee-in-Trust, that the Temple may go on, and the new translation of the Bible.

Friday, March 11—Attended the High Council, at the trial of Francis Gladden Bishop, who had set himself up as a Prophet and Revelator to the Church. After his revelations were read, which were a bundle of nonsense and folly, they were committed to the flames, and he was cut off from the Church, and delivered over to the buffetings of Satan.

Sunday, March 20—Attended meeting, and heard Joseph preach on the ordinances of the Gospel and the resurrection of the dead, after which he baptized eighty in the river. I officiated with the Twelve at the font, in baptizing and confirming for the dead. We wrote a long Epistle to the Saints in Europe, which was signed by ten of the Twelve, and published.

Wednesday, Thursday and Friday, April 6, 7, and 8—I attended a special Conference.

On the 8th, in company with Elders Kimball, O. Pratt, Richards, Woodruff, George A. Smith, and Wight, we ordained 275 Elders, being the most ordained in one day since the foundation of the Church.

Sunday, April 24—I called upon Elder Woodruff, who was sick with the chills and fever, and laid hands upon him and he was healed, when he accompanied me in a wagon to the prairie, where we laid hands on others of the sick.

Wednesday, May 4—I met with Joseph, Hyrum, Heber, Willard, Bishops Whitney and Miller, and Gen. James Adams, in Joseph's private office, where Joseph taught the ancient order of things for the first time in these last days, and received my washings, anointings and endowments.

Thursday, May 5—I attended Council as yesterday, and we administered to brother Joseph the same ordinances.

Saturday, May 14—Attended City Council during the day. In the evening attended Council of the Twelve, and silenced B. Winchester until he make satisfaction.

Sunday, May 15—I attended meeting at the Grove, and addressed the Saints in the forenoon; brother Woodruff preached in the afternoon. At the close of the meeting I repaired to the font, with several of the Twelve. Brothers Woodruff and Rich baptized about 100 for the remission of sins and for their dead. I confirmed those baptized, assisted by other Elders.

Thursday, May 19—I attended City Council. Joseph Smith was elected mayor, John C. Bennett having resigned.

Saturday, June 18—A special meeting was held, at which several thousands of the citizens of Nauvoo assembled, near the Temple. They were addressed by the Prophet on the subject of the impositions practiced upon our immigration by land speculators, who frequently sold them lands to which they had no title, and other subjects. I was appointed, in connection with brothers H. C. Kimball, Hyrum Smith and Geo. A. Smith, as a committee to wait upon the immigrants, and give them counsel and aid in procuring them places on which to settle.

Sunday, June 26—I addressed the Saints on the principle of union in building up the city, and sustaining the poor by providing labor for them. Six, p.m., I attended Council at brother Joseph's, to take into consideration the situation of the pine country and lumbering business, and other subjects of importance to the Church; after which we spent a season in prayer that the Lord would deliver us from the power of our enemies, and provide means for us to build houses as he had commanded his people.

Wednesday, June 29—Rode out with the Prophet, and looked at lands the Church had for disposal.

Sunday, July 31—Attended Council with the Prophet and others.

In the month of July I attended Councils, waited upon the immigrants; and as President Joseph Smith kept concealed from his enemies, I had continual calls from the brethren for counsel, which occupied much of my time.

Monday, August 8—Attended City Council.

Assisted by Elders H. C. Kimball and Geo. A. Smith, I spent several days laboring with Elder Orson Pratt, whose mind became so darkened by the influence and statements of his wife, that he came out in rebellion against Joseph, refusing to believe his testimony or obey his counsel. He said he would believe his wife in preference to the Prophet. Joseph told him if he did believe his wife and follow her suggestions, he would go to hell.

We reported to the Prophet that we had labored with brother Orson diligently in a spirit of meekness, forbearance and long-suffering. He requested us to ordain brother Amasa Lyman in brother Orson's stead. After receiving these instructions, we met brother Orson near my house, and continued to labor with him. He said to us, There is brother Amasa Lyman in your house, brother Young; he has been long in the ministry, go in and ordain him in my stead.

Saturday, August 20—Brother Orson Pratt was cut off from the Church, and, according to the Prophet's direction, brother H. C. Kimball, Geo. A. Smith and I ordained brother Amasa Lyman in his stead.

Friday, August 26—Met in the evening in Council with the Prophet Joseph and some of the Twelve. We received much good instruction and counsel from Joseph, relative to the situation of the Church, and the policy to be pursued in sending many Elders through the States to preach the Gospel and disabuse the public mind in relation to the false statements of Dr. J. C. Bennett.

The Prophet also directed us to call a special Conference on Monday next, and nominate the Elders to go on this important mission, and give them their instructions; and that we should also get the affidavits against Dr. Bennett published, so that the Elders might have authentic and strong testimony to lay before the public in relation to those matters.

Saturday, August 27—Engaged with brother Joseph and others, preparing affidavits for the press.

Monday, August 29—Conference convened. Presidents Joseph and Hyrum Smith addressed the Saints; 380 Elders volunteered to go immediately on the contemplated mission.

Tuesday, September 6—With Elders Kimball and Lyman, I called upon the Prophet to counsel concerning our mission to the branches and people in the States.

Friday, September 9—I attended City Council, and gave in my notification of absence, and started on my mission and went to Lima.

Saturday, September 10—I preached in Lima. Here brothers H. C. Kimball, Geo. A. Smith and Amasa Lyman overtook me. We remained over Sunday, the 11th, and preached to a large congregation at the Grove, in Lima, and showed the falsity of Bennett's statements. We ordained 19 Elders and baptized 12.

Saturday and Sunday, September 17 and 18—Elders Kimball, Smith, Lyman and myself held a Conference at Quincy, in the Court House. We exposed the course of Bennett and the mobocrats, and disabused the public mind, to some extent, of the prejudices recently imbibed. Governor Carlin attended one meeting.

Saturday, September 24 and 25—Attended Conference at Payson; Elder Kimball and myself preached.

I endeavored to get the affidavits against Dr. J. C. Bennett inserted in the *Whig* and *Herald*, at Quincy, but they refused to print them on any terms. I returned to Nauvoo, and had a number of them struck off as handbills for circulation.

I proceeded to Atlas, and found Elder Kimball. We preached in Col. Ross' brick-house.

Saturday and Sunday, October 8 and 9—Attended Conference at Pittsfield. Elders Kimball, Smith, Lyman and myself preached. We proceeded to Glasgow, and held a two-day's meeting. I sharply reproved Elder Howard Smith, the presiding Elder, for his indolence and folly. He attempted to instruct me how to preach, in a foolish, braggadocio manner.

Saturday and Sunday, October 15 and 16—We attended Conference at Apple Creek. Elders Kimball, Smith, Lyman and myself preached. Brother Kimball and I staid at Esq. Walker's.

Elder Kimball and I went to Jacksonville, and preached. We proceeded to Springfield, and preached. From thence, we returned to Jacksonville, and attended a two-day's meeting in the Court House, which Elders Geo. A. Smith and Amasa Lyman also attended. We went to Morgan City, and held a two-day's meeting; staid with brother Augustus Farnham. Nearly all these Conferences and meetings were numerously attended. We continued preaching from place to place until

Friday, November 4—when I returned to Nauvoo with Elder Kimball.

Monday, November 21—I met with the Twelve at Elder Kimball's. We unanimously decided that the printing of the *Millennial Star* and other Church publications cease on the return of Elder Parley P. Pratt from England, and I wrote a letter to that effect to the editor of the *Star*.

Saturday, November 26—I was suddenly attacked with a slight fit of apoplexy. Next morning I felt quite comfortable; but in the evening, at the same hour that I had the fit the day before, I was attacked with the most violent fever I ever experienced. The Prophet Joseph and Elder Willard Richards visited and administered unto me; the Prophet prophesied that I should live and recover from my sickness. He sat by me for six hours, and directed my attendants what to do for me. In about thirty hours from the time of my being attacked by the fever, the skin began to peel from my body, and I was skinned all over. I desired to be baptized in the river, but it was not until the 14th day that brother Joseph would give his consent for me to be showered with cold water, when my fever began to break, and it left me on the 18th day. I laid upon my back, and was not turned upon my side for eighteen days.

I laid in a log-house, which was rather open; it was so very cold during my sickness, that brother Isaac Decker, my attendant, froze his fingers and toes while fanning me, with boots, greatcoat and mittens on, and with a fire in the house, from which I was shielded by a blanket.

When the fever left me on the 18th day, I was bolstered up in my chair, but was so near gone that I could not close my eyes, which were set in my head—my chin dropped down and my breath stopped. My wife, seeing my situation, threw some cold water in my face; that having no effect, she dashed a handful of strong camphor into my face and eyes, which I did not feel in the least, neither did I move a muscle. She then held my nostrils between her thumb and finger, and placing her mouth directly over mine, blew into my lungs until she filled them with air. This set my lungs in motion, and I again began to breathe. While this was going on I was perfectly conscious of all that was passing around me; my spirit was as vivid as it ever was in my life, but I had no feeling in my body.

1843

Wednesday, January 11—The Quorum of the Twelve wrote a proclamation to the Saints, to observe the 17th inst. as a day of humiliation, fasting, prayer and thanksgiving for the great blessings which our heavenly Father has conferred on us in the deliverance of our beloved President, Joseph Smith, who has been honorably discharged from his arrest under the Missouri writ by the U. S. District Court of Illinois; Judge Pope presiding.

Wednesday, January 18—I had the pleasure of attending a feast, to which brother Joseph had invited his friends, as a memento of his release from the Missouri writ by the U. S. District Court of Illinois. This was the first time that I had been out of my house since my sickness.

Friday, January 20—I attended Council with the Prophet and the Twelve at my house, in regard to Orson Pratt, who had confessed his sins and manifested deep repentance, which resulted in his baptism and re-ordination, by the Prophet, to his former standing in the Quorum of the Twelve. Brother Joseph Smith said that he would find another place for brother Amasa Lyman.

Monday, February 6—I was re-elected a member of the City Council.

Tuesday, February 7—There was a Council of the Twelve at my house. Brother Joseph Smith attended and gave us instructions.

Saturday, February 11—I started at 9 a.m., in company with the Prophet Joseph, for Ramus.

Sunday, February 12—Joseph preached in the morning, and I in the afternoon.

Monday, February 13—Attended a Church meeting. Staid at brother B. F. Johnson's.

Tuesday, February 14—Returned home in a severe snow storm.

Tuesday, February 28—I visited Elder George A. Smith, who was sick.

Saturday, April 1—Elder Taylor and I went to La Harpe, preached four times, and returned on the 3rd.

Friday, Saturday and Sunday, April 6, 7 and 8—Attended the annual Conference of the Church, and was appointed, with my brethren of the Twelve, to collect funds for the Temple and Nauvoo House. We were required to give bonds that we would pay over all the funds we received for that purpose.

Tuesday, Wednesday and Thursday, April 10, 11 and 12—Attended special Conference, when 115 Elders were sent on missions throughout the States, and appointed their several fields of labor. Twenty-two brethren were ordained Elders. I instructed the missionaries at length on the duties required at their hands, and was followed by several of the Twelve.

Wednesday and Thursday, April 18 and 19—Met in Council with the quorum of the Twelve at Joseph's office, when Joseph gave us much instruction pertaining to our labors the ensuing summer, and also gave us directions to wake up the people in relation to the importance of building the Nauvoo House, as there was a prejudice against it, in favor of the Temple.

Saturday, April 29—I, in company with Elders Kimball, Woodruff, George A. Smith and Joseph Young, rode to Augusta, and held a meeting on Sunday, 30th; about 200 Saints were present. We preached on the subject of the building of the Nauvoo House; many promised us assistance in building it; had a good time.

Friday, May 26—Met with the Prophet Joseph, the Patriarch Hyrum, brothers Kimball and Richards, Judge James Adams; and Bishop N. K. Whitney, receiving our endowments and instructions in the Priesthood. The Prophet Joseph administered to us the first ordinances of endowment, and gave us instructions on the Priesthood and the new and everlasting covenant.

Sunday, May 28—I met with brothers Joseph, Hyrum, Heber, Willard, Bishop Whitney and Judge Adams, when we administered to brother Joseph the same ordinances of endowment, and of the holy priesthood which he administered unto us.

Monday, May 29—Met at 9 a.m., with the same brethren, when Joseph instructed us further in principles pertaining to the holy Priesthood.

Six p.m., attended Council with the Twelve, and wrote to the Saints in Philadelphia, who were desirous of observing the counsel of God, to remove, without delay, to Nauvoo: also appointed a few more Elders on missions.

Tuesday, May 30—Met in Joseph's office with the Twelve, and executed bonds for $2,000 as an agent to sell stock for the Nauvoo House: Doctor J. M. Bernhisel was my security. I received 300 shares in stock certificates, value $15,000.

Wednesday, May 31—I moved out of my log cabin into my new brick house, which was 22 feet by 16, two stories high, and a good cellar under it, and felt thankful to God for the privilege of having a comfortable, though small habitation.

Sunday, June 25—Two p.m., brother William Clayton having brought news of President Joseph Smith's arrest at Dixon, brother Hyrum Smith went to the stand and requested the brethren to meet him in half an hour at the Masonic Hall, when three hundred volunteered to go in pursuit of President Joseph Smith and prevent his being taken to Missouri, out of which number several companies were selected to go. The companies agreed to meet in the evening at

William Law's, which they did, when Hyrum reported he could not raise means. Wilson Law said, if means were not raised he would not go. I told the brethren to get in readiness and the money would be forthcoming, although at the time I knew not from whence, but in two hours I succeeded in borrowing $700 to defray the expenses of the expedition.

Friday, June 30—Brother Joseph returned to Nauvoo with the brethren who were sent after him. On his entrance into the city, multitudes of the brethren and sisters turned out to meet and greet him, and on this occasion the officers who arrested him, who were still with him, witnessed the devotion and good feeling in the hearts of the Saints towards their Prophet.

Saturday, July 1—Hyrum Smith, Parley P. Pratt, Lyman Wight, Sidney Rigdon and myself were duly sworn before the municipal court, and gave in our testimony as witnesses in the case of Joseph Smith, who had obtained a writ of *habeas corpus* from the municipal court of Nauvoo, he having been demanded by a requisition from the Governor of Missouri to the Governor of Illinois, who issued a writ for his arrest as a fugitive from justice.

We embodied in our testimony an account of the persecutions of Joseph Smith and the Saints from Jackson county to the time of the expulsion of the Saints from the State of Missouri by force of arms, under the exterminating order of Governor Boggs.

It was certainly a rehearsal of the most heart-rending scenes that ever saluted the ears of any tribunal in a civilized government on earth; it would have been a disgrace to Arabs, cannibals, or the most brutal savages. Not only theft, arson, burglary, imprisonment, chains, expulsion, rape and murder were practiced on the Saints without any redress, but even the Prophet, Joseph Smith, with his companions in prison, were loaded with chains, were fed a portion of the time on the flesh of their murdered brethren, which was cooked and given them to eat by their inhuman persecutors.

The recital of this part of the testimony was sufficient to curdle the blood in the veins of all who heard it; even the lawyers were shocked to the soul, and at the close of the testimony, in their speeches, before the Court, exhorted the Saints to maintain their rights, "stand or fall, sink or swim, live or die."

This testimony of the unparalleled persecutions of the State of Missouri against the Saints of God in the last days, will stand on history's page to future generations.

Monday, July 3—The Twelve, having been directed by the Prophet to call a special Conference to choose Elders to go into the different counties of Illinois to preach the Gospel, and disabuse the public mind with regard to his late arrest, met at the Grove with the Elders, and appointed 82 missionaries to the several counties. I addressed the Elders at length upon their duties.

Friday, July 7—I started on my mission to the east at 4 p.m., accompanied by Elders W. Woodruff, George A. Smith and E. P. Maginn, on the steamer "Rapids:" arrived in St. Louis on the 8th, and called on the Saints.

Sunday, July 9—Left St. Louis at half-past 9 a.m., for Cincinnati, on the steamer *Lancet,* and had conversation with various gentlemen who were inquiring after "Mormonism," one of whom, a professor in a Southern University, said, "I have heard and read much of your people, and of Joseph Smith, but I have no confidence in newspaper stories, and, if it would be agreeable, I would like to ask a few questions." I told him I would answer any questions he might propose, so far as I was able.

He then asked me if Joseph Smith had more wives than one. I told him I would admit he had. In order to explain the principle, I asked the gentleman if he believed the Bible, and was a believer in the resurrection. He said he was a believer in the Old and New Testament and in the resurrection.

I then asked him if he believed parents and children, husbands and wives would recognize each other in the resurrection. He said he did.

Also, if parents and children would have the same filial feeling towards each other which they have here; and he said he believed they would, and that their affections would be more acute than they were in this life.

I then said, "We see in this life, that amongst Christians, ministers, and all classes of men, a man will marry a wife, and have children by her; she dies, and he marries another, and then another, until men have had as many as six wives, and each of them bear children. This is considered all right by the Christian world, inasmuch as a man has but one at a time.

Now, in the resurrection this man and all his wives and children are raised from the dead; what will be done with those women and children, and who will they belong to? and if the man is to have but one, which one in the lot shall he have?"

The Professor replied, he never thought of the question in this light before, and said he did not believe those women and children would belong to any but those they belonged to in this life.

"Very well," said I, "you consider that to be a pure, holy place in the presence of God, angels, and celestial beings; would the Lord permit a thing to exist in his presence in heaven which is evil? And if it is right for a man to have several wives and children in heaven at the same time, is it an inconsistent doctrine that a man should have several wives, and children by those wives at the same time, here in this life, as was the case with Abraham and many of the old Prophets? Or is it any more sinful to have several wives at a time than at different times?"

He answered, "I cannot see that it would be any more inconsistent to have more wives in this life than in the next, or to have five wives at one time than at five different times. I feel to acknowledge it is a correct principle and a Bible doctrine, and I cannot see anything inconsistent in it."

After conversing with him upon the organization of the Church, the Gospel, and order of the Priesthood, he remarked that such an organization possessed within itself all the elements of permanent success and prosperity, and the system of such a government could not be overthrown.

Reached Louisville on the 12th. While passing the locks, we visited Mr. Porter, "the Kentucky Baby," a thin, spare man, 7 feet 7 inches high. We walked through and took a view of the city of Louisville, and then proceeded to

Cincinnati, where we arrived on the 13th, at 5½ p.m., and staid with the brethren. I dreamed that brother Joseph called us home.

Friday, July 14—We visited several of the brethren in the morning, travelled about the city, and wrote letters to our wives.

Saturday, July 15—Staid at brother Pew's with brother Woodruff.

Sunday, July 16—Attended meeting in the morning at father Hewitt's; Elder Woodruff and I preached. In the afternoon we visited the Licking Branch, in Kentucky, where the Saints were in a very backward state, their hearts being more engaged in the welfare of 10 or 15 acres of strawberries and raspberries which they were cultivating than in the things of the kingdom of God.

Monday, July 17—Started back for Cincinnati, viewed the strawberry and raspberry fields. We met brother Colins Pemberton, who advised us to turn off our way a couple of miles and visit a number of families of Saints in a deep valley, which they called Piedmont, which advice we complied with, and preached to them, and blessed eight of their children. The day was excessively hot, but a shower of rain fell in the evening and cooled the atmosphere.

Tuesday, July 18—Brother Pemberton took us in a skiff down the Licking River, and across the Ohio to Cincinnati.

Wednesday, July 19—Visited brother David Martin, who never asked our names: we staid with him over night, and lay on a bedstead that creaked so dreadfully that we could neither sleep nor dream.

Thursday, July 20—Visited brother Jackson, who received us kindly and gave us a sovereign to assist us on our mission. We walked fifteen miles back to Cincinnati.

Saturday, July 22—We took the steamer "Adelaide" for Pittsburgh, and on the 27th left the "Adelaide" on a sand bar and took stage at Bridgewater for the city; stopped at the town of Economy, founded by Mr. Rapp, upon the common stock principle.

On our arrival at Pittsburgh brother Small informed us there was a Latter-day Saint meeting at the Temperance Hall; we went there, and found Elders H. C. Kimball, O. Pratt and J. E. Page. Elder Page was preaching; he hammered the sectarian churches unmercifully. He informed the people of our arrival, which made six of the quorum of the Twelve in that city.

Friday, July 28—We met in Council at 2 p.m., at Richard Savary's. I inquired concerning the proceedings of the Twelve in Cincinnati, and found that Elders H. C. Kimball, O. Pratt and J. E. Page had held a Council and organized that Branch. Elders Kimball and Pratt left Cincinnati, when Elder Page remained for a few days and annulled their proceedings and reorganized the Church as it was before. I reproved Elder Page for undoing alone what three of the Twelve had done together. I exhorted him to be mild and gentle in his teachings and not fight the sects, but endeavor to win the affections of the people.

Sunday, July 30—Six of the Quorum of the Twelve met in the Temperance Hall, Pittsburgh, with the Saints. Brothers W. Woodruff and Geo. A. Smith preached in the forenoon, and brothers Page and O. Pratt in the afternoon. I followed brother H. C. Kimball in the evening, and bore testimony to the Work of the Lord.

I asked the following questions, and reasoned thus,—"Why do the people oppose the gifts and graces of the Gospel?

If a man can get faith by the power of God, and the gift of the Holy Ghost, so as to lay hands upon his wife and children or friends, when they lie sick and languishing nigh unto death, and command the fever or disease, or the power of the Destroyer, or even death itself, to cease its work and be still, and the person is relieved, I ask what harm is there in all this? Or if a man, by faith and humility before God, can get the testimony of Jesus Christ, and prophesy of things to come, or be able to speak in tongues or cast out devils, I ask what harm is there in all this? Does it do any harm? No, it does not.

I know the New Testament is true, for I have proved it according to the pattern given—namely, by believing in Christ and obeying the Gospel; and I know that the signs do follow the faithful believers; then I ask, Do these things harm anyone? No, they do not.

Again, the kingdom of God must be concentrated—the people must be together and gathered into one place. How would the King of France or England look undertaking to reign over a kingdom, when their subjects were scattered all over the world, except in France or England? So with the Saints, they must be gathered together, and this work has already commenced.

Who is the author of this work and gathering? Joseph Smith, the Prophet, as an instrument in the hands of God, is the author of it. He is the greatest man on earth. No other man, at this age of the world, has power to assemble such a great people from all the nations of the earth, with all their varied dispositions, and so assimilate and cement them together that they become subject to rule and order. This the Prophet Joseph is doing. He has already gathered a great people who willingly subject themselves to his counsel, because they know it is righteous."

Wednesday, August 2—Elder Charles Beck gave us $48 to help us to Baltimore. On the 3rd we started at 6 a.m., by stage, and rode all day and night, and arrived in the morning of the 4th at Cumberland.

While in the stage we had a very interesting conversation with two Campbellite preachers, who attacked us on "Mormonism." They contended that that which was in part had been done away, and that which was perfect had come, and that there was now no need of tongues, interpretations, &c. Elder Woodruff replied,—"You then have no need to contend, for if that which is perfect has come, you certainly should all see eye to eye, being in possession of perfect knowledge."

As we commenced to descend the mountain, one of the irons which held the springs gave way, letting the coach on to the horses, which frightened them. The coachman, at first, attempted to hold them in; but as that only drew them up against the body of the coach, it increased the fright of the wheel horses until they became unmanageable. I told the coachman to keep them in the road, and let them go until they reached the bottom of the hill; he did so, and I assisted in holding him upon his seat, until we got to a piece of ascending ground where we were enabled to stop the team without any damage. We then lifted up the coach into its place, put a pole under and held it there until we reached a blacksmith's shop and got it repaired.

From Cumberland we took the cars to Baltimore, where we arrived at 6 p.m., and at 7 took steamboat to Frenchtown; from thence by railroad to Newcastle, and thence by steamboat to Philadelphia, where we arrived at 4 o'clock on the morning of the 5th.

The brethren took lodgings among the Saints in various parts of the city. I stopped with brother Peter Hess. During the afternoon there was a very severe storm and rain; much damage was done, houses unroofed, cellars filled with water, streams suddenly rose, the iron suspension bridge, the canal bridge, and fifty other bridges in the vicinity, were reported to be washed away, and thirty persons drowned.

Sunday, August 6—In the afternoon the Twelve met with about three hundred Saints in the Canaanite Church. I preached at considerable length, and said that a man or woman may ask of God, and get a witness and testimony from God concerning any work or messenger that is sent unto them; but if a person ask for a thing that does not concern him, such as governing the Church, as a member of the Church, inquiring concerning the duty of a Presiding Elder, what the Prophet or the Twelve ought to do, &c., he will not get an answer; if he does, it will not be from God.

I also remarked that if any in the Church had the fulness of the Melchizedec Priesthood, I did not know it. For any person to have the fulness of that Priesthood, he must be a king and a priest. A person may have a portion of that Priesthood the same as governors or judges of England have power from the king to transact business; but that does not make them kings of England. A person may be anointed king and priest long before he receives his kingdom.

Tuesday, August 8—In company with the Twelve and about 150 Saints, I left Philadelphia on an excursion on the Delaware River to Gloucester Point. We partook of a picnic dinner, and the day was spent in harmonious recreation. The following subject was taken up for discussion,—"Is the prosperity of any religious denomination a positive evidence that they are right?" Elder J. E. Page contended for the affirmative, and Elder J. M. Grant for the negative. Elder Page contended for his position very sharply and warmly. Elder Grant, in meeting his arguments, also manifested great earnestness in sustaining his position, and it appeared to the Saints like contention, and caused a dampness of feeling to rest upon the company.

At the end of the discussion I was called upon to decide the question, and perceiving the feeling among the Saints, I told them I was reminded of the anecdote of the negro's attempt at shooting a squirrel. His master having occasion to be absent from home, charged him to be sure and not meddle with his guns and ammunition; but no sooner had the master got fairly out of the way, when the negro's curiosity prompted him to try one of his master's guns; he accordingly took one down which had been loaded for some time, and went into the woods. He soon saw a squirrel, and crept up a hill behind a log and fired, but the gun being heavily charged, it knocked the negro over, and he rolled down the hill.

Upon gaining his equilibrium, and realizing his defeat, he looked up from the ground where he lay, and seeing the squirrel jumping from tree to tree as if conscious of victory, he cried,—"Well, well, cuffy, if you had been at the other end of the gun you would have known more about it." This excited laughter, in which all the company joined, and I then gave my decision, which was, that the prosperity of any people was not positive evidence of their being right.

After supper we returned by the steamer to Philadelphia.

Thursday, August 10—In company with Orson Pratt, Wilford Woodruff and Geo. A. Smith, I visited the State House and the Independence Hall, where the patriots signed the Declaration of Independence. We sat in the chair which John Hancock occupied when he signed that instrument. We saw a statue of Washington, the portraits of La Fayette and others, and the painting presented by Benjamin West to the city corporation, representing the situation of Paul and Barnabas when they were set apart to the ministry. This building was erected in 1733.

Friday, August 18—Brother Kimball accompanied me to Burlington, by steamer, and from thence by coach to Mount Holley, New Jersey, where we staid with Judge William Richards and preached.

Saturday, August 19—We rode with Judge Richards in his carriage to the Rising Sun, near Bordentown, where we attended a woods meetings, and met with brothers William Smith, J. E. Page, Geo. A. Smith and W. I. Appleby. Brother George A. and I staid over night with brother Atkinson, who lived in a very large frame house, said to have stood 150 years, which was so infested with bedbugs that we could not sleep. Brother George A. Smith gave it as his legal opinion that there were bedbugs there which had danced to the music at the battle of Trenton, as their heads were perfectly grey. We took our blankets and retreated to the further end of the room, and, as the bugs followed us, I lit a candle, and as they approached, caught them and burnt them in the candle, and thus spent the night.

Sunday, August 27—Attended Conference. The Twelve continued to occupy the time in preaching, morning, afternoon and evening. We blessed several children and administered to the sick. My health was feeble, never having wholly recovered from my last winter's illness.

Monday, August 28—I attended a Council of the Twelve this morning in relation to our future movements.

Tuesday, August 29—Went to the Arlington House, Long Island, in company with brother L. R. Foster, and had a pleasant visit with General James Arlington Bennett and family, with whom I staid all night.

Wednesday, August 30—Rode with General Bennett and brother Foster to Coney Island, where we bathed in the Atlantic. He requested me to baptize him, which I did, and we confirmed him and returned to his house, where we remained over night and spent a pleasant time.

Monday, September 4—Accompanied by H. C. Kimball, Orson Pratt, Geo. A. Smith and John E. Page, we crossed the Sound from New York to

Providence, Rhode Island; from thence to Boston, where we arrived on the 5th, and called on Mr. Tewkesbury, 82, Commercial-street, who directed us to brother Dudley's, sister Dudley received us kindly. The brethren were distributed among the Saints in Boston.

Saturday, Sunday and Monday, September 9, 10 and 11—Attended Conference at Boylston Hall, Boston; there were eight of our Quorum present. Elders and members were present from most of the Branches in New England. Many of the citizens also attended, some of whom were very rude and unmannerly in their behavior; it was evident that either their parents had not taught them good manners, or they had made bad use of their early education. I gave them several sharp reproofs for their meanness and unbecoming conduct, which I accompanied by lessons of instruction which, if heeded, would have a tendency to improve their manners materially; but I must say that I never saw more of a spirit of rowdyism manifest in any congregation where I ever preached, than was manifested in the good, Christian city of Boston. I visted Lowell and instructed the Saints.

I counselled Elder Addison Pratt to engage passages for himself, Elders Noah Rogers, Knowlton F. Hanks and B. F. Grouard, to the Pacific Islands, although they had not means wherewith to pay for them.

Wednesday, September 20—At the request and expense of Elder L. R. Foster, I visited Mr. O. S. Fowler, the phrenologist, at Marlborough Chapel, with Elders Kimball, Woodruff and Geo. A. Smith. He examined our heads and gave us charts. After giving me a very good chart for $1, I will give him a chart gratis. My opinion of him is, that he is just as nigh being an idiot as a man can be, and have any sense left to pass through the world decently; and it appeared to me that the cause of his success was the amount of impudence and self-importance he possessed, and the high opinion he entertained of his own abilities.

Friday, September 29—I left Boston for New York. Brother Woodruff and I staid at brother L. R. Foster's on the 30th.

Sunday, October 1—Proceeded to Philadelphia and attended meeting in the evening.

Tuesday, October 3—In company with Elders Kimball, Hyde, Woodruff, G. A. Smith and J. M. Grant, visited the Saints in Philadelphia; dined at brother J. B. Nicolson's, and in the evening partook of an oyster-supper at Mr. Jeffrey's, who undertook to get us drunk, but only succeeded in intoxicating himself. We consecrated several bottles of oil.

Wednesday, October 4—We left Philadelphia for Nauvoo by way of Pittsburgh, by canal and railway. While on the canal boat, which was crowded with well-behaved passengers, I was attacked by a Campbellite preacher, who was very anxious for a debate, and at the request of the passengers I delivered an address on the principles of our religion, which was very satisfactory to them, but discomfited the Campbellite preacher so much that he would not reply.

In the evening a gang of about a dozen Baptist ministers came on board, returning to Pittsburgh from a Conference. The Campbellite preacher told them there were "Mormons" on board; they immediately surrounded brother Geo. A.

Smith, and challenged him to debate, which he declined on the ground that it was not a proper place to discuss on religious subjects. They accused him of pretending to have the truth and not being willing to preach it to them. He proposed to preach in their churches in Pittsburgh any time they would open them, to which they would not consent. He then told them he considered that they not only refused to hear the truth themselves, but shut the gate against their congregations, like the Scribes and Pharisees in the days of Jesus. They commenced a tirade of abuse against him, half a dozen talking at once, and making use of every foul epithet their clerical learning had put them in possession of, and so crowded round him that he was prevented from going to supper, they having taken theirs before coming on board.

After supper, brother Kimball went to George A's. assistance, and told them that he had been a Baptist himself three weeks, but when he was a Baptist, Baptist ministers were gentlemen. Brother Kimball made several quotations knowing they were not from the Scriptures. The ministers would frequently interrupt him and say,—"That quotation is not in the Bible." Brother Kimball frequently turned to brother George A. and said,—"Will you find that passage?" He opened his Bible as if to search, when the ministers all remembered the passages.

I came up and inquired what was the meaning of this loud talk? The ministers answered that they had challenged the "Mormons" to debate, but they would not debate with them; they understood there had been gambling on the boat, and they wished to banish such wickedness. I told them if there had been gambling, the gamblers had minded their own business and behaved like gentlemen, for there had been no disorder on board, since starting from Philadelphia, except what was made by a tip-o-tail of a Campbellite minister; and if *they* pretended to be ministers of the Gospel of Jesus Christ, their conduct belied their profession, for they had abused Elder Smith ridiculously for an hour, and prevented him from getting his supper by blocking up the door, while he had submitted to their abuse with commendable patience; upon which the passengers told the captain, if he did not stop that gang of Baptist preachers from insulting the "Mormon" Elders who had shown themselves gentlemen all the way, they would put them in the canal. The captain then dispersed them.

We arrived at Pittsburgh on the 8th, at ten a.m., and at eleven shipped on board the *Rariton* for St. Louis. We found brother Bradford W. Elliot and two sisters on board.

We arrived at Cincinnatti on the 12th. The river being low, the boat lay on sand-bars some time. Sister Cobb, who accompanied us from Boston, had a child very sick, who died in Cincinnatti; she had it put in a tin coffin and took it with her. We were transferred to the steamer *Nautilus* which left on the 14th and reached St. Louis on the 19th, where we reshipped for Nauvoo, and arrived on the 22nd, and went into council with Joseph, Hyrum and others, when ordinances were administered to William Marks and wife.

Monday, October 23—With Elders H. C. Kimball and Geo. A. Smith I visited the Prophet Joseph, who was glad to see us. We paid him every cent of the means we had collected for the Temple and Nauvoo House. He taught us many principles illustrating the doctrine of celestial marriage, concerning which God had given him a revelation, July 12th.

Tuesday, November 7—Met in Council with the Twelve, when Elders P. P. Pratt, W. Woodruff, John Taylor and myself were chosen a committee to raise $500 to procure paper on which to print another edition of the *Doctrine and Covenants.*

Monday, November 27—I attended prayer-meeting in the evening at President Joseph Smith's. Bishop N. K. Whitney and wife were anointed.

Saturday, December 2—Met in the Assembly Room with Joseph, Hyrum and the Twelve, when the ordinances of endowment were administered to Elders Orson Hyde, Parley P. Pratt, W. Woodruff, Geo. A. Smith and Orson Spencer. We received instructions on the Priesthood from Joseph.

Sunday, December 10—I attended prayer-meeting in the Assembly Room. President Joseph Smith being absent, I presided and instructed the brethren upon the necessity of following our file leader, and our Savior, in all his laws and commandments, without asking any questions why they were so. I was followed by P. P. Pratt and others, who expressed their minds freely. Several sick persons were prayed for.

Monday, December 25—I married Dr. Levi Richards and Sarah Griffiths.

Thursday, December 28—I attended meeting with brother Woodruff; had a full house. I exhorted the Saints to be subject to the powers that be; said our sufferings are permitted that we may learn by experience the contrast between good and evil, in order to obtain power; "never suffer anger to find a seat in your breast, never get angry, treat all mildly, govern yourselves, control your passions, and it will give you power. When the Temple is done I expect we shall be baptized, washed, anointed, ordained, and receive the keys and signs of the Priesthood for our dead, that they may have a full salvation, and thus we shall be saviors on Mount Zion according to the Scriptures."

Saturday, December 30—I attended a meeting with the Quorum in the Assembly Room. President Joseph Smith preached on the principles of integrity, and showed that the lack of sustaining this principle led men to apostacy.

1844

Monday, January 1—Visited at brother E. D. Woolley's.

Wednesday, January 3—Attended the City Council. William Law came before the Council and complained that Joseph had administered a secret oath to the police and instructed them to kill him; but the police came forward and unanimously testified under oath to the falsity of Law's statements.

Friday, January 5—I went to La Harpe, and counselled with and preached to the Saints.

Saturday, January 13—Attended City Council.

Sunday, January 14—Preached in the city. In the evening attended prayer-meeting at the Assembly Room. My wife Mary Ann and I received our second anointing.

Monday, January 15—The Twelve having invited the brethren to cut and haul wood for President Joseph Smith, the citizens to the number of 200, with 40 teams turned out and cut 200 loads and drew 100 to his house.

Saturday, January 20—Met with the Quorum: Heber C. Kimball and his wife Vilate received their second anointing.

Sunday, January 21—I met in the Assembly Room with the Quorum, and administered to Parley P. Pratt his second anointing.

Monday, January 22—I met with the Quorum of the Twelve at my house, for prayer and conversation.

Thursday, January 25—The Quorum met at my house: Orson Hyde received his second anointing.

Friday, January 26—The Twelve met at my house: Orson Pratt received his second anointing.

Saturday, January 27—We met at the Assembly Room: Willard Richards and his wife Jenetta were sealed and received their second anointing.

Sunday, January 28—The Quorum met in the Assembly Room. Wilford Woodruff and his wife Phebe W. were sealed and received their second anointing.

Tuesday, January 30—The Quorum met at my house. John and Leonora

67

Taylor were sealed and anointed.

Wednesday, January 31—I met with the Quorum at my house. George A. and Bathsheba W. Smith were anointed, having been sealed on the 20th inst.

Tuesday, February 6—Partook of supper at brother John Taylor's, with Joseph, Hyrum, Sidney and the Twelve and their wives. The Twelve discussed the propriety of establishing a moot Congress for the purpose of investigating and informing ourselves on the rules of national intercourse, domestic policy and political economy. Joseph advised us not to do it, lest we might excite the jealousy of our enemies.

Tuesday, February 20—Met with the Presidency and Twelve, the subject of Lyman Wight's preaching to the Indians in Wisconsin was discussed; the matter was left to brother Wight's own judgment.

Wednesday, February 21—I met in Council. Brother Joseph directed the Twelve to select an exploring company to go to California to select a location for the settlement of the Saints: Jonathan Dunham, David Fulmer, Phinehas H. Young and David D. Yearsly volunteered to go, and Alphonzo Young, James Emmett, George D. Watt and Daniel Spencer were selected to go.

Friday, February 23—I met with the Presidency and Twelve in relation to the Rocky Mountain Expedition, eight more volunteers gave in their names. Brother Joseph gave instructions in relation to the fit out needed. It was agreed that the company should number twenty-five.

Saturday, February 24—Went to Knowlton Settlement on Bear Creek and preached twice; my brother Phinehas H. accompanied me. Information was received concerning the death of Ex-Governor Joshua Duncan of Illinois; and Reynolds of Mo., who shot himself through the head; they were two of the most inveterate enemies of the Saints.

Thursday, March 7—Attended a general meeting at the stand; there was a large assembly present. Brothers Joseph and Hyrum spoke at length, and I followed them and said,—

"I wish to speak upon the duty of lawyers, as they have been spoken of this morning.—They were first among the children of Israel to explain the laws of Moses to the common people.

I class myself as a lawyer in Israel. My business is to make peace among the people; and when any man who calls himself a lawyer, takes a course to break peace instead of making it, he is out of the line of his duty.—A lawyer's duty is to read the law well himself, then tell the people what it is, and let them act upon it, and keep peace; and let them receive pay like any laboring man.

It is desirable for justices of the peace, when men call for writs, to enquire into the merits of the case, and tell the parties how to settle it; and thus put down lawsuits. To cure lawing, let us pay attention to our own business.

When we hear a story, never tell it again; and it will be a perfect cure. If your brother mistreats you, let him alone; If your enemy cheats you, let him go; cease to deal with men who abuse you; if all men had taken the straight-forward course that some have, we should not have such disorderly men in our midst.

I have no objection to any man coming here, but I will have nothing to do with men who will abuse me at midnight and at noon day.—Our difficulties and persecutions have always arisen from men right in our midst.

It is the lust of individuals to rob us of everything, and to take advantage of divisions that may arise among us to build themselves up. I feel that I want every man should stay, and lift up holy hands without dubiety, wrath, or doubting.

To the men who own land here I would say, do not think you can sell your lands here, and then go off and spend it somewhere else in abusing the "Mormons." I tell you nay; for know it, ye people, that Israel is here, and they are the head, and not the tail; and the people must learn it; all those who have gone from us, have gone from the head to the tail.

The grand object before us is to build the Temple this season.

We have heard the effects of slander, and we want to cure and balm; and I carry one with me all the while, and I want all of you to do the same. I will tell you what it is, it is to mind our own business, and let others alone; and suffer wrong rather than do wrong; if any one takes your property away, let them alone, and have nothing to do with them.

A Spirit has been manifest to divide the Saints; it was manifest in the last election: it was said if they did not look out, the Saints on the flat, would beat the Saints on the hill.

Great God! how such a thing looks! that the Saints should be afraid of beating one another in the election, or being beat. I would ask who built up this city? Would steamboats have landed here, if the Saints had not come? Or could you, even the speculators, have sold your lands for anything here, if the Saints had not come? They might have sold for a few bear and wolf skins, but not for money.

If any of you wish to know how to have your bread fall butter side up, butter it on both sides, and then it will fall butter side up. Oppose this work and it will roll over you.

When did this work ever stop since it began? Never? The only thing the Saints now want to know is, what does the Lord want of us, and we are ready to do it.

Well, then, build the temple of the Lord—keep the Law of God, ye Saints, and the hypocrite and scoundrel will flee out of your midst, and tremble, for the fire of God will be too hot for them.

I expect the Saints are so anxious to work, and so ready to do right, that God has whispered to the Prophet, 'Build the Temple, and let the Nauvoo House alone at present.' I would not sue a man if he owed me five hundred or a thousand dollars, should he come to me and say he would not pay me."

Monday, March 11—Joseph commenced the organization of a Council for the purpose of taking into consideration the necessary steps to obtain redress for the wrongs which had been inflicted upon us by our persecutors, and also the best manner to settle our people in some distant and unoccupied territory where we could enjoy our civil and religious rights, without being subject to constant oppression and mobocracy, under the protection of our own laws subject to the Constitution.

The Council was composed of about fifty members, several of whom were not members of the Church.

We prepared several memorials to Congress for redress of grievances, and used every available means to inform ourselves of the unoccupied territory open to settlers.

We held a number of sessions, and investigated the principles upon which our national government is founded and the true foundation and principles of all governments.

Joseph Smith was appointed chairman, William Clayton, clerk, and Willard Richards, historian of the Council.

Tuesday, Wednesday and Thursday, March 12, 13 and 14—Attended special Councils.

Sunday, March 17—Attended prayer meeting.

Tuesday, March 19—I attended the Council of Fifty.

Thursday, March 21—I met in Council in the Assembly Room.

Friday, March 22—Attended prayer-meeting with the Prophet and the Twelve in my house.

Sunday, March 24—I attended meeting at the Stand and heard President Joseph Smith deliver an address concerning a conspiracy entered into by Chauncey L. Higbee, Dr. Robert D. Foster, Mr. Joseph H. Jackson, William and Wilson Law, and others for the purpose of taking his life.

Thursday, April 4—I attended Council.

Friday, April 5—I attended the dedication of the Masonic Hall.

Saturday, Sunday, Monday and Tuesday, April 6, 7, 8 and 9—I attended a special Conference in Nauvoo, the stand was occupied by the Presidency, the Twelve and others, among whom were eleven Lamanite chiefs and braves, it was estimated there were about 20,000 persons present, the Conference was addressed by Presidents Joseph, Hyrum and Sidney, myself and Elders H. C. Kimball, John Taylor and A. Lyman. The Prophet declared that all North and South America was the land of Zion. At the close of the Conference 344 Elders volunteered to go on missions.

Wednesday, April 10—I attended Council with the Twelve, arranging appointments for Conferences the ensuing season through the United States.

Thursday, April 11—Spent the day in the Council of fifty, we had an interesting time, and closed the Council with shouts of hosannah.

Wednesday, April 17—Spent the day in Council; William and Wilson Law and Robert D. Foster were cut off from the Church.

Monday, April 22—Rainy morning, in the afternoon we harnessed up our horses and rode on to the city plot, brother Woodruff and I bought a lot each, and started for home but on reaching brother William Draper's had to take shelter for the night in consequence of a tremendous storm of hail and rain.

Tuesday, May 21—I started on my mission to the East in company with Elders H. C. Kimball and L. Wight on board the steamer Osprey; Captain Anderson. On our way to St. Louis brother Wight preached.

Wednesday, May 22—We arrived in St. Louis; I preached in the evening; the Branch numbered about 700 members.

Thursday, May 23—We left St. Louis on board the Louis Phillippe Captain J. J. Worman, with about two hundred passengers; many of them were from the Osprey, I was called upon to deliver a lecture on the principles of the Church, which allayed some prejudice which had been manifested against the Elders on board.

Friday, May 24—William Smith preached: the passengers treated us respectfully: good captain and mate.

Wednesday, June 5—Arrived in Warren and took on a large company going to Akron to an abolition convention, some of whom manifested a spirit to put down every body but themselves.

Thursday, June 6—Brothers F. D. Richards, L. Brooks and I found brother Salmon Gee's family in Shalorsville; they desired us to remain with them over night, which we did, and addressed the people in the town house in the evening, on Joseph Smith's views of the powers and policy of the government.

Friday, June 7—Lawyers and doctors called to converse with us, and obtain copies of General Smith's "Views." Afternoon, with brother Richards I went to Mantua, where we met brother Lorenzo Snow and others. We proceeded to Hiram and held a meeting in sight of the house where Joseph and Sidney were dragged out by the heels and tarred and feathered.

Arrived in Kirtland on the 8th; found my brother John Young and my sister Nancy Kent well.

Sunday, June 9—I preached in the Temple in the morning, and brother F. D. Richards in the afternoon. I lectured in the evening on the subject of the location of Nauvoo; the Saints were dead and cold to the things of God.

Thursday, June 27—Spent the day in Boston with brother Woodruff, who accompanied me to the railway station as I was about to take cars to Salem. In the evening, while sitting in the depot waiting, I felt a heavy depression of Spirit, and so melancholy I could not converse with any degree of pleasure. Not knowing anything concerning the tragedy enacting at this time in Carthage jail, I could not assign my reasons for my peculiar feelings.

Tuesday, July 9—I heard to-day, for the first time, the rumors concerning the death of Joseph and Hyrum.

Tuesday, July 16—While at brother Bement's house in Peterboro', I heard a letter read which brother Livingston had received from Mr. Joseph Powers, of Nauvoo, giving particulars of the murder of Joseph and Hyrum. The first thing which I thought of was, whether Joseph had taken the keys of the kingdom with him from the earth; brother Orson Pratt sat on my left; we were both leaning back on our chairs. Bringing my hand down on my knee, I said the keys of the kingdom are right here with the Church.

Received a letter from brother Woodruff confirming the news of the death of the Prophets. I started for Boston; staid at Lowell all night.

Wednesday, July 17—Arrived in Boston; found brothers Kimball and Woodruff.

Thursday, July 18—I met in Council with Elders H. C. Kimball, O. Pratt and W. Woodruff, preparatory to returning to Nauvoo.

Sunday, July 21—Elder Kimball and I attended meeting in Boston and preached to the Saints.

Tuesday, July 23—We attended meeting in the evening and ordained thirty-two Elders. Lyman Wight (for whom we had waited in Boston about a week) arrived.

Wednesday, July 24—I left Boston for Nauvoo in company with brothers Kimball and Wight, and on our arrival at Albany were joined by brothers Orson Hyde, Orson Pratt and W. Woodruff, who had just arrived from New York. We continued to journey night and day by railroad, stage and steamboat via Buffalo, Detroit, Chicago and Galena, and arrived in Nauvoo on the 6th day of August, where we were received with joy by our families and friends.

Wednesday, August 7—Attended meeting at the Seventies' Hall with the Twelve and High Council, where we heard Sidney Rigdon tell his story and deliver the message he said he had for us. I followed him and showed the brethren the errors and follies which brother Rigdon manifested on the occasion.

Thursday, August 8—I attended a meeting of all the authorities of the Church at Nauvoo, when the Twelve Apostles were sustained at the Presidency of the Church, and we organized and set in order the Church as far as was necessary for the furtherance and prosperity of the kingdom, as recorded in the Church History.

Friday, August 9—I met in council with Elders Heber C. Kimball, Parley P. Pratt, Orson Pratt, Wilford Woodruff, Willard Richards, George A. Smith, Amasa M. Lyman and eleven others at my house.

On motion of Elder Heber C. Kimball, Bishop Newel K. Whitney and George Miller were appointed to settle the affairs of the late Trustee-in-Trust, Joseph Smith, and be prepared to enter upon their duties as Trustees of the Church of Jesus Christ of Latter-day Saints.

The Nauvoo House committee were instructed to wind up their business and report.

Patriarch John Smith [local] had the privilege of appointing another president at Macedonia in his stead and locating in Nauvoo at his option.

Conversation ensued relative to the affairs and liabilities of the church and the building of the Nauvoo House.

Sunday, August 11—Forenoon meeting. At the stand Elder Lyman Wight preached about leading a company away into the wilderness. Afternoon, Elder Wm. Hyde preached. At 3 p.m. a few of the authorities met at my house to pray for deliverance from the mob.

Wednesday, August 14—I attended meeting of the Twelve, Temple and Nauvoo House Committees and the stonecutters for the Temple at the Seventies' Hall. Agreed to raise the wages of the windlass men to $1.50 per day. The meeting terminated in a feeling of renewed determination to prosecute the work upon the Temple.

Thursday, August 15—The Quorum of the Twelve Apostles met at my house. Many matters were talked over.

The council resolved to bear off the kingdom of God in all the world, in truth, honesty, virtue and holiness, and to continue to set their faces as a flint against every species of wickedness, vice and dishonesty in all its forms.

I met in a prayer circle with the Twelve and a few others in the afternoon and prayed for the sick.

Saturday, August 17—In company with Elders Kimball, Woodruff and others I went on to the Temple walls, viewed the country, encouraged the workmen and counseled Brother Woodruff in relation to his mission to England.

Afternoon, spent considerable time in the Tithing Office.

Sunday, August 18—I preached to the saints in the morning. The following synopsis of my discourse and minutes of the meeting were reported by Elder Woodruff:

I have learned some things I did not know when I came home. I discover a disposition in the sheep to scatter, now the shepherd is taken away. I do not say that it will never be right for this people to go from here or scatter abroad; but I do say wait until the time comes, or until you are counseled to do so. The report has gone forth through the city that the Twelve have a secret understanding with those men who are going away and taking companies with them, that they shall take away all they can; and although the Twelve will blow it up in public, yet privately they wish it to go on, but if they were the last words I had to say before going into the eternal worlds I would swear by the Holy Trinity that such a report is utterly false, and there is not a word of truth in it. There is no man who has any right to lead away one soul out of this city by the consent of the Twelve, except Lyman Wight and George Miller, they have had the privilege of taking the 'Pine Company' where they pleased, but not another soul has the consent of the Twelve to go with them. There is no man who has any liberty to lead away people into the wilderness from this church, or to lead them anywhere else, by the consent of the Twelve or the church, except in the case above named—and I tell you in the name of Jesus Christ that if Lyman Wight and George Miller take a course contrary to our counsel and will not act in concert with us, they will be damned and go to destruction—and if men will not stop striving to be great and exalted, and lead away parties from us, thereby weakening our hands, they will fall and not rise again—and I will destroy their influence in this church with the help of God and my brethren. I wish you to distinctly understand that the counsel of the Twelve is for every family that does not belong to the Pine Company to *stay here in Nauvoo*, and build up the Temple and get your endowments; do not scatter; 'united we stand, divided we fall'. It has been whispered about that all who go into the wilderness with Wight and Miller will get their endowments, but they cannot give an endowment in the wilderness. If we do not carry out the plan Joseph has laid down and the pattern he has given for us to work by, we cannot get any further endowment—I want this to sink deep into your hearts that you may remember it. If you stir up the flame of dissension, will you get an endowment? No! You get a party to run here and another there, to divide our strength, and weaken our hands, and our enemies will flock around us and destroy us—in that case you will not get your endowments, but will sink and not rise;—go to hell and not to the bosom of Abraham. Do the people leave here because they are afraid? Are you cowards? Do you fear those who have power to kill the body only? If you leave this place for fear of the mob, before God tells you to go, you will have no place of rest, but you will flee from place to place and go like the Jews, until God raises up some other people to redeem you, for if the devil scares you from this place he will scare you from all other places. Let no man go from this place but the pine country brethren, but stay here and sow, plant, build, and put your plowshares into the prairies: one plowshare will do more to drive off the mob than two guns. Let us stay here where the bones of Joseph, Hyrum, Samuel, Don Carlos, and Father Smith are. While Joseph was alive he said 'If I am slain in battle or fall by the hands of my enemies I want my body brought to Nauvoo and laid in the tomb I have prepared.' I would rather have the dead body of the Prophet than some men who are alive and I would rather have the clothes of the Prophet stuffed with straw for president of the United States than any man whose name is now before the nation as a candidate, for the straw would not do any harm.

We want to build the Temple in this place, if we have to build it as the Jews built the walls of the Temple in Jerusalem, with a sword in one hand and the trowel in the other. How easily some men are scared! I have not been frightened yet, and I know of other men who have not.

Do you suppose the mouth of God is closed, to be opened no more unto us? If this were the case I would not give the ashes of a rye straw for the salvation of the church. If God has ceased to speak by the Holy Ghost, or to give revelation, there is no salvation; but this is not the case.

There seems to be a disposition by many to leave Nauvoo and go into the wilderness or somewhere else. Suppose we should all go into the wilderness and then ask God to give us an endowment, and he should ask if we were driven from Nauvoo, and who drove us? The devil drove us would be the answer; he might say, well, did you not know that I had power over the devil? Yes, but one said I would not give a jackknife for all Nauvoo, and another said, I would not give a pair of mules for the best farm in Hancock county and I was afraid; would the Lord give an endowment to a people who would be frightened away from their duty?

Concerning those who are wishing to lead away parties contrary to counsel, I would not wish them damned worse, than to have a company after their own liking go with them, for they will soon quarrel among themselves; and if we should go to the wilderness and ask the Lord to give us an endowment, he might ask us, saying, Did I not give you rock in Nauvoo to build the Temple with? Yes. Did I not through my providence furnish men to quarry and cut the stone and prepare it for the building? Yes. Did I not give you means to build the Temple there? Yes. Very well, had you died in Nauvoo, on the walls of the Temple, or in your fields, I would have taken you to myself and raised up men to officiate for you, and you would have enjoyed the highest glory. Did you make a sacrifice by tithing? No. Well I do not wonder you did not believe I had power over the devil.

Such may go away but I want to have the faithful stay here to build the Temple and settle the city. We shall require the tenth of all your property as a tithing for the building of the Temple and for the poor and for the priesthood. I want my support and living by the church hereafter, so that I can give my whole time to the business of the church. I have always supported myself heretofore in all my travels and labors, with the aid of my brethren.

Joseph has always been preserved from his enemies, until now, but he has sealed his testimony with his blood, and his testament is now in force. While the testator lived it was all in his hands, but now he is dead.

There is no remission of sins without the shedding of blood.* You will soon wake up and know things as they are—there has been a great debt paid; there will be no need of more blood of the saints being shed at present, by and by you will understand and see that all is right.

Woe! woe! woe! unto all who have shed the blood of the saints and the Lord's anointed. It must needs be that offenses come, but woe unto that man through whom they come.

To those who want to go away from this place, I would say wait until the time comes. I will give you the key. North and South America is Zion and as soon as the Temple is done and you get your endowments you can go and build up stakes, but do not be in haste, wait until the Lord says go. If you have the Spirit of God you can discover right from wrong—when all is right with the priesthood and a man rises up and speaks by the Spirit of God and just right, all will say, Amen, but when a man rises up and talks as smooth as oil, if he is not right, there will be many queries about it, it will not edify the body [i. e. the people]. I give this as a key. You may go all over North and South America and build up stakes when the time comes. The whole continent of America must be organized into districts and presiding elders appointed over each district: the time has come when all things must be set in order.

I wish the saints to let their bickerings cease, and a strict order of things be introduced: we shall not harbor blacklegs, counterfeiters and bogus-makers; we know all about them, they have been in our midst long enough. I advise all the saints to have no dealings with such men; let them alone. The time has come that they should be wiped out of our midst, let the ungodly dealers alone; and as to the doctors who are in our midst, who are our enemies, I say let them alone, for I have no doubt but that three to one who have died in this place had a doctor. I say woe unto you lawyers, for your whole study is to put down truth and put a lie in its stead. I want the lawyers to know that we have common sense. They want to make you believe that when you spell 'baker' it means cider or whiskey. Now let the lawyers and doctors alone and leave off bitterness and evil speaking, and you will build the Temple and get an endowment. All ye lawyers go away and let us alone and when we get full of the devil and want you, we will send for you, we may then have a more convenient season.

I want to say to all who profess to be saints, do not harbor blacklegs, counterfeiters and bogus-makers, wipe them away; it is time to carry out the design of our Prophet; do cease to employ doctors, lawyers, and merchants who will empty your purses and then mob you. Store your grain in Nauvoo for you will

*Heb. ix:22.

want it here to eat while you are building the Temple. I say to the hands on the Temple, be united; and to the Temple Committee, do not turn away any person because he is an Englishman, Scotchman, Irishman or of any other nation; but employ every man you can and build the Temple and your homes. I would rather pay out every cent I have to build up this place and get an endowment, if I were driven the next minute without anything to take with me. As to the doctors, let them go. I can prove that a doctor in this place doctored a woman that was in the family way, and did not know it until she was delivered, and both woman and child died, and if you will employ them, you will all die.

There is a distinction between the law of the land and the law of the church. You have the privilege of keeping all shops that do not come in contact with the law of the state, county, or city; so I will evade the law of the land, says the dealer, and give away whiskey and sell a little tobacco or something else and charge enough for both; but the law of the church will reach such men and if they are members they should be cut off. I dreamed that I saw a fruit tree in which I went in search of fruit. I soon discovered that some of the main branches on the top were dead. It seemed to me necessary to cut off the dead branches in order to save the tree so I told some person to help me cut them off. The person stepped on to a large green limb and was afraid it would break so I put my shoulder under it and held it up till the dead branch was cut off, the green limb cracked but did not break. After all the dry limbs were cut off the wounds healed up and the tree grew finely.

Let us cut off the dead branches of the church that good fruit may grow and a voice will soon be heard, go and build up Zion and the Temple of the Lord.

Monday, August 19—Elder Willard Richards called on Emma Smith, widow of the Prophet, for the new translation of the *Bible*: She said she did not feel disposed to give it up at present.

Tuesday, August 27—I met with the officers of the Nauvoo Legion in council; six of the Apostles were present. The council decided that they would carry out all the views of our martyred Prophet: the brethren felt very spirited on the subject.

Wednesday, August 28—Elders Wilford Woodruff, Dan Jones, and Hiram Clark with their families started this afternoon for England.

Thursday, August 29—The Quorum of the Twelve Apostles met at my house, having notified Elders Rigdon and Marks to attend. This was fast day and I attended meeting at the stand and laid hands on several of the sick.

Friday, August 30—In company with my brethren of the Twelve, Father John Smith and many others I visited at Father Mikesell's, partook of dinner and an abundance of peaches from his orchard: the family were glad to see us and we spent a pleasant day. Many of the brethren in the city being apprehensive that we might fall into the hands of the mob, took their guns and went a 'hunting' around and below Mikesell's along the timbered bluffs on the Mississippi River.

Saturday, August 31—Visiting the sick. Afternoon attended general meeting of the officers of the Nauvoo Legion. I was unanimously elected lieutenant-general and Charles C. Rich, major-general of the Nauvoo Legion.

Evening, attended a school meeting.

Sunday, September 1—I went to the stand in the forenoon. Elder Sidney Rigdon preached. His discourse was complicated and somewhat confused; he said he had all things shown to him from this time to the winding-up scene, or the great battle of Gog and Magog; there were great things to take place, but he did not tell what the saints should do to save themselves.

I met with the high priests' quorum in the afternoon and spoke at some length to the brethren.

Tuesday, September 3—I had an interview with Brother Sidney Rigdon. He said he had power and authority above the Twelve Apostles and did not consider himself amenable to their counsel. In the evening, the Twelve had an interview with Brother Rigdon, who was far from feeling an interest with the Twelve. His license was demanded, which he refused to give up, and said the church had not been led by the Lord for a long time, and he should come out and expose the secrets of the church.

Wednesday, September 4—Elder Willard Richards sick. The Twelve Apostles and a few others met at my house in the evening and prayed for the preservation of the church and ourselves; and that the Lord might bind up the apostates and preserve the honest in heart.

Thursday, September 5—Brother Wm. Marks came to see me in relation to President Rigdon and his revelation. Afternoon, attended public prayer meeting and exposed the false prophets. Evening, Elder Hyde preached in the Masonic Hall on Elder Rigdon's conduct since his return to Nauvoo.

Friday, September 6—Elder Heber C. Kimball and I visited the sick till two p.m.

Brother Alonzo W. Whitney informed us of the proceedings of Elder Rigdon and others.

Elder Orson Pratt preached in the Seventies' Hall.

Saturday, September 7—Accompanied by Elder Kimball I waited upon Elder John P. Greene, and attended to ordinances for him: he was on his deathbed.*

Leonard Soby was disfellowshipped by the high council for following Elder Rigdon.

Monday, September 9—I attended council with the Quorum of the Twelve at Elder Heber C. Kimball's; thence I went in company with Elder Kimball through the city, attending to business and visiting Elders John P. Greene and Parley P. Pratt who were sick.

Elder Heber C. Kimball and George A. Smith labored diligently with James Emmett that he might be persuaded to desist from his intended course of taking away a party of misguided saints into the wilderness.

Tuesday, September 10—Elder John P. Greene died.

I attended council with the Twelve and others when orders to the mob given by Colonel Levi Williams were read. General Deming [sheriff of Hancock

*These were doubtless the usual ordinances for the sick and dedicating him to the Lord.

county] said he did not consider that a mob large enough to do any mischief could be raised.

Evening, attended a meeting of officers of the Legion, when a resolution was passed to build an arsenal and gunsmith's shop: one hundred and thirty dollars was subscribed towards the erection of the building.

Friday, September 13—I went to the parade ground where the officers were drilling. Jonathan Dunham was elected brigadier-general of the second cohort of the Nauvoo Legion: I addressed the officers.

In company with Brother Heber C. Kimball and his wife, Vilate, I visited Mother [Lucy] Smith.

There are many reports concerning the movements of the mob; who are making preparations for what they call a 'wolf hunt' on the 26th and 27th of this month; but the general apprehension is that they design coming and attempting to drag some more authorities of the church out to Carthage to murder them.

Saturday, September 14—In company with Elders Heber C. Kimball and George A. Smith I called on Sister Hyrum Smith.

Elder Amasa M. Lyman being very sick and reported to be dying, Brothers Kimball, George A. [Smith] and I retired to my upper room and prayed for him; he was healed from that very hour.

Monday, September 16—At six a.m., accompanied by Elder Heber C. Kimball, Generals C. C. Rich, Jonathan Dunham and other officers of the Legion, I went to the ground secured for the arsenal, near the Temple. We uncovered our heads and lifted our hands to heaven and I dedicated the ground, by prayer, to the God of the armies of Israel. I took the spade and broke the ground for the cellar.

Wednesday, September 18—It was voted that the profits arising from the publication of the *Book of Mormon* and *Book of Doctrine and Covenants* be devoted to the priesthood for the building up of the kingdom of God.

Thursday, September 19—At home waiting upon my wife who was very sick. The saints called upon me for counsel and direction.

Friday, September 20—Attending to ordinances in behalf of the saints, and laying hands on the sick. The Lord is with me continually.

Saturday, September 21—I visited the saints accompanied by Elders Kimball and Lyman. Received a letter from Elder Jedediah M. Grant relating the slanderous course pursued by Elder B. Winchester against the Twelve, and informing us that at the Philadelphia conference he refused to vote to sustain the Twelve asserting that they gagged him while on his trial at Nauvoo.

Sunday, September 22—I preached to the congregation of the saints on the priesthood: had a good time.

Monday, September 23—The first capital weighing about two tons was raised on to the walls of the Temple.

This evening, Sheriff Deming came into Nauvoo for a Mormon *posse* to take Sharp and Williams. The Twelve decided that it was imprudent to take [use] Mormons for that purpose and advised him accordingly.

Received some arms and ammunition from the brethren in St. Louis, by the hands of Thomas McKenzie.

Thursday, September 26—I attended a council held at my house. Benjamin Winchester and wife were cut off from the church.

The Quincy militia escorted about town by the Nauvoo Band.

Held a council at the Temple Office and appointed four watchmen to watch the Temple tonight, some of Wight's company have come to town and they report that they have come to deface the capitals, and burn the lumber round the Temple.

Friday, September 27—This was the day set apart by the anti-Mormons for the great 'wolf hunt'.

A little before noon the governor and two of his aids arrived in Nauvoo. After viewing the Temple they went down towards the Mansion. About two p.m. his troops marched into the city, about five hundred in number. They had three six-pounders with them, two of which were brass. The whole company halted on the first vacant block on the flat and tarried there some time. Many of the men visited the font and the Temple; they appeared astonished, but were civil.

I received my commission as lieutenant-general, and Charles C. Rich his as major-general.

Governor Ford said he had come to execute the law and was ready to proceed against the murderers of Joseph and Hyrum Smith as fast as the people get out writs. He issued a Proclamation offering a reward of two hundred dollars each for the arrest of Sharp, Jackson and Williams, and announced his intention of taking all the arms from this part of the state. His troops numbered four hundred and seventy, all that would volunteer in nine counties to help maintain the supremacy of the laws in Hancock and bring murderers to justice.

Saturday, September 28—I reviewed the Legion. The governor, General J. J. Hardin and staff were present. Appropriate salutes were fired on the occasion.

The Legion made a creditable and soldier-like appearance. Several of the staff officers of the Legion appeared in uniform without arms, which the governor regarded as a hint to remind him of his disarming the Legion previous to the massacre of Joseph and Hyrum Smith.

Four p.m., the governor marched his militia force about three miles down the river and camped in the woods.

The governor called upon General George Miller to furnish boats to convey his command in the night to Warsaw, who after making the necessary arrangements, accompanied by Cyrus H. Wheelock, two other brethren and one of the governor's officers, started to inform his Excellency that the boats were ready. On reaching the neighborhood of the camp the officer requested the brethren to wait until he would go in and speak to the governor; after waiting a few minutes the brethren attempted to go in and see the governor for themselves but were prevented by a sentinel who cocked his gun. Soon after three rounds of musketry were discharged by a detachment of the governor's troops, the bullets whistled all around Brother Miller and party, one ball taking effect upon the sentinel who cried out very loudly, 'I am a dead man': the officers subsequently remarked that they had forgotten to call in their sentinel. Brother Miller and party rendered the wounded sentinel all the assistance they could until comrades from the camp came to his relief, when Brother Miller learned the boats were not wanted; whereupon, accompanied by his party he started back for Nauvoo, when they got a few rods off twenty or thirty guns were fired after them; some of the balls skimmed the road near their feet; but they were preserved by the hand of God.

Sunday, September 29—I made a few remarks endorsing the sisters' penny subscription for the purpose of procuring glass and nails for the Temple and requested the saints to prepare themselves to entertain the elders who may be in attendance at conference.

Afternoon, I went to the Seventies' Hall and ordained the sixty-three members of the First Quorum of the Seventy to be presidents over the quorums from the second to the tenth inclusive.

Considerable sickness reported throughout the city and many deaths.

Monday, September 30—I breakfasted at Elder Heber C. Kimball's. We laid hands on the sick and visited Mother Smith.

Evening, went to the military school held at the Masonic Hall. Afterwards attended council with the Twelve and concluded to use our influence to prevent the brethren and sisters from attending the ball which William Marks, landlord of the Nauvoo Mansion was making arrangements for; the same to come off on Wednesday evening in the dining room of the Mansion, which was still stained with the blood which flowed from Joseph and Hyrum, as their bodies lay in said room preparatory to burial.

Tuesday, October 1—Evening, attended a meeting of the quorum for prayer: a very interesting session.

Wednesday, October 2—Governor Ford disbanded his troops. Sharp and Williams have given themselves up and gone to Quincy under a contract with the governor.

Friday, October 4—I went up to the Temple in the forenoon. Attended council with the Twelve, the bishops and the Temple Committee at Sister Emma Smith's and expressed our feelings and intentions to her.

Tuesday, October 15—Accompanied by Elder Heber C. Kimball and my brother Lorenzo D. Young I started for Ottoway. We traveled to Ramus and stayed with Brother Erastus Bingham, where Parley P. Pratt joined us.

A meeting of delegates from Trades Committees was held in the Masonic Hall, Nauvoo, John Taylor chairman; at which it was reported that enough had been made manifest to ensure the practicability of making Nauvoo a great manufacturing depot.

Wednesday, October 16—Accompanied by the brethren before named I traveled to Brother Justus Ame's near Galesburg, forty miles. Next day, we traveled to LaFayette and stayed with Brother Austin Grant, and on the following day traveled to Providence encountering a wet snowstorm from which I took cold and suffered from diarrhea: we stayed at a tavern.

Saturday, October 19—We drove forty-four miles and arrived at Ottoway.

Sunday, October 20—We held two meetings at Brother Busard's.

Elders Heber C. Kimball and Parley P. Pratt and I preached: we had a profitable time.

The seventies met in their hall at Nauvoo.

After ordaining presidents who had been selected to preside over the quorums, a call was made by request of the major-general for thirty wagons and teams to be in readiness at the hall by daylight tomorrow, with three days' provisions and horse feed sufficient for the journey. This call was made to convey witnesses to Carthage in safety, and for protection during the trials at court: as two of our best men were murdered in Carthage in June and that too under the faith and pledge of the state and since caution is the parent of safety, it was deemed inadvisable to venture upon the pledges and promises of others.

Monday, October 21—About one hundred and fifty brethren went from Nauvoo to Carthage early this morning and encamped near Crooked Creek; although they exhibited no arms their appearance created much excitement. The company consisted of the city council, police and those concerned in abating the *Nauvoo Expositor* nuisance with the witnesses and others who had business in Carthage: by encamping they avoided the necessity of paying hotel bills to enemies and the risk of being murdered in their beds.

Wednesday, October 23—In company with Elder Heber C. Kimball, Parley P. Pratt and Lorenzo D. Young, I called the brethren together as a conference of the Norwegian branch. We taught the principles of the gospel to them and appointed George P. Dykes, high priest, to preside over the Norwegian branch and the saints in that vicinity of country, and ordained Reuben Miller a bishop.

We bought one hundred acres of land from Brothers Goodman and Anderson, and thereupon laid out a city. We selected the ground for a meeting-house and drove the southeast corner stake. We called the city Norway and dedicated it to the Lord. Evening, we ordained Brother Phillip Hammond Busard a high priest and set him apart as a counselor to Brother Dykes.

Thursday, October 24—We left Ottoway and drove forty-three miles to Brother Parley P. Pratt's farm. We found his brother, Anson Pratt, and family well: they were glad to see us.

The brethren who went to Carthage returned home to Nauvoo. The members of the city council who were not indicted by the grand jury, were released from their bonds; eleven brethren were indicted for riot: the judge and attorney advised the brethren to return to Nauvoo to allay the excitement. The trials are continued until next spring term of court: the Nauvoo Legion is a terror.

Brother Hyrum Smith prophesied that the governor would call upon the Nauvoo Legion to maintain the supremacy of the law, which has been fulfilled according to [by] the governor's late order.

Willard Richards was subpoenaed to appear before the grand jury, but being unable and unwilling to go to Carthage application was made to the court to get an attachment for his person, the attorney averring that it was necessary to have someone to prove that Joseph and Hyrum were dead, and he presumed that Richards was in possession of that knowledge; the court however refused the attachment as they considered that fact could be proved without bringing a sick man out of his bed. The Twelve all left Nauvoo during the court except Elder Willard Richards who was confined to his bed, and Elder George A. Smith who gave such counsel as the excitement of the times required.

Monday, October 28—I returned to Nauvoo with my brethren, we found our families well. During our absence it was unknown to the people whither we had gone.

The Neighbor announced that true bills of indictment had been found against several persons of Hancock county, for the murder of Joseph and Hyrum Smith on the 27th of June last. Among the most conspicuous are, Colonel Levi Williams, Thomas C. Sharp, Mark Aldrich and Jacob C. Davis. The latter a senator in the legislature of Illinois.

I attended a council with my brethren of the Twelve, the Trustees, the Temple Committee and Brother William Weeks the architect at the Temple Office, settling the differences existing between the Temple Committee and Brother Weeks.

Friday, November 8—I went out to Fisher's Brick Yard and laid hands on the sick.

Saturday, November 9—I met with the city council. They passed an ordinance to prohibit the vending of spirituous liquors in the city under a penalty of not less than $25.00.

Sunday, November 10—I preached about two hours to the saints at the meeting ground; many present; had a good time.

Tuesday, November 12—I went to the Temple; called on Elders Kimball and Richards and found them recovering. I attended and addressed a meeting of the various trades of the city; a committee of three were appointed to see to the erection of a cotton factory, inasmuch as the machinery could be obtained. Elders John Taylor and Orson Spencer addressed the meeting.

Wednesday, December 25—I spent an agreeable time at Brother Coolidge's, in company with Elders Heber C. Kimball, George A. Smith, A. M. Lyman, John Taylor and their ladies. The band was in attendance. We partook of a substantial dinner; after which I made a few remarks expressive of my good feelings and love to my brethren. I remarked that the Lord would never suffer us to overcome our enemies while we cherished feelings of revenge, when we prevailed over our enemies it must be from a sense of duty and not of revenge.

Friday, December 27—I went to the Trustee's Office.

Evening, there was a meeting in the Seventies' Hall of the city council, the high council and leading authorities of the church.

Governor Ford's special message to the legislature was read. It was a very meager attempt to excuse himself from participation in the assassination of Joseph and Hyrum Smith, being full of misrepresentations, exaggerations and contemptible falsehoods.

1845

Wednesday, January 1—Accompanied by Elder Heber C. Kimball I went to Bishop David Evans' ward south of Nauvoo City, and solemnized a marriage.

In company with Elders Heber C. Kimball, Orson Pratt, George A. Smith, Willard Richards and Amasa M. Lyman, I spent the afternoon and evening, with our wives, at Hiram Kimball's; had a pleasant time: the propriety of settling a new country was discussed.

Sunday, January 5—I went to the stand and addressed the saints on the necessity of having more order and putting down iniquity, and exhorted the brethren to rise up *en masse*, and put down the thieving, swearing, gambling, bogus-making, retailing spirituous liquors, bad houses, and all abominations practiced in our midst by our enemies, who, after they could not live among us any longer would go out to the world and publish that these things were practiced by us. I severely rebuked the civil authorities of the city for their want of energy in the discharge of their duty, and censured parents and guardians for not keeping their children from prowling round the streets at night; and remarked that if we did not as a people uproot such things, they would uproot us, and we would have to leave before we had done the things the Lord had commanded us to do. Elder Kimball followed me, treating on the same subject: a large congregation—pleasant day.

Tuesday, January 7—I met in council with my brethren of the Twelve. The subject of sending a company to California was further discussed; also the propriety of sending to the branches of the church abroad for teams to help the expedition.

Wednesday, January 8—I attended a meeting which was got up by my brother, Joseph Young, of all our relatives and connections. Elder Phineas Richards, John Haven, myself, Joseph Young, Heber C. Kimball, John Taylor, John Smith and Lucy Smith, mother of the Prophet, severally addressed the meeting.

Evening, I met with the Twelve, bishops, high council, and city officials in relation to the election of city officers: the members of the Quorum of the Twelve present declined accepting any nomination.

Friday, January 10—The Twelve, the Temple Committee, the surveyors (Sherwood and Ripley) and Bishop Whitney, Trustee, met with the Committee of the Nauvoo Manufacturing Association respecting erecting the contemplated dam in the Mississippi.

The lesser priesthood met at the Music Hall. Bishop N. K. Whitney presided. He stated the object of the meeting was to fill up the quorums in order that the saints might be visited by the lesser priesthood; he recommended that the bishops establish in their respective wards the manufacturing of palm leaf and straw hats, willow baskets and other business that children are capable of learning, that they may be raised to industrious habits; he further stated his determination to have a feast prepared for the poor that their hearts might be made to rejoice. Bishops Edward Hunter, Isaac Higbee and others made some very interesting remarks. Bishop Whitney gave the lesser priesthood a faithful charge in relation to ferreting out iniquity. Four priests and ten teachers were ordained.

Saturday, January 11—City council met and transacted much business. Passed an ordinance authorizing and licensing Brigham Young to run a ferry across the Mississippi at Nauvoo in place of Joseph Smith, martyred.

With Elders Taylor, Richards and Phelps, I spent the evening writing an epistle to the churches on the gathering.

Wednesday, January 15—I went to the Temple, afterwards to the stone quarry; Brother Albert P. Rockwood reported sixty-two hands and six teams engaged today in the quarry.

Evening, went to the Seventies' Hall. The brethren of the Twelve, the high council, Trustees-in-Trust, many high priests and seventies were present. The elders appointed on missions were assigned to their respective districts. Elder Kimball instructed the elders to be fathers and not masters, and to be wise in their requirements of tithing from the saints abroad. I gave some general instructions, and counseled the elders to gather all to Nauvoo who could leave their families and especially the young men to help complete the Temple. Heavy thunder, lightning and rain.

Evening of Friday, January 17—Elder H. C. Kimball, John Taylor and George A. Smith met with me in my upper room: we counseled and prayed.

Monday, January 20—I called on Elder Willard Richards and found him engaged on the History.

Tuesday, January 21—Forenoon, with Elders Kimball and Richards at the Historian's Office. Wrote a letter to my brother, Phineas H., with counsel for the saints in Kirtland to come to Nauvoo, that all who have faith in the latter-day work may be united with us in building the Temple.

Evening, I met in council with Elders Heber C. Kimball, Willard Richards, George A. Smith and Amasa M. Lyman; we wrote to Elder Jedediah M. Grant, Philadelphia, counseling him to forward all the young men and other available help he could to build the Temple.

Thursday, January 23—I wrote to Elder Ezra T. Benson: called at the Trustees' Office; went to the Temple; called at Elder Richards', Kimball's,

Taylor's and Hyde's. Found Brother John Scott at my house who said Brother Aaron Smith had just returned from Appanoose and said Wilson Law was there lecturing to the mob; counseling them to drive the 'Mormons' from Nauvoo before the Temple was done or they never could.

Sunday, January 26—I attended the regular meeting of the high priests' quorum at the Masonic Hall. George Miller presiding, who introduced the subject of building a hall for the use of the quorums of high priests one hundred and twenty feet long by eighty wide, and about thirty-three feet high. I asked all that were in favor of having such a hall built, and were willing to do something towards building it, and not merely look on and see their brethren build it, to raise their hands; all hands were raised. I told them such a building as had been proposed would not cost less than fifteen thousand dollars.

I proposed to the quorum to finish off the upper story of the Temple in which they could receive their washings and anointings and endowments instead of undertaking a building from the commencement: this proposition was received by unanimous vote.

Elder Heber C. Kimball preached in the Concert Hall.

The seventies met in their hall. President Joseph Young presiding, James M. Munroe expressed his willingness to teach the seventies English grammar. Elder George A. Smith spoke on the benefits arising from education; he said, the saints should improve and be diligent in acquiring knowledge, this people and their gathering together has been made a political question, and we are a bone for all the world to pick at; Lawyer Babbitt had written that the legislature had repealed the city charter of Nauvoo, and there was a great rejoicing among the priests at their victory.

President Joseph Young spoke of the importance of being able to speak correctly. He lectured the youth who joined the quorums as to obedience; said, if he knew of a man belonging to these quorums stealing he would be cut off the church and published in the *Neighbor*. The saints had always taught honesty, virtue and uprightness—the lives of thousands were jeopardized by rascals and hypocrites, who would call you brother and pilfer your property; such were neither fit to be called saints nor decent human beings, they would go to hell. The names of several suspected of stealing were mentioned. James Dunn was cut off, two members were called in question for drunkenness.

Evening, I attended prayer meeting.

Monday, January 27—Attended to sending off fifty missionaries and forwarding letters to Elders Parley P. Pratt, Wm. Smith and J. M. Grant. Elder Kimball preached the funeral sermon of Sister Perrygrine Sessions.

Tuesday, February 11—Elders Kimball, Page, Taylor, Smith, Lyman and myself met with the Trades Committee.

Afternoon, attended meeting at Elder Taylor's with a Committee of the Agricultural and Manufacturing Society. It was proposed that the citizens be invited to subscribe twelve thousand days work, which it was estimated would put a sufficient dam in the Mississippi to propel machinery.

Mr. John C. Elliott, one of the murderers of Joseph and Hyrum Smith was arrested by John Kay.

Wednesday, February 12—Mr. Elliott was examined before Justices Aaron Johnson, Daniel H. Wells, Isaac Higbee and committed to Carthage jail to await his trial at the next term of the circuit court.

Friday, February 14—Father Morley arrived from Yelrome near Lima, Adams county, bringing word that five of the brethren there had been arrested charged with larceny; he says that property had been concealed on their premises and recovered by a search warrant, on the principle "those that hide can find". These proceedings were had to produce excitement, and a warrant is said to be out for Father Morley. I met with the Twelve and others and prayed for the deliverance of these brethren. Father Morley was counseled to remove his family to Nauvoo and Solomon Hancock was appointed to preside over that branch. Dr. John M. Bernhisel was appointed a Traveling Bishop to visit the churches. Some conversation ensued on the subject of sending six brethren with Brother Lewis Dana to the west and especially to Texas.

Monday, February 24—In company with Elders Heber C. Kimball, Orson Pratt, Amasa M. Lyman, George Miller, William Clayton, George D. Grant, E. D. Woolley, John Kay and John L. Smith; I went to Macedonia: we were armed with forty-six rounds, loaded pistols.

After the company partook of refreshments, we met at Brother Benjamin F. Johnson's and enjoyed a pleasant evening; Brother Kay sang a number of songs.

Evening, the Presidents of Seventies met in their hall. The charges against James Carrol and Hiram Gates, were investigated and they were expelled from the church. The brethren agreed to trade with those merchants who sustained good order and honored the laws of the city.

Tuesday, February 25—I spent the day in Macedonia, settling the church business with Elder B. F. Johnson. The company from Nauvoo dined at Elder Wm. G. Perkins'.

Afternoon, visited the saints. Evening. Elders Orson Pratt, Amasa M. Lyman, George Miller and I preached. Chatted at Brother Johnson's till after midnight. I told the brethren that all was not right and that we would have some of the brethren from Nauvoo before daybreak; George D. Grant and John Kay agreed to watch during the night. A rumor having reached Nauvoo that Elder Kimball and I were in Carthage jail, Elders John E. Page, John Taylor, Willard Richards, George A. Smith, and Charles C. Rich, met in Nauvoo at Elder Taylor's and investigated the report, and though they did not believe it, they deemed it prudent to dispatch Brother Hosea Stout and seven of the old police to Macedonia, as a protection for us.

Wednesday, February 26—Brother Hosea Stout and company arrived in front of Brother Johnson's house; we at first thought it was the mob, but when Wm. H. Kimball cried out 'Father don't you know me', we immediately recognized the brethren and had a joyful meeting; they brought us word of the rumor which had arisen in Nauvoo from two suspicious persons who had been at Brother Turley's inquiring for Elder Kimball and me.

At ten a.m. we started for Nauvoo, twenty-three of the brethren from

Macedonia accompanying us through the timber about seven miles when we halted and Howard Egan recited a negro sermon; I made a few remarks by way of counsel to the Macedonia brethren and blessed them in the name of the Lord; they returned home; we proceeded and arrived in Nauvoo about three p.m.

Saturday, March 1—I met with the "General Council" at the Seventies Hall. We decided to send nine brethren westward, to search out a location for the saints; many eloquent speeches were made on the present position of affairs: had a good meeting, which continued all day.

The high council met: no business.

The overflowing of rivers in the north of China submerged whole provinces with populations respectively larger than some of the second class kingdoms of Europe. When the waters receded thousands of corpses were left on the ground. Upwards of seventeen millions of human beings who have escaped from the inundations have spread over the adjacent provinces, beggared of all things and crying for bread.

Monday, March 3—I accompanied Elder Heber C. Kimball at his request on to the hill to transact some business: returned home quite sick and went to bed.

Evening, the Presidents of Seventies met, and investigated the characters of several of their members. The choir had a concert at the Music Hall; Elders Taylor and Kimball addressed the assembly spiritedly.

Tuesday, March 4—Continued sickly. General Council met at Seventies Hall; Elder Kimball presided; the subject of the western mission was discussed.

Thursday, March 6—Elders Kimball and Richards called on me this evening. I sat up a little and felt better.

Friday, March 7—I walked over to my brother Joseph's: felt considerably better. I had no doctor in my sickness, but the Lord, my wife, and the laying on of hands of the elders.

Tuesday, March 11—I attended the General Council. The subject of writing to Governor Ford; also the present movements of the mob were discussed. It was considered best for those who are hunted with writs to go on missions; as the policy of commencing a mob persecution has always been to get out vexatious writs in order to provoke resistance to the form of legal authority and thereby produce a collision between us and the state; so that we may, if possible, evade the blow until we can finish the Temple and the Nauvoo House. It was also decided that the workmen on the walls of the Temple commence work tomorrow.

Wednesday, March 12—The sheriff is here with writs for several of the brethren. He says that the mob have sent messengers to the governor to inform him that the Mormons have resisted the officers and requesting him to order a *posse comitatus* to come and take Brackenbury: Mr. Brackenbury was a witness against the murderers of Joseph and Hyrum Smith.

Wm. Marks left town suddenly.

A dreadful earthquake occurred in the city of Mexico at fifty-two minutes past three p.m., which caused a great amount of suffering and great destruction of property.

Thursday, March 13—Several brethren accompanied Mr. Brackenbury to Augusta.

Friday, March 14—I attended meeting in the Masonic Hall and proposed that deacons be appointed to take care of the poor, in every neighborhood, with bishops at their head: agreed to meet the bishops and their counselors at the Masonic Hall on Monday morning to organize.

Sunday, March 16—Elder Amasa M. Lyman preached at the stand.

I said: "I will give a few of my own ideas in short. Living poor, being in the wilderness, etc., is nothing to me when I am called to endure it, but people who run headlong into misery and bring upon themselves suffering, do not arrive at anything but darkness and despair. There is not one of Emmett's company that can claim the protection of heaven or any blessing of the everlasting gospel; their sufferings add nothing to their exaltation, but if the Lord had called them to pass through trials, they would have visions, revelations and faith (if necessity required) to cause him to feed them like the children of Israel. We told James Emmett, if he went, he would get into trouble: this congregation can be led by a thread. Religion is one thing and fanaticism is another.

Spring is here; we covenanted to labor on the Temple until it was finished and do all we could towards its completion; but we have not done it; if the brethren had continued, they might have worked on those walls four days a week. The stonecutters and joiners have been at work; the joiners have far exceeded our expectations this winter. The timber holds out, we keep using and there is enough left; there will be no lack of timber. If the brethren will go to work now, there will be no lack of provisions. We want the brethren to pay up their tithing. If you will haul wood, timber, etc., and help on the Temple you will find that it will be made up to you in your crops.

Since N. K. Whitney and George Miller have taken charge of the business, no man has needed anything but what has been supplied. I can call scores of men around me, who would sooner sacrifice every dollar they have, than the work on the Temple should stop. We can set four hundred men to work on the Temple. I do not want any man to go to preach till he is sent. If the world want to hear preaching let them come here, and if they really want the gospel, let them clean [up] Carthage jail.

I have proposed to the leading men of the Water Power Company, to put their work on the Temple. I will call the stockholders together, and give my reasons to them. We want to press forward the work on the Temple. I now proclaim to all saints who control means, to go to the Trustees and see if they want means to procure provisions, etc., for the hands; and I ask you to use all your influence to strengthen the hands of the Trustees.

I swear by the God of heaven that we will not spend money in feeing lawyers. All the lawsuits that have been got up against the saints, have been hatched up to fee lawyers, tavernkeepers, etc. I would rather have a six-shooter than all the lawyers in Illinois. I am sworn not to pay lawyers, but to pay our debts, and it will relieve us from an immense tax. Do not let there be a lot laying vacant in this town, join fences, for there is land enough in this city without going on to the prairie. I am going to drop the name Nauvoo and call this the 'City of Joseph'. Tomorrow evening we want the bishops at the Masonic Hall, and we will organize them according to our notion of things. We have no police; the legislature has repealed our charter, and we mean to have the 'City of Joseph' organized. The streets shall be kept clear; and the poor cared for.

Brother Wm. Marks has gone without being 'whitled' out. He would hire a man for twenty-five cents a day and would make a man work two days in the harvest field for one bushel of wheat, which is one of the most low, dishonest, mean things a person can do."

Monday, March 17—One hundred and five extra laborers and about thirty teams commenced work at the Temple this morning in obedience to the call of yesterday to hasten its completion.

Wednesday, March 19—Colonel Hosea Stout, who was on duty this evening at my house [i. e. as watchman] called upon me and I had some conversation with him in regard to the saints settling the country near the headwaters of the Colorado of the west.

Monday, March 24—In company with the Twelve Apostles I attended a meeting at the Concert Hall in the evening. We ordained bishops who were directed to set apart deacons in their wards to attend to all things needful and especially to watch; being without any city organization, we deemed it prudent to organize the priesthood more strictly that the peace and good order hitherto sustained by the city might still be preserved.

Wednesday, March 26—Elder Amos Fielding with about fifty saints arrived this evening, being a portion of the company who left Liverpool, England, on the ship *Palmyra*; many of the company were unable to get further than St. Louis. At nine p.m., I rode to the upper landing and welcomed the saints, and directed the schoolhouse to be opened for the use of the company during the night.

Brother Perkins from Macedonia, brought word that the mob were making active preparations to make a break upon us about court time, which is the third Monday in May: they were collecting artillery and organizing themselves for a general raid.

Thursday, March 27—I attended council with the Twelve, the Trustees, the Temple committee and Brother Amos Fielding at Father Cutler's. Church matters and the plans of the mob were canvassed.

At three p.m., Brother Wm. W. Player finished setting the last trumpet stone on the capitals of the pilasters of the Temple. All the capitals and trumpet stones are now safe on the walls, which is a matter of rejoicing to all who love to witness the prosperity of the work. The weather has been sometimes very cold and at other times very windy, so that it has been impossible for the hands to continue on the walls, much of the time of late.

Friday, March 28—I attended a party at the Mansion; most of the Twelve and their families and about one hundred and forty others were present: the brass band performed some good pieces.

Tuesday, April 1—I commenced revising the History of Joseph Smith at Brother Richards' office: Elder Heber C. Kimball and George A. Smith were with me. President Joseph Smith had corrected forty-two pages before his massacre. It afforded us great satisfaction to hear Brother Richards read the history of the infancy of the church. Adjourned at eleven p.m. having read one hundred and forty pages in Book 'A'.

Thursday, April 3—Accompanied by Elders Heber C. Kimball, Willard Richards and George A. Smith, I went to the Temple.

Evening, the brethren of the Twelve and others met at Elder Richards' office and prayed; we remembered our enemies and prayed that their designs against Zion might fail; we felt the power of God.

Friday, April 4—I visited Brother Moore, who had been accidentally shot. Dr. Bernhisel decided that the wound was mortal; but by the blessing of God he recovered.

Elder Benjamin L. Clapp reported that he left Nauvoo on the twenty-third day of October, 1844, on a special mission to collect tithing throughout the southern states. He returned about this date, having held many meetings, baptized fifteen persons and collected one thousand and forty-seven dollars which he delivered to the Trustee-in-Trust.

The mob left notice with Sheriff Backenstos of Carthage to leave by three p.m. today. The Jack-Mormons (the name attached to those friendly to Mormonism), say they will defend him and are gathering a company for that purpose. Backenstos says he will not be driven, but will stand his ground: report says the mob are divided among themselves.

Brother William W. Major exhibited a painting of the assassination of Joseph and Hyrum Smith by the mob at Carthage.

Tuesday, April 8—I had a conversation with Dr. W. G. Goforth on the principles of the gospel and baptized him, and in company with Brothers Heber C. Kimball and George A. Smith confirmed him a member of the church and ordained him a high priest.

Brother Elijah Fordham returned from New York and brought twelve hundred and sixty-three dollars for the Temple.

Wednesday, April 9—I met in council with the Twelve and bishops at the Trustees' Office. We agreed to advise Peter Maughan and Jacob Peart to return from Rock river whither they had been to work a coal mine; Reuben McBride to put the Kirtland property in the best state possible, without paying out money and to come to Nauvoo bye and bye. The bishops were instructed to sell the steamboat *Maid of Iowa* for what they could get for it.

Elder Lorenzo Snow returned to Nauvoo and brought some money and property and a six-pounder cannon on tithing.

Thursday, April 10—I met in council with Elders Heber C. Kimball, Orson Hyde, John Taylor, George A. Smith, Willard Richards and Amasa M. Lyman. We decided to print our own works at Nauvoo; remove the printing office into the Masonic Hall, and print the *Book of Doctrine and Covenants, Hymn Book* and *History* as soon as possible.

A resolution was passed to disfellowship George J. Adams and Sam Brannan, and a letter was written to Elder Parley P. Pratt on the subject.

The trustees of the Nauvoo House Association met and examined their books.

Evening, the Twelve and bishops met at the Historian's Office and prayed for rain; an abundant harvest; deliverance from our enemies and blessings on the saints.

Saturday, April 12—The old police invited the Twelve and their families to a party at the Masonic Hall, when a comfortable repast was partaken of. The police performed a new piece entitled, 'Father Marks' Return to Mormonism'. Evening, the U. S. deputy marshal for the district of Illinois arrived in town with writs for myself and others.

Sunday, April 13—Meeting at the stand. Elders Heber C. Kimball and John Taylor preached. Several officers attended meeting. Elder Taylor gave them to understand that if they made an attempt to serve writs on him it would cost them their lives, and said, if they wished to magnify the law and make it honorable they should bring to justice the murderers of Joseph and Hyrum, two of our best men, who were treacherously butchered while in the custody of officers pledged for their safety; and that he would not submit any more to such outrages on our lives and liberties, for under present circumstances the law is only powerful to hold men still while the lawless massacre them.

Monday, April 14—The public hands commenced the foundation of the wall around the Temple block.

Elder Richards and I attended the deacons' meeting. The deacons have become very efficient looking after the welfare of the saints; every part of the city is watched with the strictest care, and whatever time of night the streets are traveled at the corner of every block a deacon is found attending to his duty.

Friday, April 18—As the workmen on the Temple had raised a large stone about fifteen hundred pounds weight, the chain broke and it fell fifty feet, but without injury to the building or any person.

Monday, April 21—Elder Wm. W. Player put up the first star on the southeast corner of the Temple. Elders Heber C. Kimball and William Clayton were watching the progress of the stone towards its destination: the 'stars' will add much to the beauty of the Temple.

Wednesday, May 7—Brother Orson Hyde reported that a mob of about two hundred men were collected at Appanoose who had prevented some of the brethren from going to work on the Island. The mob captain told the brethren that they had arranged matters so as to cut off all communication with the governor.

The officers of the Legion met at the Masonic Hall.

Evening, attended prayer meeting with the Twelve, N. K. Whitney, and Levi Richards.

Saturday, May 10—Brother George A. Smith called upon me this morning and I accompanied him to the Historian's Office where we read and revised Church History.

Tuesday, May 13—With Elders Heber C. Kimball, W. Richards and George A. Smith reading and revising Church History at Brother Edward Hunter's where we had retired to keep out of the way of writs reported to have been issued against us.

Wednesday, May 14—Continued at Brother Edward Hunter's as yesterday; my health, and that of Brother Richards poor; but we read and revised history all day.

Thursday, May 15—I was quite unwell, Brother George A. Smith called in the forenoon and read the *Neighbor* to me: Brothers W. Richards and Amasa M. Lyman sick.

Fast day: all works were stopped. Meetings were held in the several wards and donations made to the bishops for the poor; enough was contributed to supply the wants of the poor until harvest. Evening, met at Brother Richards' for prayer.

Saturday, May 24—A large number of the saints assembled to witness the laying of the capstone on the southeast corner of the Temple. Of the Twelve there were present, besides myself, Heber C. Kimball, John Taylor, Willard Richards, Amasa M. Lyman, George A. Smith, John E. Page, Orson Hyde and Orson Pratt, also Newel K. Whitney and George Miller the Presiding Bishops and Trustees-in-Trust, Alpheus Cutler and Reynolds Cahoon, Temple Committee, William Clayton, Temple recorder, John Smith, patriarch and president of the stake and several members of the high council. The brass band arranged themselves and played the 'Nightingale'.

At six o'clock and eight minutes a.m., Brother Wm. Player commenced spreading the mortar, perfect silence prevailing; the stone being lifted to its place. I stepped on the same and fitted it precisely to its position with the large beetle, at twenty-two minutes past six a.m., the capstone was pronounced set; the band played the 'Capstone March' composed for the occasion by Wm. Pitt. I said:

"The last stone is now laid upon the Temple and I pray the Almighty in the name of Jesus to defend us in this place and sustain us until the Temple is finished and we have all got our endowments."

The whole congregation then shouted, 'Hosanna, Hosanna, Hosanna, to God and the Lamb, Amen, Amen, and Amen,' which was repeated a second and third time. I concluded by saying, "So let it be, O Lord Almighty. This is the seventh day of the week or the Jewish Sabbath. It is the day on which the Almighty finished his work and rested from his labors; we have finished the walls of the Temple and we may rest today from our labors."

I dismissed the workmen for the day and requested them to spend the day in giving thanks to God; and dismissed the congregation, and with the brethren of the Twelve retired to our places of retreat, out of the way of constables and officers who are prowling around the city from Carthage.

The morning was wet and cold, but those present were highly interested with the morning's services, and felt well in consideration that the walls of the Temple were completed, notwithstanding the prophecies of our enemies and apostates.

Elder Orson Pratt preached the funeral discourse of Caroline, the daughter of Joshua and Thalia Grant and wife of Elder Wm. Smith, to a large assembly at the stand; her remains were deposited in the tomb of Joseph: she has left two children to mourn her loss.

At three p.m., a council of the Twelve met at Elder Taylor's and took into consideration the case of Elder Samuel Brannan who had been disfellowshipped; an investigation was entered into and Elder Brannan introduced testimony to prove his innocence of the charges made against him: he was restored to fellowship.

The brethren present expressed their feelings towards Elder Wm. Smith to which he responded. The Twelve then laid their hands upon him and ordained him to be a Patriarch to the whole church: there was a warm interchange of good feeling between William Smith and the quorum.

Tuesday, May 27—I received a respectful letter from Governor Drew in reply to our Memorial to him as governor of Arkansas; stating his inability to protect us in the state of Arkansas, and suggesting the propriety of our settling in Oregon, California, Nebraska or some other country where we will be out of the reach of our persecutors.

Wednesday, May 28—This morning the workmen commenced to raise the attic story of the Temple.

Thursday, May 29—Evening, met at Brother Richards' for prayer in company with Brothers Heber C. Kimball, Orson Hyde, Orson Pratt, Willard Richards, John Taylor, Amasa M. Lyman, N. K. Whitney, George Miller, Joseph Young and Levi Richards. Prayed that the Lord would overrule the movements of Wm. Smith who is endeavoring to ride the Twelve down; also that the Lord would overrule the proceedings of the mob so that we may dwell in peace until the Temple is finished.

The court at Carthage heard the lawyer's pleas on the defense in the case the state of Illinois *vs.* the murderers of Joseph and Hyrum Smith; the counsel for the defense exhibited a cruel and mendacious spirit. Calvin A. Warren of Quincy made the most inflammatory speech.

Friday, May 30—I attended council with the Twelve at Elder Taylor's

The jury at Carthage brought in a verdict of acquittal in favor of Levi Williams, Thomas C. Sharp, Mark Aldrich, Jacob C. Davis and William N. Grover—as we had anticipated: the court, attorneys, jury and bystanders being all fully satisfied of their guilt.

Saturday, May 31—Brother George D. Watt returned from Carthage. Threats were made that his minutes should never go to Nauvoo, but he succeeded in passing them out of the court room about every hour.

Calvin A. Warren [counsel for the defense] said that if the prisoners were guilty of murder he himself was guilty alleging that it was the public opinion that the Smiths ought to be killed, and public opinion made the laws consequently it was not murder to kill the Smiths. [!]

Sunday, June 22—Meeting at the stand; Elder Orson Pratt preached, but as it rained heavily, the meeting was dismissed. Evening, I met with the Twelve and others for prayer; Sister Jennetta Richards being very sick was administered to.

Monday, June 23—The sheriff came in with writs for a number of brethren and succeeded in arresting O. P. Rockwell and J. P. Harmon, but Rockwell got away from him. A constable from Le Harpe came in with writs for Brother Taylor, myself and others, but we kept out of the way.

Tuesday, June 24—I examined Church History with the brethren. Evening, Hiram Kimball and D. H. Wells returned from Carthage and brought word that Sheriff Deming had shot Sam Marshall.

Wednesday, June 25—At three p.m., I met with the Quorum of the Twelve for prayer; and in council in relation to a difficulty between William Smith and Brother Elbridge Tufts.

After council the Twelve met with the police at the Masonic Hall when Wm. Smith delivered a very pathetic speech, delineating in a sectarian tone, the wrongs that his brothers and himself had sustained; asserting that we were all dependent upon his family for the priesthood, and pronouncing the most fearful anathemas upon all those who should not sustain him in his course, justifying his assault upon Brother Tufts, and demanding of the Twelve to inform the police that it was their duty to take his counsel in relation to the manner they discharge their duty. I told him that as an officer Brother Tufts was subject to the magistrates, and had no right to discharge a prisoner only by the order of the proper officer; that he (Brother William Smith) had no more right to interfere with the police than I had; that when he beat Brother Tufts for refusing to discharge his prisoner, he was doing wrong, and meddling with that which was not his business and should make satisfaction; that we received the priesthood from God through Joseph Smith and not through William, and that he had no authority or power to curse the Twelve Apostles who received the priesthood from Joseph; that we were not influenced by his curses, and that his prayers and imprecations upon the heads of those who were seeking to fulfill the instructions of Joseph to the letter would rise no higher than the smoke from a dung hill.

Brother William appeared humbled and agreed to make ample satisfaction to Brother Tufts.

Received a letter from James Arlington Bennett of New York, in which he applies to be consecrated a general of the Nauvoo Legion, that he may "fight Napoleon's battles over again, either in Nauvoo or elsewhere." This wild spirit of ambition has repeatedly manifested itself to us by many communications received from various sources, suggesting schemes of blood and empire, as if the work of the Lord was intended for personal aggrandisement.

Thursday, June 26—The Twelve met for council and prayer: several children were blessed. The first stone for the new font was laid in the Temple.

Saturday, June 28—A number of brethren met and removed the stand and benches to the ground west of the Temple.

I rode out to the prairie with several of the Twelve: we felt thankful to God to see the crops looking so well.

Some of our wealthy brethren went to Carthage and became sureties on the bond upon which General Deming was set at liberty: the sum required was ten thousand dollars. Each signer was required to swear to the lowest cash value of his property and that it did not lie in the City of Nauvoo and he was then taken for one-half the sworn amount, so that twenty thousand dollars in property at its lowest cash value was held in security for General Deming's appearance at court. This contrasts strangely with the clemency extended by the court to Sharp, Williams, Aldrich, Grover, and Davis who were admitted to bail at the last court for one thousand dollars each on their own security; Deming having killed Marshall in self-defense, while the others violated the solemn faith of the state, pledged by its executive, and murdered innocent, unoffending men while confined in helpless condition in a prison awaiting examination!

Father John Smith and Brother George A. Smith called upon William Smith in relation to his mother's visions. William evinced a very bitter spirit and declared himself President of the Church, and said that he would have his rights: his uncle reasoned with him and endeavored to show him the falsity of his position.

Sunday, June 29—Elder Ezra T. Benson and I preached in the forenoon and Elders John Taylor and Amasa M. Lyman in the afternoon, at the grove west of the Temple. Evening, I met with the Twelve and others for prayer.

Monday, June 30—Visited Mother Smith in company with the Twelve and Bishops Whitney and Miller. William Smith was invited but did not attend. Mother Smith expressed herself satisfied with the Twelve and the course they were pursuing.

Tuesday, July 8—Brother Joseph Toronto handed to me $2,500 in gold and said he wanted to give himself and all he had to the upbuilding of the church and kingdom of God; he said he should henceforth look to me for protection and counsel. I laid the money at the feet of the bishops.

Wednesday, July 9—Sister Jennetta Richards, wife of Dr. Willard Richards, died at 10:15 a.m.

At 2 p.m., the Smith family attended a public dinner at the Mansion which was given by Bishops Whitney and Miller in behalf of the church; seven widows and about fifty of the family were present. Brothers H. C. Kimball, John Taylor, Bishops Whitney, Miller and myself, assisted in waiting on the table; the band and a few friends attended: Mother Smith addressed her kindred and the audience in a feeling and pathetic manner.

Saturday, August 2—In council with several of the Twelve and bishops. Brother Emmett desired in behalf of his company to be retained in the fellowship of the church. I informed him that if he and his company would follow the counsel of the Twelve we would fellowship them, but not otherwise.

Afternoon, I rode out in the new church carriage with Brother Kimball and the bishops to look at two [city] blocks of Emma Smith's which she has agreed to sell the Trustees for $550.00. We selected blocks 96 and 97 and then went to Mother Smith's and brought her in the carriage to choose which of the two blocks she would have deeded to herself and her daughters. She selected block 96, and desired to have the church build her a house like Brother Kimball's. She asked for the carriage we rode in, a horse and a double carriage harness. We gave her the use of the carriage during her lifetime.

Tuesday, August 12—9 a.m., the Twelve, presiding bishops and others met in council, and wrote letters for H. G. Sherwood and John S. Fullmer, with authority to lead, direct and instruct Emmett's company who are now encamped among the Sioux on the Missouri river about thirty miles above the mouth of Big Sioux river. We laid our hands upon the heads of Brothers Sherwood, Fullmer and Emmett and blessed them for the mission. Brother Emmett declared he would be subject to counsel.

Sunday, August 17—I dreamed this morning I saw Brother Joseph Smith, and as I was going about my business, he said, "Brother Brigham, don't be in a hurry", which was repeated the second and third times with a degree of sharpness.

Wednesday, August 20—A severe thunderstorm this morning, Brother Ralph was killed by lightning on Parley Street. Others were knocked down.

Governor Ford ordered the state arms in the possession of the Carthage Greys to be delivered to Sheriff Backenstos.

Tuesday, September 9—Forenoon, unwell.

Two p.m. General Council [Council of Fifty] met. Resolved that a company of 1500 men be selected to go to Great Salt Lake valley and that a committee of five be appointed to gather information relative to emigration, and report the same to the council.

Wednesday, September 10—I dreamed last night that I was chased by a mob to a place like a barn full of corn or grain, one chased me so close that he got into the same room with me and it was Thomas Ford, who appeared only two and one-half feet high. I took his wrist between my fingers and stepped to the door and knocked down one after another of the mob with him till I discovered he was dead.

News arrived that the mob are burning the houses of the brethren at Yelrome.

Thursday, September 11—I received a letter from Sheriff J. B. Backenstos announcing the death of General Miner R. Deming, who died at half past ten o'clock yesterday of congestive fever; during his illness his life was repeatedly threatened by the mob, he was prevented from sleeping at night by their yells and hideous screams, as they kept up a continual row in the streets of Carthage near the general's residence which greatly aggravated his fever, and doubtless caused his death.

I answered Sheriff Backenstos' letter assuring him of our regret at the loss the cause of liberty, law, and order had sustained in the unexpected death of General Deming, and informed him of the burning of the houses of the citizens of Morley Settlement by the mob yesterday, and requested him to take immediate steps to suppress the mob, advised him to inform the governor that he may take the necessary measures to protect the lives and property of the people in this country.

A messenger from Lima reports eight houses burned.

The Twelve met in council; it was agreed to dispatch a messenger to the Lima branch and counsel the brethren to propose to sell their property to the mob and bring their families and grain here, and to send a messenger to Michigan to advise the brethren to sell their farms for stock, sheep, etc., also to Ottawa and recommend the brethren there to gather all the hay they can.

Prayers were offered up that the Lord would give us wisdom to manage affairs with the mob so as to keep them off till we can accomplish what he requires at our hands in completing the Temple and Nauvoo House, also for wisdom to manage the affairs in regard to the western emigration.

A selection was made of members of the council to start westward next spring.

Friday, September 12—By letter from Solomon Hancock, Yelrome, we learn that the mob have burned all the houses on the south side of the branch [brook], and left last evening for Lima, said they would return this morning as soon as light, and swear they will sweep through and burn everything to Nauvoo. Colonel Levi Williams is at the head of the mob.

Saturday, September 13—Brother H. C. Kimball and Andrew Perkins visited me. Brother Perkins wanted to know something about our going west; I told him that those who went must expect to go on the Apostles' doctrines and no man say aught that he has is his own, but all things are the Lord's: and we his stewards, and every man receive his stewardship.

George W. Lang reported that he had been among the mob at Green Plains and Lima. Esquire Hill of Lima told him they did not design gathering in large bodies, but go on as they had done and finish burning Yelrome, then attack some other place and drive the Mormons all into Nauvoo, then they had further plans to move them from there by help from abroad.

Afternoon, I visited the sick and met the Committee on Emigration and others at Brother Daniel Spencer's. Father Bent was instructed to organize a company of 100 families.

George Miller said he went to Carthage with his wife and was transacting business at the county clerk's office, when he was arrested by Michael Barnes, constable, and taken before Captain Robert F. Smith, justice of the peace; was charged with treason and as the state was not ready for trial, and the offense not bailable, Captain Smith ordered him to be committed to jail, upon which Miller told him there was not enough men in the little town to put him in jail. Said he had served the United States government in two wars—had made the roads into this country and had killed snakes, and it was an imposition for these slinks that followed his tracks to charge him with treason, but if they wished to have an examination, he would come and attend court, but would not go into that jail alive. Upon which Esquire Smith took his verbal recognizance for his appearance at Carthage the next Saturday.

Sunday, September 14—I prophesied we would have a winter of peace in Nauvoo.

I said, in relation to the mob burning houses, I was willing they should do so, until the surrounding counties should be convinced that we were not the aggressors, peradventure they may conclude to maintain the supremacy of the law by putting down mob violence and bringing offenders to justice.

I counseled the brethren to bring their families and grain here, and called for volunteers with wagons and teams to aid in removing the saints to this place; one hundred and thirty-four teams were procured and started forthwith. The brethren agreed to continue until they had brought in all their families, effects and grain of the saints in the settlements attacked by the mob.

Monday, September 15—Seven a.m., the police met at my house and put me up a stable.

Sheriff Backenstos went to Warsaw and tried his best to summon a *posse* to stop the burning but could not raise one.

Forty-four buildings have been burned by the mob. Several houses have been burned in the Prairie branch, Green Plain precinct.

Michael Barnes a constable from Carthage, and his brother came into Nauvoo with writs for H. C. Kimball, Willard Richards, John E. Page, Daniel Garn, Wm. and George A. Smith, and myself, issued by Captain Smith of the Carthage Greys, on the complaint of _____ Backman. The charges were for aiding and abetting Joseph Smith in treasonable designs against the state, for being officers in the Nauvoo Legion, for building an arsenal, for keeping cannon in times of peace, for holding a private council in Nauvoo, and for holding correspondence with the Indians.

I received a letter from J. B. Backenstos, dated, Carthage, September 15th, in which he stated his inability to raise law and order citizens to quell the mob and requested us to hold two thousand well armed men in readiness for immediate service at any hour that he may call for them and added: that if we will not defend our own lives and property that we cannot reasonably expect any considerable support from those citizens commonly called "Jack-Mormons". "Colonel Levi Williams has ordered out his brigade of militia, I am certain the turnout will be slim, we must whip them."

In reply I advised him to wait a few days and see if there are any law and order citizens in the county that are not Mormons, and if it proved there were none else to stand up for the Constitution and laws of the state, it would then be time enough for us, as the old citizens had heretofore advised us to "hold still"! "Keep cool"! "Be quiet"! etc., etc., we were determined to do so.

The first regiment, second cohort of the Nauvoo Legion met and organized, choosing the old officers, to place themselves in readiness to act at the sheriff's call.

Tuesday, September 16—Sheriff Backenstos arrived in great haste and somewhat excited, said that the mob had driven him from his house in Carthage yesterday, and he went to Warsaw and stayed over night. He soon ascertained that the people were so enraged at him for trying to stop the house-burning that there was little probability of getting away alive, but finally prevailed on an influential mobocrat to escort him out of Warsaw this morning, who came with him about three and a half miles and on leaving cautioned him that if he saw two men together to avoid them for there were deep plans laid to kill him. Soon after he was pursued by a party of the mob on horseback, three of whom took the lead, one of the three had a swifter horse and gained a hundred yards in advance of his party in a short time when his horse stumbled and threw his rider. Backenstos maintained his speed, driving as fast as his horse could go.

The mob took the nearest road to cross his track and on his arrival at the old railroad crossing, the mob were within about 200 yards, they being on horseback and he in a buggy, they had gained on him considerably.

Orrin P. Rockwell and John Redding were refreshing themselves near the crossing as they had been out to bring in some of the burnt-out families who were sick, and on looking up saw Backenstos coming down the hill at full speed, and asked what was the matter. Backenstos replied the mob were after and determined to kill him and commanded them in the name of the people of the state to protect him. Rockwell replied, fear not, we have 50 rounds (two fifteen-shooter rifles besides revolvers).

Sheriff Backenstos then turned to the mob and commanded them to stop, and as they continued to advance raising their guns, he ordered Rockwell to fire; he did so aiming at the clasp of the belt on one of the mob, which proved to be Frank Worrell, who fell from his horse and the rest turned back and soon brought up a wagon and put his body into it.

Tuesday, September 30—Met in General Council at the Seventies' Hall.

Parley P. Pratt said he had made a calculation for an outfit that every family of five persons would require: one good wagon, three yoke of cattle, two cows, two beef cattle, three sheep, one thousand pounds of flour, twenty pounds of sugar, one rifle and ammunition, a tent and tent poles; and that the cost would be about $250.00 provided the family had nothing to begin with, only bedding and cooking utensils; and the weight would be about twenty-seven hundred including the family, and calculating them to walk considerably would reduce it to about nineteen hundred weight.

It was decided that all the council [i. e. of the Twelve] were to go west with their families, friends and neighbors.

General C. C. Rich reported that General J. J. Hardin with his troops had arrived in the city and were on the square northeast of the temple, waiting an interview with the Twelve and authorities of the place. Also that sheriff Jacob B. Backenstos and Judge Stephen A. Douglas were at Elder Taylor's and wished to see me as soon as possible. Council adjourned.

I went with the Twelve to Elder Taylor's and saw Judge Douglas and Sheriff Backenstos.

They said it was hard to make the people, the other side of the Illinois river, believe that it was not the Mormons that were burning houses in Hancock county.

They wished us to go and see General Hardin. In company with H. C. Kimball, W. Richards, John Taylor, George A. Smith and Amasa M. Lyman, I went on to the hill and met General Hardin and staff surrounded by his troops, four hundred in number. He read us his orders from the governor to come here and keep the peace if he had to keep the county under martial law: said he wished to search for the bodies of two dead men who were last seen in Nauvoo and it was supposed they had been murdered.

I told him he was welcome to search for dead bodies or anything else he pleased. He inquired if I knew anything about them or of crimes having been committed in Nauvoo. I replied I knew nothing of the kind, but that I had reliable information that some hundred houses had been burned in the south part of the county and probably if he would go there, he would find the persons who had done it.

I tendered him the hospitality of the city and a home at my house, to which he replied drily, "I always stay in camp."

General Hardin marched his troops to, and searched the Temple, Masonic Hall, Nauvoo House, and the stables of the Mansion.

There were deposited some forty barrels of wild grape wine in the Masonic Hall which attracted the attention of some of the searchers and caused some delay.

While searching the Mansion stables, they found where a horse had been bled and sent for the landlord and demanded an explanation; after being shown the horse, the General and Judge Douglas ran their swords into the manure, as though they expected to prick some dead bodies and make them squeal. Almon W. Babbitt told them they must think we were fools to bury dead men in a stable when it was so easy to throw them into the Mississippi river, which was only a few rods off. They then marched off and camped on the south side of the city.

Caleb Baldwin was arrested and taken into camp, and examined as a witness. Most of the questions asked were designed to find out where the bodies of Joseph and Hyrum Smith were buried.

Wednesday, October 1—Met in council at Elder Taylor's. General John J. Hardin, Hon. Stephen A. Douglas and J. A. McDougal were present.

E. A. Bedell, Esqr., asked General Hardin for three or four men to go to Warsaw and make arrests, which request was granted.

I asked the gentlemen present as to their feelings as friends and neighbors, and in relation to our propositions for removal.

General Hardin said he would do all in his power by counsel, etc., to help us, and approved of our proposed location at Vancouver's Island. He thought it desirable for our sakes that we should remove, also for the peace of the county.

Judge Douglas said Vancouver's Island was claimed by the United States, and he felt sure there would be no objection to its settlement, or to the settlement of Oregon.

General Hardin proposed that we should appoint trustees-in-trust to sell our property.

I proposed a committee of the whole on both sides, and informed them that we were not sowing any winter wheat, and a greater testimony of our intentions to remove should not be asked.

Judge Douglas said, all competent men must admit that the propositions of the committee of citizens of Nauvoo were just and fair.

General Hardin said he was satisfied we intended to remove but had not the assurance we could go if our property could not be sold.

Saturday, October 4—Attended General Council at Seventies' Hall. While riding to the hall with Elders H. C. Kimball and W. Richards, Elder Richards prophesied that we should have means to move all the poor and want for nothing. Elder Kimball said, amen.

The correspondence from General Hardin and suite, the governor, and the Resolutions by the citizens of Quincy were read to the council.

I proposed that we cease publishing the *Nauvoo Neighbor* and save our paper inasmuch as our papers rarely get beyond the hands of our enemies. Any information we want to send abroad we will publish in circulars and extras.

Sunday, October 5—I opened the services of the day by a dedicatory prayer, presenting the Temple, thus far completed, as a monument of the saints' liberality, fidelity, and faith, concluding: "Lord, we dedicate this house and ourselves, to thee." The day was occupied most agreeably in hearing instructions and teachings, and offering up the gratitude of honest hearts, for so great a privilege, as worshiping God within instead of without an edifice, whose beauty and workmanship will compare with any house of worship in America, and whose motto is:

"HOLINESS TO THE LORD".

Thursday, October 9—The seventies met in general conference. President Joseph Young counseled the seventies to pay strict attention to the call of their presidents and strongly exhorted them to pray unto the Lord day and night, and trust in him for deliverance, for the fervent prayers and faith of the saints would accomplish more than the strength of their arms, for the Lord holds the destinies of all men in his hands and he will control them according to his will and he has power to deliver us.

General Hardin has pledged himself to the mob that he will come to Nauvoo with his troops and either arrest Orrin P. Rockwell and some others of the brethren or he "will unroof every house in Nauvoo". Three hundred of our enemies have volunteered to come with him from Quincy and they expect to be joined by others on the way.

There seems to be no disposition abroad but to massacre the whole body of this people, and nothing but the power of God can save us from the cruel ravages of the bloodthirsty mob.

We concluded to plead with our heavenly Father to preserve his people, and the lives of his servants that the saints may finish the Temple and receive their endowments.

Saturday, October 11—The council met at Elder Taylor's. We joined in prayer, and wrote a circular for the agents to take abroad with them.

Afternoon, I remained at home being worn down with fatigue.

Tuesday, October 14—Major Warren came into the city with a detachment of the troops.

We prayed that they might not be permitted to do any injury to any of the saints; nor to interrupt our peace; they stayed but a short time.

Sunday, October 19—The congregation met in the Temple, Elder Orson Hyde preached.

William Smith who has published a pamphlet against the Twelve was excommunicated from the church by unanimous vote.

4 p.m., I met with the first Emigrating Company and proceeded with the organizaton by appointing captains of fifties and tens.

Wednesday, October 22—General J. A. Bennett and Mr. Booth, editor of the *Quincy Herald*, called at Dr. Richards' and tarried till noon. The conversation turned upon the saints going west. General Bennett asked Mr. Booth "why don't you go with them"? Mr. Booth replied, "To tell you the truth, that is my business here and I am not alone, for a number of others in Quincy are thinking of the same thing."

Mr. Booth offered to publish in his paper anything to help the saints in the sale of their property, and any other communication from us which would not conflict with public opinion so far as to drive away his subscribers.

Evening, I met with the Twelve at Elder Taylor's. A letter was read from Reuben McBride, Kirtland, stating that the apostates were doing everything they could to injure the saints. S. B. Stoddard, Jacob Bump, Hiram Kellogg, Leonard Rich, and Jewel Raney are the leaders of the rioters; they have broken into the House of the Lord, and taken possession of it, and are trying to take possession of the church farm.

Jesse P. Harmon and John Lytle who were charged with destroying the *Expositor* press were tried before Judge Purple.

The court decided in his charge to the jury, that the defendants acting under the municipal authorities of Nauvoo, were acting without authority, and if it could be proven that they had taken any part in the destruction of the press they were to be found guilty.

Rollison was the principal witness for the prosecution and gave a minute detail of the manner in which the nuisance was abated and stated that Mr. Harmon took the lead of the police on the occasion. On being asked if it was Appleton M. Harmon or Jesse P. Harmon, he replied it was the policeman and on being informed they were both policemen, he became confused and said he could not tell which it was.

The witness was asked whether it was John Lytle or Andrew Lytle, he replied, it was the Policeman Lytle, on being informed that they were both policemen, he answered it was the Blacksmith Lytle and on being told they were both blacksmiths, he declared that he could not identify the persons. The jury brought in a verdict of 'not guilty' and the defendants were acquitted accordingly.

Thus were the words of the Prophet Joseph fulfilled, who told the police (when they reported to him that they had abated the nuisance) that not one of them should ever be harmed for what they had done, and that if there were any expenses consequent he would foot the bill.

Thursday, October 23—A detachment of the governor's troops came in from Carthage to search for a bogus press. They searched Lucien Woodworth's house in vain.

Friday, October 24—Evening, council met at Elder Taylor's. Some of the mob went to Nathan Bigelow's near Camp Creek and ordered him to leave before Thursday for they were coming to burn his house, he sent his son to Nauvoo for counsel, and he was advised to go to Carthage and make the facts known to Major Warren.

He accordingly went and told Warren who replied, that the troops were gone elsewhere and he had nobody to send. But told the young man to tell his father to defend his house, and call on his neighbors to assist him. It appears that on Thursday the young man did not get back to tell his father that night. Soon after this, Warren sent five of his men to Father Bigelow's to defend his house. They missed their way and did not get there till 11 o'clock at night. On arriving they tied their horses; and their commander, Lieutenant Edwards from Quincy, went straight to the door and undertook to go in without knocking. Father Bigelow expected it was the mob coming and asked who was there, but the man did not answer but still attempted to open the door. Father Bigelow again asked who was there, and what he wanted, but could get no answer. He then told the man if he opened the door he should shoot him. The man finally opened the door and Father Bigelow discharged a pistol at him loaded with buckshot; he then snatched up a musket and shot that. The shot took effect on Edwards' hip and three balls entered his breast. He fell and called to the others to come and help him. They then told Father Bigelow they were the governor's troops and had come to protect him. Father Bigelow said if that was the case he was sorry, and went to work and made a fire and got the man in and took care of him. This morning they brought Father Bigelow to Carthage a prisoner, but his case was not disposed of when the brethren left. Warren justified the act.

Saturday, October 25—4 p.m., A. W. Babbitt arrived from Carthage and stated that when the brethren went in yesterday as witnesses of the house-burning the grand jury refused to hear their testimony, or to admit any of them into the jury room, which effectually shields the house-burners from justice and blockades the way for the sufferers to obtain redress.

The steamer *Sarah Ann* passed up the river, Doctor Foster and Lyman E. Johnson were on board. When the boat landed Jackson Redden was standing by and L. E. Johnson stepped up to him to counsel concerning his father and brother's case. Dr. R. D. Foster got a number of men from the boat and undertook to haul Redden on board and take him off with them. Redden knocked the first man down that undertook to lay hands on him; a few of the brethren who were not far off ran to Redden's assistance and with sticks and stones soon drove the whole crew on board; the captain started immediately, without unloading; the clerk left the bills of lading with a man who handed them to Albert P. Rockwood, but appeared not to know what he did. After the boat started Doctor Foster shot his pistol at the brethren but hurt no one. One of the brethren was cut on the back of the neck with a stone.

This morning Hosea Stout and John Scott stationed themselves at the mound, seven miles east of Nauvoo, and extended a few men for miles north and south to ascertain and express any hostile movements which might be made towards Nauvoo.

Major Warren, Judge Purple, J. B. Backenstos, Judge Ralston and Mr. Brannan with a detachment of troops came into town and Warren demanded an explanation in relation to seeing some fifteen or twenty of our express men on the prairie.

I went to the Mansion and in plain but mild language stated the reason why our men were there. Warren in a great rage declared he would issue his manifesto on Monday morning and put the county under martial law. After this Elder John Taylor made some very just and spirited remarks in relation to the foul treachery or criminal imbecility of the governor's protection, telling Mr. Warren that we had placed our express men in a position to communicate the earliest intelligence should any mob violence be attempted upon our brethren while at Carthage and further said: "We lack confidence in the governor's troops under your command while hundreds of murderers, robbers and house-burners roam at large unwhipped of justice. We shall take measures to protect ourselves. I, Sir, have been shot all to pieces under the 'protection' of the governor's troops. Our leading men have been murdered in Carthage and we shall not trust ourselves unprotected again until the state gives some evidence more than it has done of its justice and humane intentions to enforce its laws."

Judge Purple said: "Mr. Taylor do not talk on such an exciting topic."

Elder Taylor ordered wine for the company, Judge Purple and all except Warren drank.

Elder Hyde commenced to make an apology for Elder Taylor. Elder Taylor interrupted him, saying, "Do not offer any apology for me". Judge Purple said, "We accept the wine for Mr. Taylor's apology."

Evening, I met with the council at Elder Taylor's. We prayed that the Lord would overrule the matter and remove from Warren's heart the disposition to declare martial law or otherwise let his hand be heavy upon him with judgment that he may not be able to bring trouble upon the saints.

Brother Hedlock called upon Dr. Richards with a message from General Bennett, saying that he had left Carthage and gone to Quincy that he would write Dr. Richards soon, and that he would cross the Rocky Mountains with us in the spring.

Sunday, October 26—I conversed with Judge Ralston in relation to selling our property to the Catholics. He advised us to sell to them and said he would use his influence with them in Quincy to come and settle here.

Major Warren said this morning that no man would be permitted to go into Carthage [to attend trial of the Prophet's murderers] with any kind of arms. He swore he should search every man. It was thought best that about one hundred of the brethren should go and about twenty advance into town without arms, and the balance remain behind until they could ascertain Warren's movements; and if he declared martial law, all return, as in that case there can be no court held.

Monday, October 27—Elder A. W. Babbitt returned from Carthage and reported that Backenstos had obtained a change of venue to Peoria to have his trial in five weeks. He is in the hands of the coroner who has permission either to take bail or select his own guard, at the expense of the state. The court adjourned until next May. The grand jury found bills of indictment against several of our brethren, none of the witnesses who had been burned out by the mob were admitted into the jury room, or allowed any opportunity to testify of their sufferings and so the farce ended with adding insult to injury. All Governor Ford, General John J. Hardin, Major Warren and Mr. Brayman's promise of administering justice and punishing the house-burners simply ends in compelling the sufferers to leave their destitute and helpless families and bear the loss of time and expense of spending several days at court to be told: "You d_____ Mormons shall not be admitted into the jury room to testify against the old citizens who have burned your houses, barns and grain, and turned your sick and helpless families out of doors to perish without food or shelter on the eve of winter."

Babbitt states that Dr. Abiather Williams has been before one of the judges of Iowa and sworn that the Twelve made bogus at his house in Iowa.

They have taken out a United States writ and made a demand on the governor of this state for them, and the deputy marshal of Iowa (Silas Haight) is at Carthage with writs for all the Twelve. Warren is coming with the troops tomorrow, to aid the marshal in making the arrests. They had these writs with them on Saturday evening and this deputy was also with them, but when Elder Taylor made his speech it bluffed them off and they were afraid to serve them; since then Warren has sent to some of the eastern counties for volunteers to join his ranks.

The brethren in council expressed their feelings and all felt satisfied that the Lord would overrule this matter also for our good. The brethren of the Twelve all concluded to leave their homes tonight, so that if the *posse* come in during the night there will be no danger.

Tuesday, October 28—Ten a.m., President John Smith, Elders Newell K. Whitney, Joseph Young, Wm. W. Phelps, Orson Spencer, Joseph C. Kingsbury, and Lucien Woodworth met at Elder Taylor's and prayed.

The Twelve being apprehensive of treachery hid themselves until towards evening, when I received word from Major Warren that he wished to have an interview with us.

Wednesday, October 29—I remained incognito at Brother A. P. Rockwood's, Brothers George A. Smith and Amasa M. Lyman came to see me; also Brothers Henry G. Sherwood and John S. Fullmer who had just returned from their misson westward; Bishop Whitney and Brother Wm. Clayton also came to see me. Elder Sherwood made a report of their late mission, which was very satisfactory and gave us some very interesting information concerning our best route to the west.

Thursday, October 30—Bishop George Miller and E. A. Bedell returned from Springfield at 10 a.m. and reported their interview with Governor Ford and informed us that the governor would be at Carthage today, and intends to see to matters himself and try to preserve peace until we can get away.

Friday, October 31—At the Tithing Office, writing a letter to Brother V. Shurtliff to receive tithing in the east, and donations to help away the poor.

I received a letter from Charles A. Lovell, Mass., October 20th recommending us as a community to remove to California. Another from Thomas J. Farnhaus, New York, October 20th, on the same subject. Also one from Edward Warren, Boston, October 22nd portraying the Bay of San Francisco and country round as one well adapted for our location in the west.

Saturday, November 1—I paid William Clayton one hundred and fifty dollars to purchase instruments for the brass band.

Sunday, November 2—The first Emigration Company [for the west] organized by appointing captains of tens.

The second quorum of seventies held a festival at the Seventies Hall.

Monday, November 3—Brother Heber C. Kimball and I visited Dr. Willard Richards who was sick.

Evening, council met at Elder John Taylor's, Brothers Sherwood, Fullmer and Butler made a further report of the country west.

Abraham C. Hodge stated that he had some conversation with Robert D. Foster, who told him his feelings on the subject of Mormonism. He said, "Hodge, you are going to the west—I wish I was going among you, but it can't be so, I am the most miserable wretch that the sun shines upon. If I could recall eighteen months of my life I would be willing to sacrifice everything I have upon earth, my wife and child not excepted. I did love Joseph Smith more than any man that ever lived, if I had been present I would have stood between him and death." Hodge inquired, "Why did you do as you have done? You were accessory to his murder." He replied: "I know that, and I have not seen one moment's peace since that time. I know that Mormonism is true, and the thought of meeting (Joseph and Hyrum) at the bar of God is more awful to me than anything else."

Tuesday, November 4—Emigrating Company No. 1 met in the Temple, eighteen companies of ten families each were filled up and Parley P. Pratt and Amasa Lyman appointed captains over the first and second hundreds.

Joshua Smith died. He was poisoned by the militia while at Carthage where he was summoned to attend court; the militia searched for him and found a knife under his arm and arrested him, and while under arrest they gave him dinner, where no doubt he received the poison, he soon became very thirsty, and vomiting followed until death. He said, he had been poisoned by the militia and at a post mortem examination by Drs. John M. Bernhisel, Lucius P. Sanger and Jesse Brailey the suspicion was confirmed; he was a good man and his name will be registered among those who wear a martyr's crown.

He was second counselor to Samuel Williams, president of the elder's quorum, at the time of his death.

Wednesday, November 5—Attended council with the Twelve to direct the arrangement of the seats in the Temple.

Sunday, November 9—No public meeting; the floor of the first story in the Temple having been taken up to put in new timbers, the sleepers which were put in at the commencement of the Temple having become rotten.

The brethren belonging to the different Emigrating Companies assembled in and around the Temple, and received instruction concerning emigration.

Eleven a.m., I addressed the saints.

Wednesday, November 12—Brother Rice's farmhouse on Camp Creek was burned by about thirty men of the mob who swore they were Governor Ford's troops, which was probably false, John M. Finch and Rollison were with them.

Thursday, November 13—Forenoon, I rode out to the prairie with Dr. Richards, my brothers John and Joseph, E. T. Benson and G. D. Grant, and dined at Brother Chamberlain's.

4 p.m., attended council with the Twelve. It was decided that Mother Lucy Smith should be furnished with food, clothing, and wood for the winter.

We prayed as usual.

Dr. Richards and I visited Stephen Markham who was cutting and sawing wagon spokes, at his place in the woods. We helped him to cut and saw a while, and then took his rifle and shot at a mark, with my second shot I cut the pin that fastened the two-inch paper mark to a tree.

I wrote a lengthy communication to Noah Rogers giving him the general items of church news since he left on his mission to the Pacific Islands.

Saturday, November 15—A considerable party of the mob set fire to a stack of straw near Solomon Hancock's barn and concealed themselves. Hancock and others went out to put out the fire which was the only way to save the building, when they were fired upon by the burners, and Elder Edmund Durfee killed on the spot, many balls flew around the rest of the brethren, but none of the rest were hurt.

Elder Joseph B. Brackenbury died at Pomfret from the effects of poison secretly administered to him by opposers, who afterwards boasted that Mormon elders had not faith enough to stand poison. The night after his burial there was a heavy snowstorm, about half past eleven o'clock Joel H. Johnson dreamed that some persons were digging up Brother Brackenbury's body, and was so exercised about it that he called up some of the brethren and went to the spot, about one mile distant, and found a party of doctors at work, who had nearly cleared the grave of earth; the men fled with utmost precipitation. David Johnson took after the largest one who was caught and bound over in one thousand dollar bonds for his appearance at court, but was never tried.

Tuesday, November 18—The Twelve met in council at Dr. Richards'.

Mr. Brayman, attorney for the state, wrote a letter to the council desiring witnesses against the murderers of Durfee to be sent to Carthage, also affidavits forwarded in relation to the burning of Rice's house, and advising us of the arrest of George Backman, Moss and Snyder, who were charged with the murder of Elder Edmund Durfee, Sen.

The council replied immediately and requested the witnesses to start in the morning for Carthage to perform their part in another judicial farce.

I received a letter from James Arlington Bennett urging me to appoint him military commander-in-chief in the church, the spirit of the letter shows a thirst for personal aggrandizement unbecoming a servant of God.

Friday, November 21—Sheriff Backenstos came into council about 7 p.m., and said that he had watched Major Warren very closely for the last four days, thought he had turned Jack-Mormon, that he had been very busy and energetic in arresting the murderers of Durfee and the burners of Rice's house, that he had several of them under guard at Carthage and was in pursuit of more and had chased one of them into Missouri and forced him back at the point of the pistol without any requisition from the governor.

Saturday, November 22—The Twelve met with thirty-eight of the brethren who were expelled from Jackson county, Missouri, in 1833. Several of them spoke, some of them saying they thought they were neglected and cast off poor.

I made a few remarks, and showed that many had been slothful and had not preached nor magnified their callings in the church.

The plasterers finished the attic story of the Temple.

Sunday, November 23—Eleven a.m., seventies met in the Concert Hall.

I met with the captains of Emigrating Companies and gave them appropriate counsel.

Families organized, 3285.

Wagons on hand, 1508.

Wagons commenced, 1892.

Afternoon, the Council of the Twelve met. Several letters were read. Many threats by our enemies were afloat.

Monday, November 24—We have learned that the persons who murdered Edmund Durfee as also those who burned Rice's and Hick's houses were discharged by the magistrate without examination. Our brethren went according to Major Warren and Mr. Brayman's request as witnesses thereby fulfilling their part towards magnifying and making the laws honorable, but returned unheard, and the farce closed sooner than he had anticipated, without even a grand jury on the case.

Afternoon, council met for prayers.

Thursday, November 27—At the Trustees' Office, arranging business.

Afternoon, Erastus H. Derby called upon Dr. Richards and informed him that Silas Haight, a deputy United States marshal of Iowa and another suspicious fellow were loitering about the streets, and endeavoring to see some of the Twelve to serve writs on them.

Saturday, November 29—I met with the Twelve, Bishops Whitney and Miller and a few others in the Temple and laid the carpet on the main floor of the attic story, and also on several of the small rooms ready for the First Quorum [of the Seventy] to meet in.

Sunday, November 30—At ten a.m. I went to the attic story of the Temple with Elders Heber C. Kimball, Willard Richards, Parley P. Pratt, John Taylor, Orson Hyde, George A. Smith, and Amasa Lyman, of the Quorum of the Twelve; also Newel K. Whitney and George Miller, Presiding Bishops; John Smith, Patriarch and President of the Stake, Joseph Young, President of the Seventies, Alpheus Cutler and R. Cahoon, Temple Committee, Cornelius P. Lott, Levi Richards, Joseph C. Kingsbury, Orson Spencer, Wm. W. Phelps, Isaac Morley, Lucien Woodworth. At about 12 o'clock, sang "Come All Ye Sons of Zion".

I requested Wm. Clayton to keep minutes. I then offered up prayer and dedicated the attic story of the Temple and ourselves to God, and prayed that God would sustain and deliver us his servants from the hands of our enemies, until we have accomplished his will in this house. Elder Taylor then sang "A Poor Wayfaring Man of Grief", after which Elder Heber C. Kimball prayed, that the Lord would hear and answer the prayers of his servant Brigham, and break off the yoke of our enemies and inasmuch as they lay traps for the feet of his servants that they may fall into them themselves and be destroyed—that God would bless his servant Joseph Young, heal his wife, and bless his family—that God would bless and heal his own [Elder Kimball's] family and asked for the same blessings on all our families which he had asked for Joseph Young and himself.

Hans C. Hanson, the doorkeeper reported that there were two officers waiting at the foot of the stairs for me. I told the brethren that I could bear to tarry here where it was warm as long as they could stay in the cold waiting for me. Elder Amasa Lyman requested hands to be laid on him that he might be healed; five of the brethren laid hands on him.

Every hundred have established one or more wagon shops; wheelrights, carpenters and cabinetmakers are nearly all foremen wagon makers, and many not mechanics are at work in every part of the town preparing timber for making wagons. The timber is cut and brought into the city green; hub, spoke, and felloe timber boiled in salt and water, and other parts kiln dried; shops are established at the Nauvoo House, Masonic Hall, and Arsenal, nearly every shop in town is employed in making wagons.

Teams are sent to all parts of the county to purchase iron; blacksmiths are at work night and day and all hands are busily engaged getting ready for our departure westward as soon as possible.

Very few sales of property are being made, the citizens of the country around instead of aiding us to sell our property, are using their influence to discourage sales and the authorities constantly haunt us with vexatious writs, efforts are making to bring us into collision with the authorities of the United States by means of vexatious writs from the federal courts. The brethren are doing their utmost to prepare amidst all the discouragements that surround us for a general exodus in the spring; but from the manner that our neighbors have kept their faith, it is very apparent that as soon as the strength of Israel is gone, that the remainder will be in danger of violence, from our cruel persecutors, the promises of governors, generals, judges, conventions of citizens, and mob leaders, and their hounds to the contrary notwithstanding; but we trust in God, we praise him that we have been thus far able to prepare his Temple for the ordinances of the priesthood, and we feel full of confidence that he will hear our prayers and deliver his unoffending people from the power of their enemies, and lead us to a land where we can enjoy peace for a season.

Monday, December 1—Elder Almon W. Babbitt made a report of his mission to St. Louis, Cincinnati and Chicago, relative to the disposition of property in Hancock county; and said the Catholics were making considerable exertions to have the members of their church purchase our property. They were very anxious to lease the Temple, but were not able to buy it. Mr. Quarters, the bishop at Chicago, has sent an agent who may probably enter into some arrangements for our property, he is expected tomorrow.

Brother Albert P. Rockwood was instructed to rent the upper stream mill for four months.

Bishop Miller answered a letter from Thomas H. Owen, giving him an estimate of lands for sale in the several settlements in Hancock county under cultivation.

Tuesday, December 2—I received a letter from Messrs. Duncan and Co. of Bloomington, stating that a heavy firm in Philadelphia wished to know the condition and situation of our property, terms, etc., as they wished to buy, and for their ability to do so, referred us to Sheriff Backenstos and others; they proposed to pay specie for the whole, if a bargain were concluded.

The council returned answer by letter that if their agent or agents would come here and examine the property, that we would sell the whole or any part of the city of Nauvoo, owned by our people, or the farms in the county, for fifty per cent under the valuation of like property, similarly situated in this country.

I spent the day in the Temple making preparations for the endowments.

Spent an hour in prayer.

Thursday, December 4—I was with several of the Twelve fitting up the Temple preparatory to administering the ordinances of endowment.

Evening, the council met for prayer in the Temple.

Friday, December 5—Eight a.m., Brother Heber C. Kimball and I called on Dr. Richards who was sick, we proceeded to the Temple and were engaged in fitting up the upper rooms.

Sunday, December 7—I met with the Twelve and others in the Temple. We partook of the sacrament, exhorted each other and prayed.

Monday, December 8—I have been actively engaged in the Temple since the painters finished, fitting up the apartments and preparing the rooms for administering endowments.

Tuesday, November 9—Forenoon, in the Temple.

Four p.m., Elders Heber C. Kimball, Orson Hyde, Parley P. Pratt, Willard Richards, John Taylor, George A. Smith, Amasa Lyman, Joseph L. Haywood, and I met at the Historian's Office with Father Tucker from Quincy and Father Hamilton from Springfield.

Father Tucker stated that Father Hamilton and himself had come here by direction of the bishop of Chicago, to see and inquire into the situation of the land and property for sale in and around Nauvoo.

I informed them that we would so reduce the value of the property as to make it an object for a society or speculators; and we wish to hand it over to the Catholics and so keep out those who want to have our property for nothing.

Evening, we wrote out propositions for the sale of our lands for the benefit of the Catholic deputation.

Wednesday, December 10—Nine a.m., I went to the Temple, weather fine, but cold.

I fitted up the curtains on the east windows, Brother Heber C. Kimball and wife, Sisters Parley P. Pratt and N. K. Whitney assisted me.

Eleven a.m., Messrs. Tucker and Hamilton, Catholics, were admitted into the Temple to an audience with the Quorum of the Twelve and a few other brethren.

The propositions for sale of our lands were handed, by Brother Orson Hyde, to Father Tucker, who perused them, and handed them to Father Hamilton, his colleague. I gave him an explanation of the design of the rooms in the Temple, with which they seemed well satisfied.

Father Tucker said he thought it would be wisdom to publish our propositions in all the Catholic papers and lay the matter plainly before their people.

He should also think it advisable for the Catholic bishop to send a competent committee to ascertain the value of our property, etc., etc. At the same time they will use all their influence to effect a sale as speedily as possible.

Father Tucker thought they had men in St. Louis, New York and other cities, who could soon raise the amount we want, but the time is so very short he does not know whether it can be done so soon.

He asked if we would be willing to have our propositions published in their papers.

I answered that we would have no objections, providing it was understood that we reserved the right to sell when we had an opportunity.

Father Hamilton wished to ascertain upon what conditions they could obtain two of our public buildings, one for a school and one for a church. They intended to write to the bishop, and wished to be able to supply him with some information on this subject.

I said I was well aware that there were many men in the Catholic Church who could furnish all the money we wanted immediately, but I supposed it was with them as it was with a Mr. Butler, a wealthy banker, who, when asked, why he did not sign off more bills, replied it was a good deal of trouble to sign off bills!

Perhaps it is too much trouble to dig their money out of their vaults, but I wished it distinctly understood that while we make liberal propositions to dispose of our property, we must have the means to help ourselves away.

I said I would like to add a note to our proposals before they are presented for publication, to this effect, that if a party agree to them, we will lease them the Temple for a period of from five to thirty-five years, at a reasonable price, the rent to be paid in finishing the unfinished parts of the Temple, the wall around the Temple block and the block west of the Temple, and keeping the Temple in repair.

The council agreed to the amendment, which was accordingly added to the proposals, and handed to Father Tucker.

Father Tucker gave much encouragement that an arrangement would speedily be entered into to accomplish the sale of our property; both of the gentlemen seemed highly pleased with the Temple and city.

Three p.m., Sisters Mary Ann Young, Vilate Kimball and Elizabeth Ann Whitney commenced administering the ordinances in the Temple.

We consecrated oil.

News has arrived that Sheriff Backenstos, who went to Peoria in charge of Henry W. Miller, coroner of Hancock county, and was tried before Judge Purple on the charge of the "murder" of Frank A. Worrell, was acquitted. The moral atmosphere around the judge was so different, than when at Carthage, that in all his charges and rulings, he appeared like another judge, and as though he had never been afflicted with mobocratic mania.

At 3:45 p.m., we completed the arrangements of the east room, preparatory to giving endowments.

The main room of the attic story is eighty-eight feet two inches long and twenty-eight feet eight inches wide. It is arched over, and the arch is divided into six spaces by cross beams to support the roof. There are six small rooms on each side about fourteen feet square. The last one on the east end on each side is a little smaller.

The first room on the south side beginning on the east is occupied by myself, the second by Elder Kimball, the third by Elders Orson Hyde, Parley P. Pratt and Orson Pratt; the fourth by John Taylor, George A. Smith, Amasa Lyman and John E. Page; the fifth by Joseph Young and Presidents of Seventies; the sixth, a preparation room.

On the north side, the first east room is for Bishop Whitney and the lesser priesthood, the second is for the high council, the third and fourth for President George Miller and the high priests' quorum, the fifth the elders' room, and the sixth the female preparation room.

Four-twenty-five p.m., Elder Heber C. Kimball and I commenced administering the ordinances of endowment.

Five o'clock, Isaac Morley and his wife Lucy, Joseph Fielding, Joseph C. Kingsbury and Cornelius P. Lott came in.

Nine-thirty p.m., we assembled for prayers, Amasa Lyman was mouth.

We continued officiating in the Temple during the night until three-thirty a.m. of the 11th.

Thursday, December 11—Elder Heber C. Kimball and I went to Joseph Kingsbury's and ate breakfast and returned to the Temple.

Elder Orson Pratt returned from his eastern mission, bringing four hundred dollars worth of Allen's revolving six-shooting pistols (alias pepperboxes).

I officiated in the Temple with the brethren of the Twelve.

At eight a.m., we assembled for prayer, Elder John E. Page was mouth.

After which I called the Twelve and bishops together and informed them that I had received a letter from Brother Samuel Brannan, stating that he had been at Washington and had learned that the secretary of war and other members of the cabinet were laying plans and were determined to prevent our moving west: alleging that it is against the law for an armed body of men to go from the United States to any other government.

They say it will not do to let the Mormons go to California nor Oregon, neither will it do to let them tarry in the states, and they must be obliterated from the face of the earth.

We prayed that the Lord would defeat and frustrate all the plans of our enemies, and inasmuch as they lay plans to exterminate this people and destroy the priesthood from off the earth, that the curse of God may come upon them, and all the evil which they design to bring upon us, may befall themselves; and that the Lord would preserve the lives of his servants and lead us out of this ungodly nation in peace.

I said we should go out from this place in spite of them all, and the brethren all felt that God would deliver us from the grasp of this ungodly and mobocratic nation.

Brother Amasa Lyman and I tarried in the Temple all night.

Friday, December 12—In company with my brethren of the Twelve I officiated in the Temple until midnight.

Orson Pratt and his wife, Sarah Marinda, the First Presidency of the Seventy and their wives and others numbering in all twenty-eight males and twenty-seven females received the ordinances of endowment.

Several tarried in the Temple all night.

Saturday, December 13—We continued officiating in the Temple; twenty-five males and twenty females were adminstered unto.

I drafted rules for the preservation of order in the House of the Lord.

Sunday, December 14—The Twelve and others with our wives met in the attic story of the Temple.

After prayer and singing, Elders Isaac Morley and Charles C. Rich administered, and we partook of the sacrament.

I introduced the subject of establishing rules for the preservation of order in the House of the Lord which were agreed to and ordered to be printed.

There is too much covetousness in the church, and too much disposition amongst the brethren to seek after power and has been from the beginning, but this feeling is diminishing and the brethren begin to know better. In consequence of such feelings Joseph [Smith] left the people in the dark on many subjects of importance and they still remain in the dark. We have got to rid such principles from our hearts.

I refered to the manner in which the corner stones of this Temple were laid as published in the *Times and Seasons*, and said that the perfect order would have been for the presidency of the stake to lay the first or southeast corner; the high council the second or southwest corner; the bishops the northeast corner; but the high priests laid the southwest corner, though they had no right to do it.

I spoke of the brethren making objections to persons being permitted to receive the ordinances, and added, that when objections were made I should feel bound to determine whether the person making the objections was a responsible person, and if he is not, I should do as I pleased about listening to the objections; but if he was a responsible person I should listen to them.

To constitute a man responsible he must have the power and ability not only to save himself but to save others; but there are those who are not capable of saving themselves and will have to be saved by others.

When a man objects to another receiving the ordinances he becomes responsible to answer to God for that man's salvation; and who can tell but if he received the ordinances he would be saved, but if we refuse to give him the means he cannot be saved and we are responsible for it.

There is no law to prevent any man from obtaining all the blessings of the priesthood if he will walk according to the commandments, pay his tithes and seek after salvation, but he may deprive himself of them.

After much profitable instruction we united in prayer, Orson Hyde being mouth.

Meeting adjourned for one week.

Two p.m., many of those who had received their ordinances the past week met and received instructions from Elders Parley P. Pratt and William W. Phelps.

The Twelve met and read some letters, also an account of Sheriff Backenstos' travel from the *Peoria Register*.

We went down to the lower room and counseled on the arrangement of the pulpits.

I remained in the Temple all night.

Monday, December 15—The ordinances of endowment were administered to sixty-four brethren and sisters.

The Twelve and others officiated.

Tuesday, December 16—I have been busy in the Temple dictating the order of business, appointing brethren to officiate in the various departments, and giving much instruction at different intervals; Elder Kimball assisted me. Sixty-nine brethren and sisters received their ordinances.

Wednesday, December 17—We continued our labors in the Temple, administered the ordinances of endowment to sixty-nine brethren and sisters.

Ten twenty-five p.m., eighteen persons assembled in my room and joined with me in prayer.

My son, Joseph A., remained with me in the Temple all night.

Letters were written to Stephen A. Douglas, M. C., J. P. Hoge, M. C., Wm. S. Marcy, Secretary of War, John Wentworth, M. C., and John Chapman in relation to our movement to the west, in consequence of learning that attempts were made to induce government to prevent our removal.

Thursday, December 18—Sixty-six persons were administered to in the Temple. I retired to bed about midnight.

In consequence of the great pressure of business during the past week, it had been decided to devote Saturday to the purpose of washing robes and garments used, but there being a general desire in the minds of all those officiating in the ordinances that the work should not cease, it was determined that the clothes should be washed during the night.

Saturday, December 20—Beautiful morning. I dictated the arrangements for the day. Afterwards, with a few of the Twelve and others heard F. D. Richards read *Fremont's Journal*, giving an account of his travels to California.

We considered it prudent to devote today to cleaning and washing, and suspend operations in the Temple; but on account of the anxiety of the saints to receive their ordinances, the brethren and sisters volunteered to wash clothes every night. Ninety-five persons received their ordinances.

Sunday, December 21—According to appointment on Sunday last, a meeting was held in the Temple today of some of those who had received their ordinances.

Seventy-five persons were present.

Elder Heber C. Kimball presiding.

The sacrament was administered by Father John Smith and Bishop George Miller.

Elders George A. Smith and Heber C. Kimball preached, others made a few remarks confirming what had been said.

Elder John Taylor was mouth in prayer.

Meeting dismissed at 2:10 p.m.

Three p.m., many others who had been invited met according to appointment.

Elders Amasa Lyman and Heber C. Kimball preached.

At ten a.m., the seventies met in the Music Hall. The thirty-second quorum of seventies was organized; and arrangements made to finish an upper room in the Temple for the benefit of the seventies.

Monday, December 22—I stayed in the Temple last night and early this morning gave direction for the arrangements of the day, assisted by George Miller,* as the day was set apart more especially for the high priests.

One hundred and six persons received ordinances.

Tuesday, December 23—Early this morning the drying house of Captain Charles C. Rich's Emigrating Co. No. 13 was burned to the ground, consuming $300.00 worth of wagon timber.

The high council met in the Temple for prayer.

One-five p.m., Almon W. Babbitt came into the Temple and informed me that there were some federal officers from Springfield accompanied by several of the state troops in the city for the purpose of arresting some of the Twelve, especially Amasa Lyman and myself.

It was soon reported that they were at the door of the Temple and were intending to search it. George D. Grant, my coachman, went below and drove

*Brother Miller was president of the high priests.

my carriage up to the door as if he was waiting for me to come down.

William Miller put on my cap and Brother Kimball's cloak and went downstairs meeting the marshal and his assistants at the door, as he was about getting into my carriage the marshal arrested him, on a writ from the United States court, charging him with counterfeiting the coin of the United States. Miller told him there must be some mistake about it, as he was not guilty of anything of the kind, but the marshal insisted it was right. Miller desired the marshal to go down to the Mansion where he could get counsel and ascertain if the proceedings were legal. On reaching the Mansion they went into a private room where Esq. Edmonds examined the writ and pronounced it legal. Miller gave Edmonds the name of four witnesses for subpoena for him, and asked the marshal to remain until morning; he consented, but soon got uneasy and said he must go to Carthage. Miller then inquired if he would wait three quarters of an hour until he could get his witnesses, but in fifteen minutes he said he must go, and would wait no longer. Miller got into his carriage, Esq. Edmonds rode with the marshal's guard and they started for Carthage, Miller protesting there was some mistake about it, for he certainly was not guilty of any such things as were charged in the writ: on the way to Carthage the marshal was very social, and remarked that the people had got quite a joke upon him for letting Turley give him the dodge. As they approached Carthage the troops began to whoop and holloa and went into town in high glee, performing the journey which was eighteen miles in two hours.

The marshal put up at Hamilton's Tavern, and the rumor soon spread through the town that Brigham Young was in the custody of the marshal at Hamilton's. Among others, George W. Thatcher, county commissioner's clerk, who was well acquainted with Miller came into the tavern to see me. The marshal at his request took Miller into a private room. After a little conversation one of the guards came in and the marshal went out. The marshal soon returned and said to Mr. Miller, "I am informed you are not Mr. Young;" "Ah!" exclaimed Miller, "then if I should prove not to be Mr. Young, it would be a worse joke on you than the Turley affair," he replied, "I'll be damned if it won't."

The marshal asked Miller if his name was Young, he answered, "I never told you my name was Young, did I?" "No," replied the marshal, "but one of my men professed to be acquainted with Mr. Young, and pointed you out to me to be him." William Backenstos was called in and he told them William Miller was not Brigham Young. Another man came, and said he could swear Miller was not Brigham Young. The marshal said he was sorry, and asked Miller his name, he replied, "it is William Miller".

The marshal left the room and soon returned accompanied by Edmonds who was laughing heartily at him. Edmonds inquired if he had anything more to do with "Mr. Young". The marshal replied that he did not know that he had anything further to do with Mr. Miller.

Eighty-seven persons received the ordinances.

Seven-thirty p.m., I met with the Twelve in prayer, and thanked the Lord for deliverance from the snares of our enemies.

Eight-twenty, I left the Temple disguised and shortly after Brothers Heber C. Kimball, Parley P. Pratt, George A. Smith and Amasa Lyman left, to elude the vexatious writs of our persecutors.

Wednesday, December 24—All the Twelve have been absent from the Temple the greater part of this day except Orson Pratt. One hundred twenty-two persons received the ordinances.

At 11:20, Elder Heber C. Kimball and I returned to the Temple and remained all night.

William Miller remained last night at Carthage at Jacob B. Backenstos'. Miller said he could not sleep being interrupted by Edmonds' continued roars of laughter at the marshal's discomfiture.

Miller saw two of the marshal's guards, one of whom threatened his life. Miller came in with the stage, the driver told him that the officers said it would be like searching for a needle in a hay mow now, to undertake to find Brigham Young in Nauvoo.

Thursday, December 25—12:15 p.m., George D. Grant brought word that the United States marshal is in the city again.

The Twelve met in my room for counsel and prayer. After considerable conversation about the western country we united in prayer: George A. Smith was mouth.

One hundred seven persons received their ordinances. The business of the day closed at twenty minutes past ten o'clock, and notice was given that no more washings and anointings would be attended to at present. Brother Kimball and I, with some few others, remained in the Temple all night.

Friday, December 26—Elders Heber C. Kimball, Orson Pratt and I were present in the Temple this morning and a few of those who had been officiating: I called them together in the east room about 11:30 a.m., and told them there would be no business done today and that they were all dismissed except the two Brothers Hanson, and three brethren for officers.

I said we shall have no more anointing at present, and if the brethren do not get anything more than they have already received, they have got all they have worked for in building this house; and if there is any more to be received it is because the Lord is merciful and gracious.

The high council and high priests will meet together once a day as usual for prayer.

Two hundred sixty-eight high priests were reported to have received their endowments.

I further remarked, that when we began again we should pay no respect to quorums. Every man that comes in, is washed and anointed by good men and it makes no difference. Every man that gets his endowments, whether he is a high priest or seventy may go into any part of the world and build up the kingdom if he has the keys. We have been ordained to the Melchizedek priesthood which is the highest order of the priesthood, and it has many branches or appendages.

I said, my feelings were to rest a few days and let the Temple rest, and when we commenced work again I would make a selection of hands who will remain and officiate daily. No persons will be allowed to come in unless they are invited, and I shall feel insulted if they remain here. I felt it impressed upon me to rest a few days and make these regulations, and as our oil is done we cannot do much anyway.

Sheriff Backenstos informed me that the United States deputy marshal was in town with writs for the Twelve and Brother George Miller.

Eight p.m., Elder Kimball and I left the Temple.

Saturday, December 27—This morning was a very pleasant one, moderately cold, the sun shining clear and bright in the heavens.

Orson Pratt was the only one of the Twelve present in the Temple.

Ten-fifteen a.m., the United States Deputy Marshal Roberts, went to the Temple in company with Almon W. Babbitt and searched for the Twelve and others. He was freely admitted to every part of the Temple, to which he desired access; he went into the tower, on to the roof, into the attic story and while viewing the city from the tower he expressed his astonishment at its magnificence and extent and said considering the unfavorable circumstances with which the people had been surrounded it seemed almost impossible that so much should have been accomplished. He passed through the various departments into the east room where he very intently examined the portraits, and made inquiries as to whose they were.

On entering the attic hall he was requesteed to take off his boots and uncover his head, to which he complied; after remaining about half an hour he departed.

About two p.m., the marshal returned accompanied by a gentleman whom he introduced as from New Orleans, and Sheriff Backenstos. They visited the middle room and the tower and departed after about half an hour.

Lewis Robbins is cleaning and putting in order the washing rooms and furniture, Peter Hanson is translating the *Book of Mormon* in the Danish language, Elisha Averett is doorkeeper, John L. Butler, fireman, David Candland and L. R. Foster, clerks. Orson Pratt has been engaged in making astronomical calculations. From several observations he makes the latitude of Nauvoo 40°35'48" north.

Sunday, December 28—About two hundred of the brethren and sisters met at ten-thirty a.m. in the attic story of the Temple, some of the side rooms were filled, and the curtains withdrawn.

After singing and prayer, I addressed the meeting.

The sacrament was administered. Elder Kimball made a few remarks. After prayer the meeting was dismissed by benediction from Elder Orson Hyde.

Six p.m., the high council and the high priests met for prayer.

Elder Kimball and I remained in the Temple.

Monday, December 29—Elder Kimball and I assisted by our wives, and the laborers in the Temple, cleaned up and arranged the furniture in the rooms.

Four dragoons came in from Carthage and searched Nauvoo for hogs, said to have been stolen from Mr. Hibbard.

Three-forty, a company numbering twelve commenced receiving their ordinances; this makes 1000 who have received the ordinances.

The Twelve met for prayer. We prayed for deliverance from our enemies, and that we might be spared to give the faithful saints their endowments, Orson Hyde being mouth

I spent an hour reading, and with Brothers Kimball and Lyman remained in the Temple all night.

Tuesday, December 30—At eight-ten a.m., commenced to administer the ordinances. Elders Heber C. Kimball, Parley P. Pratt, George A. Smith, Amasa Lyman, Joseph Young and myself consecrated oil.

Eleven-thirty, Almon W. Babbitt reported that the marshal had left for Springfield, and there would probably be no more danger of writs for the present.

Eighty-eight persons received ordinances.

Elder Parley P. Pratt has been engaged part of the time in forming a schedule for a Pioneer Company of 1000 men to precede the body of emigrants, to find a proper location and put in seed early in the summer.

The labors of the day having been brought to a close at so early an hour, *viz.*: eight-thirty, it was thought proper to have a little season of recreation, accordingly Brother Hanson was invited to produce his violin, which he did, and played several lively airs accompanied by Elisha Averett on his flute, among others some very good lively dancing tunes. This was too much for the gravity of Brother Joseph Young who indulged in dancing a hornpipe, and was soon joined by several others, and before the dance was over several French fours were indulged in. The first was opened by myself with Sister Whitney and Elder Heber C. Kimball and partner. The spirit of dancing increased until the whole floor was covered with dancers, and while we danced before the Lord, we shook the dust from off our feet as a testimony against this nation.

After the dancing had continued about an hour, several excellent songs were sung, in which several of the brethren and sisters joined. The "Upper California" was sung by Erastus Snow, after which I called upon Sister Whitney who stood up and invoking the gift of tongues, sang a beautiful song of Zion in tongues. The interpretation was given by her husband, Bishop Whitney, and me, it related to our efforts to build this house to the privilege we now have of meeting in it, our departure shortly to the country of the Lamanites, their rejoicing when they hear the gospel and of the ingathering of Israel.

I spoke in a foreign tongue; likewise, Brother Kimball.

After a little conversation of a general nature I closed the exercises of the evening by prayer.

Wednesday, December 31—Elder Heber C. Kimball and I superintended the operations in the Temple, examined maps with reference to selecting a location for the saints west of the Rocky Mountains, and reading various works written by travelers in those regions; also made selections of names of persons to be invited to receive their endowments.

Eighty-four persons were received into the Temple.

1846

.

Thursday, January 1—At an early hour, Elder Heber C. Kimball and I went to the Temple. The plasterers have commenced to plaster the arched ceiling of the lower hall, the floor is laid, the framework of the pulpits and seats for the choir and band are put up; and the work of finishing the room for dedication progresses rapidly.

6:30 p.m., the high priests met and prayed, eighty-nine persons received ordinances.

10:20 p.m., after finishing the labors of the day, the company assembled in the large room in the attic story and united in prayer with Elder Heber C. Kimball, thanking God for his great mercy and goodness to us in granting this opportunity of meeting together in the House of the Lord, asking him that he would continue to bless us, that he would bless President Brigham Young with health and wisdom, that he might be able to lead and direct this people; and that the same blessings might be extended to all his brethren of the Twelve and all the saints; and that God would bless our wives and give unto them strength of body that they might live and administer to the servants of God, that they might see three score years and ten, and behold the kingdom of God established in the earth; and that we might be enabled to continue in Nauvoo in peace, until all the faithful saints had received their endowments; and that when the time to leave here should arrive that we might be able to sell our possessions and obtain those things that we need to enable us to go away in comfort. Also, that God would bless our children, and all that pertains to us.

Friday, January 2—Sixty-four persons received ordinances.

This morning Elder Heber C. Kimball related the following dream: Last evening, before retiring to bed he asked God to enlighten his mind with regard to the work of endowment; while sleeping he beheld a large field of corn that was fully ripe, he and a number of others were commanded to take baskets and pick off the corn with all possible speed, for there would soon be a storm that would hinder the gathering of the harvest. The hands engaged in gathering the harvest, were heedless and unconcerned and did not haste, as they were commanded; but he and the man he assisted had a much larger basket than the rest, and picked with all their might of the largest ears of the field, they once in a while would pick an ear that had a long tail on each end and but a few grains scattering over the center of the cob, which were very light.

The interpretation of the dream is, that the field represented the church, the good corn represented good saints, the light corn represented the light and indifferent saints, the laborers are those appointed to officiate in the Temple, the storm is trouble that is near upon us, and requires an immediate united exertion of all engaged in giving the endowments to the saints, or else we will not get through before we will be obliged to flee for our lives.

Elder Kimball having invited Brothers William Pitt, William Clayton, J. F. Hutchinson and James Smithies [musicians], they performed several very beautiful pieces of music.

After a short time spent in dancing, Elder Orson Hyde delivered a short address and requested the company present to unite with him in prayer.

I addressed the brethren at length, alluding to the privileges we enjoy—of the order of administering endowments: that the way to grow and thrive was to serve the Lord in all we did, exhorted the brethren to remember their covenants and not to speak evil of each other, and related some of the efforts made to arrest me and persecute the saints. If Joseph Smith had been living, we should have already been in some other country, and we would go where we would be "the old settlers", and build larger Temples than this.

Saturday, January 3—One hundred and fourteen persons received their ordinances.

I had a chill today, accompanied by fever, and felt unable to attend to business. I remained in the Temple all night.

Sunday, January 4—No public meeting was held in the Temple this day, on account of the floor being insufficient to support a large congregation.

Should Governor Ford's speculations and suppositions in relation to U. S. troops prove correct, and the government send a regular force to arrest us, we will run no risk of being murdered by them as our leaders have been; and as to fearing a trial before the courts it is all gammon for our danger consists only in being held still by the authorities while mobs massacre us as Governor Ford held Joseph and Hyrum Smith while they were butchered.

Monday, January 5—My health being better I was ready for duty at an early hour. Spent the morning in hearing letters and newspapers [read], and giving directions as to the business of the day.

8:45 a.m., commenced washing and anointing [i. e. in the Temple].

Seventeen bottles of oil were consecrated.

One hundred four persons received their endowments.

9 p.m., the labors of the day being over, Brothers Hanson and E. Averett played on the violin and flute and enlivened the spirits of the saints present: some embraced the opportunity and danced to the lively strains of music.

Elder Heber C. Kimball and I returned home about midnight.

Tuesday, January 6—Seventeen bottles of oil were consecrated.

Ninety persons received ordinances.

6 p.m., Elder H. C. Kimball and I with our wives attended a party at Elder John Taylor's.

Three companies of high priests, the high council, and the seventies met for prayer in their respective rooms in the Temple.

Several musicians were present in the evening, some of the brethren danced.

I returned to the Temple about 10 p.m. and took part in the exercises. Brothers Erastus Snow and Levi W. Hancock sang hymns.

Wednesday, January 7—This morning there was an immense crowd at the reception room waiting for admission. The brethren brought all kinds of provisions for the use of those who are attending on the ordinances of the Lord's House.

A letter was received this morning from Father Tucker, informing us that the Catholic bishop could not raise money enough to purchase our property, but would either purchase or rent one of our public buildings, but would not insure it against fire or mobs.

One hundred twenty-one persons received ordinances.

The supply of provisions brought in today has been very abundant, and much has been sent away to those families that are destitute.

The high council and three companies of high priests met for prayer.

The Presidents of Seventies met in council, in relation to keeping order in the Temple. The Twelve delegated to them the government of the Temple, while the ordinances were being administered to their quorums.

This afternoon, the new altar was used for the first time, and four individuals and their wives were sealed. The altar is about two and one-half feet high and two and one-half feet long and about one foot wide, rising from a platform about 8 or 9 inches high and extending out on all sides about a foot, forming a convenient place to kneel upon. The top of the altar and the platform for kneeling upon are covered with cushions of scarlet damask cloth; the sides of the upright part or body of the altar are covered with white linen.

The Twelve and presiding bishops with their wives were present at the dedication of the altar this afternoon.

Thursday, January 8—Eighty-one persons received ordinances.

Friday, January 9—One hundred and five persons received ordinances in the Temple. I attended to ordinances at the altar. The several quorums met for prayer.

I observed to the brethren that it was my wish that all dancing and merriment should cease, lest the brethren and sisters be carried away by vanity; and that the name of the Deity should be held in reverence, with all the due deference that belongeth to an infinite being of his character.

Monday, January 12—One hundred and forty-three persons received their endowments in the Temple. I officiated at the altar. Such has been the anxiety manifested by the saints to receive the ordinances [of the Temple], and such the anxiety on our part to administer to them, that I have given myself up entirely to the work of the Lord in the Temple night and day, not taking more than four hours sleep, upon an average, per day, and going home but once a week.

Elder Heber C. Kimball and the others of the Twelve Apostles were in constant attendance but in consequence of close application some of them had to leave the Temple to rest and recruit their health.

Tuesday, January 13—A council was held in the Temple.

The captains of fifties and tens made reports of the number in their respective companies, who were prepared to start west immediately, should the persecutions of our enemies compel us to do so: one hundred and forty horses and seventy wagons were reported ready for immediate service.

Saturday, January 17—I attended a concert in the Music Hall; while my coachman, Brother George D. Grant, was taking his last passenger home, my horses fell through a bridge on Parley Street; I was in bed when I heard of it, but immediately arose, put on my clothes and hastened to the rescue of my team; on arriving I found they had lain nearly an hour between the timbers of the bridge, totally unable to extricate themselves from their distressing situation, and notwithstanding they were dumb animals they were sensible of their condition. We soon tore the timbers away and let down the horses one at a time, and rolling them over placed them where they could help themselves. (The depth of the gully was about six feet.) I returned home and washed the horses all over with spirits, using about half a gallon of whiskey in bathing them, which prevented stiffness and colds, so that in a few days they were able for service again.

Sunday, January 18—A meeting of the captains of Emigrating Companies was held in the attic story of the Temple, to ascertain the number ready and willing to start should necessity compel our instant removal, being aware that evil is intended towards us, and that our safety alone will depend upon our departure from this place, before our enemies shall intercept and prevent our going.

A general interest in the movement was manifested by the whole council, every man felt willing to yield to the circumstances that surround us, and let their property be used for the purpose of accomplishing the removal and salvation of this people.

Monday, January 19—I administered at the altar all day with the exception of thirty minutes in which I took some refreshments.

Evening, I attended a concert in the Music Hall.

Tuesday, January 20—One hundred and ninety-five persons received ordinances in the Temple.

Public prejudice being so strong against us, and the excitement becoming alarming we determined to continue the administration of the ordinances of endowment night and day.

Wednesday, January 21—Two hundred and eight persons received ordinances.

Thursday, January 22—One hundred and ninety-eight persons received ordinances in the Temple.

Friday, January 23—One hundred and twenty-eight persons received ordinances in the Temple.

Saturday, January 24—One hundred and fifty-one persons received ordinances in the Temple. I attended a general meeting of the official members of the church held in the second story of the Temple, for the purpose of arranging the business affairs of the church prior to our exit from this place.

The meeting being organized previous to my arrival Elder Orson Pratt was appointed chairman.

I explained to the brethren the object of appointing trustees, and informed them that the trustees would act in concert with Bishops Whitney and Miller while they remained here; and that when the Twelve left the bishops would accompany them, and that the trustees now appointed would carry on the finishing of the Temple and the Nauvoo House, also dispose of our property, fit out the saints and send them westward. It is wisdom to take this course that we may have efficient men to act for and in behalf of the church and people. I want Bishops Whitney and Miller here while we are here, and when we go, they will go with us.

We intend to start a company of young men and some few families perhaps within a few weeks. This company will travel until they can find a good location beyond the settlements, and there stop and put in a summer crop, that we may have something to subsist upon, and a portion of us remain there until we can make further discoveries.

We are forced to this policy by those who are in authority [i. e. in the state]. I find no fault with the Constitution or laws of our country, they are good enough. It is the abuse of those laws which I despise, and which God, good men and angels abhor.

I hope we will find a place, where no self-righteous neighbors can say that we are obnoxious to them; I exhort you brethren not to be self-important. We have covenanted to remove the poor that are worthy, and this we intend to do, God being our helper.

Let us walk humbly before the Lord, be upright and sustain yourselves and realize that we are engaged in a great and important movement. If any want to go with us that are not members of the church bid them welcome; for I look upon every man that is a true republican as bone of my bone and flesh of my flesh; and if any wish to follow Sidney Rigdon or J. J. Strang I say let them go; we will cut them off from the church, and let them take their own course for salvation.

I know where the power of the priesthood lies and I know that the enemy of all righteousness seeks our downfall, but God is our preserver.

A set of bogus-makers who recently commenced operations in this city, who are determined to counterfeit coin here by wagonloads and make it pass upon the community as land office money; [they] are determined to be revenged upon us, because we would not permit them to pursue their wicked business in Nauvoo, they have scattered through the country circulating their bogus money and spreading lies and every species of falsehood, saying that we are engaged in bogus-making in order thereby to conceal their crimes, and screen themselves from observation and punishment, and at the same time be avenged upon us for not consenting to the establishment of their bogus mints at Nauvoo.

Nevertheless, we may have to suffer repeated wrongs in consequence of those falsehoods that are and which will be circulated about us; but my faith is that God will rule the elements, and the Prince and power of the air will be stayed, and the Lord will fight out battles, as in the days of Moses; and we will see the deliverance brought to pass. Although, there may be bloodshed frequently, still this must needs be that the scriptures may be fulfilled.

It is but a small matter for us to lay down our lives if we are prepared for the change: when we take our exit from this world we go into the society of disembodied spirits, and there become one of those who await the resurrection of the body; if humility and faithfulness has characterized our lives, our condition will be much better than the present. This nation is fearful that we will turn the world upside down and accomplish wonderful things in the land; our elders have confounded the wise men if they have not converted them. The nation are afraid that we will convert the savages of the forest; we will teach them and all with whom we may have intercourse, and further we will yet bring salvation to this nation if they will cease their hostilities against us, and repent of their sins. The Lord has said he would fight our battles, and if this nation still continues to be actuated towards us with a persecuting spirit, vengeance shall come from the Lord upon them, until they shall be utterly wasted; but I intend to preach and do all the good that I can.

When the time comes to start westward we will continue to gather, until Israel is gathered; let there be no feelings about who shall go first; those who go first will lay a foundation for those who shall come after, and none will be neglected in their time.

I have one request to make of all the saints that expect to emigrate with us, that they be subject to their leaders, with their property and means, and if this is done I can say there never will be a lack in the church. If any man can say that he has been wronged out of his money by the bishops, let him speak and it shall be restored to him again; but I am aware it is not so. Keep your money in circulation and it will enable you to do good and you will be blessed in so doing; retain your money when the poor around you are crying for bread and it will prove a curse to you. Be honorable in all your dealings, prompt and punctual to pay all your debts and restore confidence, let promptness and punctuality be the standard with you and the God of peace will pour out blessings upon you that there shall not be room enough to receive them.

We intend to finish the Temple and the Nauvoo House, as far as putting on the roof and putting in the windows are concerned, and we shall drop all political operations and church government, and by so doing we may preserve our public buildings from the torch. I propose that all the saints lay down their property to be used in building the Temple, the Nauvoo House and helping the poor away, such as must go in the first company.

I nominated Almon W. Babbitt, Joseph L. Heywood, and John S. Fullmer, trustees for the building of the Temple and Henry W. Miller and John M. Bernhisel, trustees or committee for the building of the Nauvoo House, which nominations were seconded and carried without a dissenting voice.

Two p.m., on motion, the meeting adjourned, after which I ascended the stairs—called at the dining room and partook of some refreshment, then repaired to room No. 1 where I continued administering at the altar until midnight.

Sunday, January 25—I attended to ordinances in the Temple.

Monday, January 26—Nine a.m., I went to the Temple and commenced the ordinances in the different departments which were set apart for the purpose; the washing and anointing was suspended until tomorrow.

Tuesday, January 27—One hundred and twenty-six persons received ordinances.

Elders Heber C. Kimball, Orson Hyde, Parley P. Pratt, Orson Pratt, Amasa Lyman, and I officiated in the higher ordinances. Elders George A. Smith and Willard Richards were absent, being sick.

Sheriff Backenstos has returned from Springfield, and says, that Governor Ford has turned against us, and that Major Warren is making calculations to prevent our going away.

I received a letter from Josiah Lamborn, Esq., Springfield, stating that Governor Ford was decidedly in favor of General J. J. Hardin's policy, which is, that of suspending all civil offices, the collection of taxes, and placing the county under martial law.

I officiated at the altar until 10 p.m. and remained in the Temple all night.

Wednesday, January 28—One hundred and seventy-two persons received ordinances in the Temple.

Nine-thirty p.m., the labors of the day closed. I remained in the Temple.

Thursday, January 29—I continued giving endowments in the Temple in connection with my brethren of the Twelve and others. One hundred and thirty-three persons received ordinances.

Quite a number of the governor's troops are prowling around our city; I am informed that they are seeking to arrest some of the leading men of the church.

This evening I read a letter from S. Brannan in which he said he had ascertained from Amos Kendall, the late postmaster-general, that government intended to intercept our movements by stationing strong forces in our way to take from us all firearms on the pretense that we were going to join another nation.

Brannan said this jealousy originated from Arlington Bennett's letters in relation to our movements. We ask God our heavenly Father to exert his power in our deliverance that we may be preserved to establish truth upon all the face of the earth.

Friday, January 30—One hundred and seventy-two persons received the ordinances of endowment.

Nine a.m., the [wind] vane was put upon the tower of the Temple.

The weather is stormy, yet not cold. At ten a.m., I entered the Temple where I labored until evening.

Saturday, January 31—Two hundred and thirty-three persons received ordinances.

About noon, Brother Amasa Lyman came into the Temple being quite feeble; Elder H. C. Kimball administered to him.

Monday, February 2—Two hundred and thirty-four persons received ordinances.

Ten a.m., the Twelve, Trustees and a few others met in council, to ascertain the feelings of the brethren that were expecting to start westward. We agreed that it was imperatively necessary to start as soon as possible. I counseled the brethren to procure boats and hold them in readiness to convey our wagons and teams over the river, and let everything for the journey be in readiness, that when a family is called to go, everything necessary may be put into the wagon within four hours, at least, for if we are here many days, our way will be hedged up. Our enemies have resolved to intercept us whenever we start. I should like to push on as far as possible before they are aware of our movements. In order to have this counsel circulated, I sent messengers to notify the captains of hundreds and fifties to meet at 4 p.m. at Father Cutlers'.

At four o'clock, I met with the captains of hundreds and fifties, and laid my counsel before them, to which they all consented, and dispersed to carry it into execution.

I received letters from England and the eastern states.

At sundown, I returned to the Temple and continued there until 9 p.m. Before leaving I gave instructions to my clerks not to stop recording until the records of the endowments were finished.

Elder H. C. Kimball and I went to Willard Richards' office, where we remained in council with him. In the course of our council we walked out into the garden, and examined his grove of chestnut trees, and his wife, Jennetta's grave, and after returning to the office made inquiries of the Lord as to our circumstances and the circumstances of the saints and received satisfactory answers. Retired about 1 a.m.

Tuesday, February 3—Notwithstanding that I had announced that we would not attend to the administration of the ordinances, the House of the Lord was thronged all day, the anxiety being so great to receive, as if the brethren would have us stay here and continue the endowments until our way would be hedged up, and our enemies would intercept us. But I informed the brethren that this was not wise, and that we should build more Temples, and have further opportunities to receive the blessings of the Lord, as soon as the saints were prepared to receive them. In this Temple we have been abundantly rewarded, if we receive no more. I also informed the brethren that I was going to get my wagons started and be off. I walked some distance from the Temple supposing the crowd would disperse, but on returning I found the house filled to overflowing.

Looking upon the multitude and knowing their anxiety, as they were thirsting and hungering for the word, we continued at work diligently in the House of the Lord.

Two hundred and ninety-five persons received ordinances.

Brother Player and two others altering Jennetta Richards' grave. I stayed at home until 6 p.m. I went to the Temple and returned again in an hour, busy preparing for my journey to the west.

Jennetta's coffin was opened, and the whole family looked at the corpse, which was but little decayed.

Wednesday, February 4—I continued loading up my wagons, preparatory to starting west.

Brother Player and other completed Jennetta's grave placing the inscription stone across her breast, one stone below, and another above, for a covering of the whole. It was first covered with a plank. A line passing ten feet south of the house, in a range with the west side of the building, thence west at a right angle twenty feet, thence descend at a right angle about three feet, and it will reach about the center of the vault containing the coffin.

Friday, February 6—Five hundred and twelve persons received the first ordinances of endowment in the Temple.

Bishop George Miller and family crossed the Mississippi river. They had six wagons.

Saturday, February 7—According to G. A. Smith's Journal upwards of six hundred received the ordinances [i. e. of the Temple]: One hundred and twenty-six of which were reported in the Seventies Record.

Sunday, February 8—I met with the Council of the Twelve in the southeast corner room of the attic of the Temple. We knelt around the altar, and dedicated the building to the Most High. We asked his blessing upon our intended move to the west; also asked him to enable us some day to finish the Temple, and dedicate it to him, and we would leave it in his hands to do as he pleased; and to preserve the building as a monument to Joseph Smith. We asked the Lord to accept the labors of his servants in this land. We then left the Temple.

I addressed the saints in the grove and informed them that the company going to the west would start this week across the river.

John Smith, president of the stake, and family crossed the river, accompanied by his clerk, Albert Carrington, and family.

Monday, February 9—A detachment of the governor's troops came into the city and apprehended a man named Samuel Smith, who soon escaped.

Elder George A. Smith sent his family across the river.

Three-thirty p.m., the roof of the Temple was discovered to be on fire. An alarm was immediately given, when the brethren marched steadily to its rescue. I saw the flames from a distance, but it was out of my power to get there in time to do any good towards putting out the fire, and I said if it is the will of the Lord that the Temple be burned, instead of being defiled by the Gentiles, Amen to it.

I went to the Temple as soon as I could, after the fire had been extinguished, the brethren gave a loud shout of Hosannah, while standing on the deck roof.

Willard Richards called on the brethren to bring out all their buckets, to fill them with water, and pass them on. Lines inside were formed, and the buckets passed in quick succession. The fire raged near half an hour. It was caused by the stovepipe being overheated, drying the clothing in the upper room. It burned from the west stovepipe from the ridge to the railing, about sixteen feet north and south, and about ten feet east and west on the north side. The shingles on the north were broken in several places.

By the advice of President H. C. Kimball the brethren dispersed.

Several of the troops went to the Temple and attempted to enter, but were prevented by the brethren at the door.

At the same time that the Temple was on fire a number of brethren were crossing the river in a flatboat, when in their rear a man and two boys were in a skiff in a sinking condition, on account of being overloaded and the unskilfulness of the helmsman. They hailed to the flatboat, which soon turned, and rendered them assistance. As soon as they got the three on board the flatboat, a filthy wicked man squirted some tobacco juice into the eyes of one of the oxen attached to Thomas Grover's wagon, which immediately plunged into the river, dragging another ox with him, and as he was going overboard he tore off one of the sideboards which caused the water to flow into the flatboat, and as they approached the shore the boat sank to the bottom, before all the men could leap off. Several of the brethren were picked up in an exhausted condition. Two oxen were drowned and a few things floated away and were lost. The wagon was drawn out of the river with its contents damaged.

The crossing of the river was superintended by the police, under the direction of Hosea Stout. They gathered several flatboats, some old lighters, and a number of skiffs, forming altogether quite a fleet, and were at work night and day, crossing the saints.

Sunday, February 15—I crossed the river with my family accompanied by W. Richards and family and George A. Smith. We traveled on four miles, when we came to the bluff. I would not go on until I saw all the teams up. I helped them up the hill with my own hands. At dusk started on, and reached Sugar Creek about 8 p.m., having traveled nine miles. The roads were very bad.

Monday, February 16—I was very busy in organizing the camp on Sugar Creek, Ambrosia township, Lee county, Iowa territory, where there was plenty of timber and water.

Ten a.m., I walked up the valley with Amasa Lyman and Willard Richards where we united in prayer, and I read to them a communication received two days previously, then returned to camp and continued the organization, acting the part of a father to everybody.

The night was clear and cold.

Tuesday, February 17—Nine-fifty a.m., all the brethren of the camp assembled near the bridge, when I arose in a wagon and cried with a loud voice—"Attention! the whole Camp of Israel". I proceeded to explain the cause of delay of the camp, which was, in short, that Bishop Whitney and Elders H. C. Kimball and Wm. Clayton were not ready, or were waiting to secure and bring with them church property needed in the camp. Some of the brethren have been here nearly two weeks, and if all had come on according to counsel, I should have been here sooner, if I had come without a shirt to my back.

I wish the brethren to stop running to Nauvoo, hunting, fishing, roasting their shins, idling away their time, and fix nosebaskets for their horses, and save their corn, and fix comfortable places for their wives and children to ride, and never borrow without asking leave, and be sure and return what was borrowed, lest your brother be vexed with you and in his anger curse you, and then you would be cursed according to the power of the priesthood that brother possesses, and evil will come upon you. That all dogs in the camp should be killed, if the owners would not tie them up; and any man who would keep a horse in camp, that had the horse distemper, ought to forfeit all his horses. [This because horse distemper was rife in the camp and contagious.]

We will have no laws we cannot keep, but we will have order in the camp. If any want to live in peace when we have left this, they must toe the mark.

I then called upon all who wanted to go with the camp, to raise their right hands, and all hands were up. I said we must wait here until we get the artillery, canvas, and public property; that the brethren must build a pen for corn and hay. George W. Harris was appointed commissary. That all spare men were for pioneers, guards, watchmen, and that all men of families must be organized into companies of tens, fifties, and hundreds. Wm. Clayton would be general clerk of the camp.

I requested the brethren to report all matters of history which might arise, to Willard Richards, historian.

At eleven o'clock, I returned to my tent and commenced organizing my division of the camp, consisting of four companies of tens, including the historian, his family, and teams.

Elder Heber C. Kimball arrived in camp at the same hour, and at half past one he and I dined on bean porridge in George D. Grant's tent.

Two-thirty, accompanied by Elders Heber C. Kimball, Orson Hyde, Orson Pratt, John Taylor, George A. Smith, and Willard Richards. I went up the valley east of the camp about half a mile and counseled. A letter from Samuel Brannan and a copy of an agreement between Brannan and Benson were read.

Amos Kendall, of Kentucky, who was postmaster-general from May, 1835, till May, 1840, A. G. Benson and others represented to Samuel Brannan that unless the leaders of the church would sign an agreement with them, to which the president of the United States was a silent party, the government would not permit the Latter-day Saints to proceed on their journey westward. This agreement requires the Latter-day Saints to transfer to "A. G. Berson and Company" the odd number of all the land and town lots they may acquire in the country where they may settle, and in case they refuse to sign said agreement, the president would issue a proclamation that it was the intention of the Latter-day Saints to take sides with other nations against the United States, and order them to be disarmed and dispersed. Brannan becoming fully satisfied that this was the secret intention of the government, and that the president was a principal party, signed it.

Samuel Brannan urged upon the council the necessity of signing the document.

The council considered the subject, and concluded that as our trust was in God and that we looked to him for protection, we would not sign any such unjust and oppressive agreement.

This was a plan of political demagogues to rob the Latter-day Saints of millions and compel them to submit to it, by threats of federal bayonets.

This evening was severely cold.

Wednesday, February 18—I called the brethren together and instructed the captains of hundreds to raise money in their respective companies and send for cloth for tent ends and wagon covers; and informed the Pioneer Company that it would be their duty to prepare roads, look out camp grounds, dig wells, when necessary, and ascertain where hay and corn could be purchased for the camp; that if the brethren could not bring their minds to perfect order, they had better leave the camp and I would have no feelings against them; that after dark no man must leave the camp without the countersign, nor approach the guard abruptly; that every family must call on the Lord night and morning at every tent or wagon, and we shall have no confidence in the man who does not; that the police would be night and day guard; that every captain of ten would keep one man on watch every night; that Benjamin F. Johnson be authorized to receive and preserve for the owners all the lost property found; and that when I wanted to see the brethren together, a white flag should be hoisted, and that when the captains are wanted together a blue or colored flag should be raised; the captains of hundreds were instructed to form their companies in circles, without the circle surrounding the stand; Captain Hosea Stout formed the police; Captain Stephen Markham the Pioneers.

Those not organized were instructed to join the Pioneers, and all to organize into companies of tens.

I told the brethren they were the best set of fellows in the world, still there was a great chance for improvement: I blessed them in the name of the Lord.

The artillery was brought into camp in charge of Colonel John Scott, two six-pounders carronade [cannon].

Elder Kimball, myself and a few others returned to Nauvoo: the night was moderate.

Twenty-four elders met for prayer in the Temple.

Sunday, February 22—I attended meeting at the Temple, the room was crowded and a great weight caused the new truss floor to settle nearly to its proper position. While settling, an inch-board or some light timber underneath was caught and cracked, the sound of which created great alarm in the congregation and some jumped out of the windows, smashing the glass and all before them. Philo Farnsworth smashed the northeast window while others ran out of the doors and many of those who remained jumped up and down with all their might crying Oh! Oh!! Oh!!! as though they could not settle the floor fast enough, but at the same time so agitated that they knew not what they did.

I attempted to call the assembly to order to explain the cause of the settling of the floor, but failing to get their attention I adjourned the meeting to the grove. I went below, examined the floor and found it had hardly settled to its designed position, passed on to the assembly in the grove where the snow was about a foot deep, and told the people they might jump up and down as much as they pleased.

One man who jumped out of the window broke his arm and mashed his face, another broke his leg; both were apostates.

Afternoon, Elders Heber C. Kimball, John Taylor and I started for the camp; the ice was running in the river so there was no possibility of crossing only with a skiff which we accomplished with difficulty and danger, the skiff being very heavily laden, and arrived at camp at 7 o'clock.

Monday, February 23—I met in council with the Twelve and captains of hundreds as to moving the camp.

We agreed to pass up the divide between the Des Moines and Missouri rivers.

Several guns were discharged in and about the camp. During the council Benjamin Stewart came up to the tent fire of the guards, caught up a large pistol and discharged it across the fire; it contained three small rifle balls which entered the left thigh of Abner Blackburn, son of Anthony Blackburn, two balls passed out the opposite side and one hit the bone and passed down remaining in the leg.

Evening, the Pioneers returned and reported a good camping ground ten miles from this, and corn plenty at 18¾ cents; 12¾ cents being the market price at Sugar Creek and Montrose.

Tuesday, February 24—A son was born to John Redding in camp.

The cold has been severe the past night, a snowstorm this morning which continued during the forenoon, blowing from the northwest, which prevented Captain Bent's Company from moving; the cold was severe through the day and increased as night approached.

I was busy in unloading, weighing and loading my wagons preparatory to removal.

I handed out to many of the brethren cloth for tent ends and wagon covers.

Seven p.m., thermometer 12 degrees below zero, Fah. Mississippi river frozen over above Montrose.

Wednesday, February 25—The morning was colder than any one since the encampment, but the sun rose clear, the whole camp appeared cheerful and happy.

Nine a.m., the blast of the bugle and the raising of the flag called the brethren together.

About eleven a.m., Captain Charles C. Rich arrived from Nauvoo and reported that he had walked over the Mississippi river on the ice at Montrose.

Seven a.m., thermometer at 6° Fah.; one p.m., thermometer 18° Fah. Latitude of the Camp of Israel by a meridian observation of the sun taken by Professor Orson Pratt this day was 40° 31' 50", longitude 91° 16' 0".

Bishop George Miller with about sixteen wagons and thirty or forty Pioneers started for Des Moines.

At seven p.m., thermometer stood 10° Fah.

Thursday, February 26—Six-thirty a.m., thermometer stood at 2° below zero, Fah.

The weather being so cold it was not considered prudent to remove the tents of families as had been contemplated.

John Gool let Thomas Grover, whose oxen were drowned on the 9th, have a span of horses and wagon to help him forward to be returned from the journey's end. This morning John Gool's wife came into camp and demanded the team; I tried to persuade her that it would be loss to her to take away the team under existing circumstances; but she persisted in her demand and took the team and drove off: I told Brother Grover to trust in the Lord.

About noon, someone presented Brother Grover with a team.

Mr. Prentice, U. S. marshal, and several of the governor's troops from Carthage, came into camp and inquired for a grey horse which they said was stolen from McDonough county two weeks previously; that they had traced the horse to within six miles of Nauvoo and had caught the thief in Nauvoo but he was not a Mormon.

Friday, February 27—Six a.m., thermometer 5° above zero, Fah.

This morning Captain Albert P. Rockwood slaughtered a fine ox which had been sprained, and distributed it amongst the most needy of the camp.

James Wallace came into camp and thought he ought to have pay for the timber which the brethren had cut; he was willing to leave it to them what the timber was worth.

William Clayton arrived at three thirty p.m.; having crossed the Mississippi with his teams on the ice.

The sky was clouded through the day, the wind in the southeast and very chilly, and towards night a little fine hail fell; the camp generally healthy and happy.

Six p.m., 21° above zero, Fah.

Brother McKee protested my order for corn to the amount of $15.00, which he promised to the camp yesterday; when the teams called for the corn this morning, McKee told them he had concluded to keep the corn to help off the poor with, which caused the teams in camp to be fed on five ears of corn each.

Saturday, February 28—Six a.m., thermometer 20° above zero, Fah. Wind variable, changing toward the north.

Some of the Pioneers, Daniel Spencer, Charles Shumway, and part of Captain Bent's Company moved on four miles.

I was so afflicted with the rheumatism it was with difficulty I could walk.

Some of the brethren were engaged this day in building a log house to pay James Wallace for his wood which the camp had burned on his claim.

The camp consisted of nearly four hundred wagons all very heavily loaded with not over one-half of the teams necessary to make a rapid journey. Most of the families were provided with provisions for several months. A considerable number, regardless of counsel, had started in a destitute condition, and some others, with only provisions for a few days.

Colonel Stephen Markham had about one hundred Pioneers to prepare the road in advance of the main body.

Colonel Hosea Stout with about one hundred men acted as police for the encampment; they were generally armed with rifles.

Colonel John Scott with about one hundred men accompanied the artillery.

A considerable number of the teams were to be returned as soon as an encampment could be selected for putting in spring crops; others expected to return as soon as the loads of provisions and forage which they hauled were exhausted.

Our encampment on Sugar Creek has had a tendency to check the movements of the mob, as they were generally of opinion, that our fit out was so insufficient that in a short time we would break to pieces and scatter.

The great severity of the weather and not being able to sell any of our property, the difficulty of crossing the river during many days of running ice all combined to delay our departure, though for several days the bridge of ice across the Mississippi greatly facilitated the crossing and compensated, in part, for the delay caused by the running ice.

The fact is worthy of remembrance that several thousand persons left their homes in midwinter and exposed themselves without shelter, except that afforded by a scanty supply of tents and wagon covers, to a cold which effectually made an ice bridge over the Mississippi river which at Nauvoo is more than a mile broad. We could have remained sheltered in our homes had it not been for the threats and hostile demonstrations of our enemies, who, notwithstanding their solemn agreements had thrown every obstacle in our way, not respecting either life, liberty or property, so much so, that our only means of avoiding a rupture was by starting in midwinter.

Our homes, gardens, orchards, farms, streets, bridges, mills, public halls, magnificent Temple, and other public improvements we leave as a monument of our patriotism, industry, economy, uprightness of purpose and integrity of heart; and as a living testimony of the falsehood and wickedness of those who charge us with disloyalty to the Constitution of our country, idleness and dishonesty.

Sunday, March 1—6 a.m. Thermometer 19 degrees Fah. A pleasant morning.

The Camp of Israel was enlarged by accessions of families that had been scattered among the saints through Iowa, waiting to accompany us; so that when we came to string out our company amounted to about five hundred souls.

At 8 a.m., I notified the camp to prepare for removal, to meet together at 10, and be ready to start at noon. Those in camp made the necessary preparation; but there were several teams and brethren at Nauvoo which caused considerable delay.

Half past ten, Elder Kimball went to the meeting and stated that as I was unwell, I wished him to say to the Saints, that it was my will for the Camp to remove to some other location, because while we are so near Nauvoo the brethren are continually going back and neglecting their teams and families, and running to me for counsel about a little property they have here or there or somewhere.

President Kimball said, no doubt many would be tried, but he would see the kingdom of God established and all the kingdoms of this world become the kingdom of God and his Christ—referred to his travels in Missouri—encouraged the brethren to go forward, and felt that the grass would start before long; that we were not going out of the world. If Nauvoo has been the most holy place it will be the most wicked place. He then called upon all who meant to go ahead to say, *I*, which was responded to most heartily by the brethren present. No doubt you mean to have President Young for your leader. We will do all that he says and everything will be right. A plague came upon Zion's Camp for disobedience; when on our way to Missouri and our best men fell victims, and it will be again under like circumstances; I want no man to touch any of my things without leave; if any man will come to me and say that he wants to steal, I will give him the amount; cease all your loud laughter and light speeches, for the Lord is displeased with such things, and call upon the Lord with all your might.

About noon, the Camp began to move and at 4 o'clock nearly five hundred wagons were on the way traveling in a Northwesterly direction.

Beautiful day. Encamped for the night on Sugar Creek, having traveled five miles.

My carriage did not arrive from Nauvoo till about sunset, which caused me an evening's ride, near the end of which, and while passing down the hill to my tent, the carriage would have upset had not Jesse D. Hunter upheld it.

As Brother Parley P. Pratt's team was going down another part of the same hill his neck yoke broke, his horses and wagon plunged down the hill and amongst the tents, women and children below, but no one received any injury which was very providential.

A portion of the Pioneers had taken a job of cutting and splitting three thousand rails at this encampment, and husking one hundred and fifty shocks of corn, which supplied the Camp with corn and fodder.

8 p.m. Parley P. Pratt, Heber C. Kimball and Willard Richards met with me in my tent, we concluded that the Camp move in the morning towards Farmington. The snow was three or four inches deep at this encampment.

Monday, March 2—7 a.m. Thermometer 23 degrees above Zero.

About 9 a.m. cows and ox teams began to move, those encamped in the valley passed up the creek, those on the hill passed round on the prairie, the two roads uniting at some distance ahead, which caused some derangement of the already imperfect organization, separating teams of the same company, which produced a little uneasiness in the minds of the brethren, and in striving to get together again run against and damaged several wagons. The Camp traveled ten miles and tented in a field, on the West side of Lick Creek, about half a mile from its junction with the Des Moines, where log heaps had been piled up previously for clearing.

The waters of Lick Creek and Des Moines are very clear; there were several tedious hills on this days route.

Thursday, March 3—7 a.m. Thermometer 23 degrees Fah.

About 9 the Camp came together. I told them that I wanted the Pioneers to go ahead and prepare the roads by cutting and trimming trees and filling up bad places, etc., and the Guard to carry axes instead of guns and help the teams; that it is not for the Guard or Pioneers to order the Teamsters-that I did not want a man along who was not willing to help in every place, the guard have to watch but we will help them for men cannot work night and day. We want every man to quit this Camp who cannot quit swearing. You had better go now, if you do not the law will be put in force by and bye. I felt insulted yesterday by one of P. P. Pratt's teamsters, Wm. Pratt, who would not let me pass, but hindered me unnecessarily. Men must not crowd upon each other, ox teams must give the road and let horse teams pass, when we get properly organized no two teams must come within two or more rods of each other.

We camped on the bank of a small clear creek, most of the Camp arrived before dark, the weather was very pleasant, the wind for several days variable, mostly from the North but light.

One hundred and seventy-two bushels of tithing corn had been brought into Camp, besides other corn for cutting and splitting rails. Several wagons were broken and damaged this day, occasioned mostly by the bad roads the last three miles. After the encampment, Bishop Miller introduced Dr. Jewett to Dr. Richards and me.

Dr. Jewett gave a long history of experiments on animal magnetism, and said it had nearly cured him of infidelity, and he thought the Mormons would understand the principle. I told him I did perfectly, that we believed in the Lord's magnetizing, that he magnetized Belteshazar so that he saw the hand writing on the wall.

Wednesday, March 4—8 a.m. Thermometer 43 degrees Fah.

The Council met and decided to lay by until tomorrow.

9 a.m. I called the brethren together and informed them that they would remain in Camp until tomorrow, when part of the Pioneers and the first hundred would roll out, I wanted they should be busy in repairing and greasing their wagons, shoeing their horses, mending harnesses, and seeing that everything was in readiness for an early start, each team to be provided with two days feed of corn.

Two tons of timothy hay were purchased at four dollars per ton, and brought into Camp part for cash and part for splitting rails, the day was very pleasant, the Camp very cheerful.

We were visited by many of the citizens of Farmington who invited the band to go to their village and have a concert; in the afternoon they rode down on horseback to respond to the invitation.

Captain Scott, of the artillery, engaged a job of removing dirt from a coal bed at 12½ cents per yard, and two thousand rails to cut and split payable in flour, at two dollars per hundred pounds, pork at six dollars, and cash, and fifty men commenced the job. This morning I requested the Captains of companies to number the Camp. The band returned from Farmington about 9 p.m.

Thursday, March 5—8:30 a.m., I told the Camp that three teams were wanting to draw the cannon, that there was corn to husk where we should go tonight, that the first Company (composed of the Twelve and Bishops) were enough to go out today, that when the Camp was organized every wagon must be numbered with the initials of the Captain's name, etc., that I wanted to go ahead with the Pioneers to help counsel in their arrangements, that there was one family who had no means of going and they must be divided amongst the different teams and no one be left who wanted to go, that the Camp had better eat all their provisions as they needed except biscuit, crackers, parched corn meal, which would lighten our loads and when we get to the Missouri river we would go to work and get flour, etc., and prepare for our journey over the mountains—that good economy, virtue and industry was better than Gold or Silver; at the close of the meeting individuals offered teams to draw the cannon.

Colonel Swazy and family visited the Camp and said that much good feeling was created by the music of the Band at Farmington.

I moved on with my company about 10 o'clock and forded the Des Moines river just below Buonaparte Mills, about two feet of water and passed up the West bank a short distance, arrived on the border of the Prairie about one o'clock p.m.; having travelled over a *very muddy* road the wagons frequently sinking to the axle trees in the mud; having been disappointed about teams meeting the Camp at the river with corn, and not having fed this morning the horses were let loose on the Prairie to pick at the dry grass while we sent back one mile and purchased a load of corn.

At 4 p.m., most of the teams had come up, the horses had eaten, the corn, and the Camp moved on in a westerly direction and on a pretty good road seven miles, and commenced camping about sunset on a low piece of land on the North bank of Indian Creek.

No Pioneers were to be seen or heard of, we having traveled about twelve miles. Most of the teams were exhausted by their heavy loads and short feed; the ground was found too wet to pitch tents and most of the Camp remained in their wagons; about 10 o'clock I removed my carriage and pitched my tent on the bank of the Creek. Corn was purchased for cash at 15 cents per bushel sufficient to give each beast eight ears; the citizens generally asked 18¾ and 20 cents per bushel; a few oats were engaged at 12½ cents per dozen bundles, but when payment was made the man would have the price of thirteen bundles for nine. Bishop Whitney broke an axle tree and encamped on the South bank of the Des Moines.

Elders Kimball, P. P. Pratt and Taylor encamped on the Prairie, also Father John Smith, whose wagon upset and hurt Mother Smith. Notwithstanding the uncomfortable situation of that portion of the Camp at Indian Creek, there was no murmuring, but all appeared happy; several horses were sick, some of which were fed on oats and tobacco, others on salt. One had the distemper and was removed from the Camp.

Friday, March 6—7 a.m. Thermometer 35 degrees Fah.

One of my horses died this morning. All others were well or better. The supposed distemper proved a mistake, and the horse returned into camp. Brother Parley P. Pratt and company arrived at the encampment about 11 a.m., and passed on. Elder Kimball and Father John Smith arrived about 1 p.m., and Elder Taylor about 2.

One hundred bushels of corn was purchased by the Camp at $14. In the evening Brother John S. Gleason introduced Dr. John D. Elbert to me and Dr. Richards in his tent. Dr. Elbert stated that when the first news reached them that the Mormons were about to pass through that section of country there was great excitement among the inhabitants, on account of the prejudices which had been created by false and alarming reports, fearing that they should be swallowed up alive, but the more recent reports of the honest dealing of the Camp had caused those feelings to subside and the citizens had concluded to let the Mormons pass in peace, that he had appropriated one quarter section of land seven miles ahead for an encampment, and had contracted with our agent, Mr. Gleason, for cutting and splitting rails, for three bushels of corn per hundred; also, for clearing land payable in corn; the band came up in front of the tent, and gave the Dr. a salute. Dr. Elbert said there were many families of Mormons in his vicinity that he had attended them all as physician, and that every one had paid him honestly but he could not say the same of all the citizens.

Christiana, wife of John Lytle was delivered of a son, named Charles, while encamped on Reeds Creek. North side of the Des Moines, 2 p.m.

C. W. Wandell wrote a revelation purporting to come from the Lord through J. J. Strang, to see what effect it would have upon the strangites. He sent it to Jehiel Savage, who took the article, went on to the stand, read it to the people and bore testimony that he knew it was from the Lord.

Brother Wandell seeing it was having an evil effect upon the followers of Strang, came out and acknowledged that he was the author of the article, that the Lord had nothing to do with it, and that Strang never saw it.

Brother Wandell found it unprofitable and dangerous business to use the name of the Lord falsely, that it was wrong and produced evil among the children of men; as was the case with William E. McLellan who undertook to imitate one of the Revelations of Jesus Christ and failed in the attempt, and although this article of brother Wandell's showed that Savage and the followers of Strang, who had forsaken the truth, were more ready to receive fables than truth and bear testimony that they were of the Lord; yet no man should use this means to produce such an effect.

Saturday, March 7—Indian Creek. This morning I was busy in removing a load of biscuit from russia duck sacks, which were worn through by traveling, and packed them in boxes; while thus engaged most of the carriages and teams passed on, two and a half miles, and I overtook many of them seven miles on the way near Dr. Elbert's Camp ground, where one man locked up his well bucket, and where a part of the Camp had already stopped; the traveling was so good and the day so pleasant I concluded to go farther and most of the Camp passed on five miles to a place formerly called Richardson's point, Van Buren County, and pitched their tents on a very dry spot, close by the road and near a branch of Chequest Creek, commencing about 4 p.m.

Corn was plenty at this place at fifteen cents per bushel, and timothy hay at $5. per ton, oats twelve and a half cents in work cutting and splitting rails.

Tuesday, March 10—Richardson's Point. Cloudy morning. Several warm showers this a.m.

The brethren husked more than one hundred bushels of corn for every fourth bushel, and the fodder; the Band started for Keosaugua about 1 p.m., mostly in carriages.

The Band gave a concert in the courthouse at Keosaugua this evening, and cleared $25.70, and were treated with the utmost kindness and attention by the citizens and invited to play again tomorrow evening; fifteen or twenty of the brethren held a party at Bro. Stewart's this evening.

Captain A. P. Rockwood's wife, Nancy, presented her husband with a good hat made of straw gathered from the horse feed.

This morning, George D. Grant and O. P. Rockwell left Camp with several of my horses to trade for oxen.

Wednesday, March 11—Richardson's Point.

The Band returned to Camp about 2 a.m. Rain commenced falling at sunset last evening, and continued till sunrise this morning, wind, East, since yesterday morning. The Band started to Keosaugua about 11 a.m.; Edwin Little was conveyed to a neighboring house in my carriage.

From sunrise till noon the clouds were broken with occasional slight showers. Four cases of Measles and one of mumps were reported in Camp.

Thursday, March 12—At 5 p.m., I met with Elders Kimball and Richards in council in the Historian's tent, when a challenge for a duel (by James Hemmick) on yesterday was reported.

At 6, Captain Markham dischargd Hemmick, who went forward to the next company; said he would not leave the saints, and appeared to regret his folly.

Brother Stewart brought intelligence to the Camp that brother Orson Spencer's wife died this morning at his encampment four miles back, that he is now on his way to Nauvoo for her burial.

Corn and fodder are plenty in Camp and paid for mostly in labour by the brethren; corn 13½¢ cash, oats 8¢ per dozen.

The day is very clear and fine, and the mud is rapidly converted into dry land.

Friday, March 13—Richardson's Point.

The night was cloudy with occasional showers, the morning clear after a slight shower of snow flakes. Wind northerly; so much water has fallen within three days that the small creeks in the vicinity are not fordable.

Brother Isaac Chase continues sick with the lung fever, he was removed to a neighboring house; several cases of the fever and ague, coughs, etc. are reported, but in general the Camp is much more healthy than could reasonably be anticipated, after such a severe storm of rain.

SSaturday, March 14—During the day William Hall left Camp with his team for the Des Moines to bring forward a load for Allen J. Stout; at Indian creek one of his horses sickened with bloating and colic; Elders Hall and Lluellen Mantle laid hands on him and he recovered immediately, and went on about two miles when he was again attacked more violently than before, they tried to give him medicine but could not succeed, the horse lay on his side with his forefoot over his ear, but Reuben Strong said he believed there was breath in him yet, and proposed to lay hands upon him, some present doubted whether it was right to lay hands on a horse, Elder Hall replied the Prophet Joel has said that in the last days the Lord would pour out his spirit upon all flesh and thus satisfied the brethren, and Elders Wm. Hall, Reuben R. Strong, Lluellen Mantle, Joseph Champlin, Martin Potter and one more laid hands on the horse and commanded the unclean and foul spirits of every name and nature to depart and go to the Gentiles at Warsaw and trouble the Saints no more, when the horse rolled twice over in great distress, sprang to his feet, squealed, vomited and purged, and the next morning was harnessed to a load of about twelve hundred weight and performed his part as usual.

Sunday, March 15—The day was rather cool, wind North and at times very brisk capsizing several tents.

At noon, Elders I. Cillet and H. G. Sherwood addressed the public assembly, on the first principles of the Gospel, many strangers present, and many were offering to exchange Oxen for horses—purchase harness; sell corn and offering to let various jobs of work, some of the brethren declined trading on the Sabbath.

Monday, March 16—The Council wrote to the Trustees to give Thomas Bullock an immediate outfit. I was frequently in the Post Office, wrote several letters and signed several orders; the remainder of the day I was particularly engaged in counseling the brethren, changing loads in my wagons, and preparing my company for traveling; the day was more pleasant than any day since we started, wind North in the forenoon, and South West in the afternoon. In the evening the people assembled in great numbers in and about the Post Office to hear a Methodist sermon, it having been reported that there was such a Preacher in Camp, but the people returned disappointed.

The Band passed through the Camp and played us a few tunes.

Tuesday, March 17—I was frequently in the Post Office; wrote an order and signed others; and related how that in my dream of the past night I was pursued by a beast which threatened my life, and I fled into a house for safety, the beast following me appeared to change into a human being which I attempted to shoot with a seven shooter, to save my own life but it would not go off, then to bluff off the person I drew my small six shooter which went off contrary to my expectations, the ball passed through the brain of the individual, soon as the blood started the man came to his senses and was sorry for what he had done. I felt so bad because I had shot a man, that I awoke and was thankful that it was but a dream.

In the p.m., Elder Kimball and I rode three miles to the next encampment, to ascertain the state of the traveling, found it passable and concluded to roll on in the morning.

James Monroe, son of Sidney Tanner, died at 5 a.m. of inflammation of the brain, aged fifteen months.

Wednesday, March 18—Richardson's Point. At 7:20 a.m., Edwin Little died, and was buried at dusk on the divide between Fox and Chequest rivers.

I was very busy through the day in preparing for the burial of Brother Little, and rolling out in the morning.

Dr. Richards rode out with his family below the next encampment and found the road dry and good, on his return called on Isaac Chase (who had been sick) and found him better. Between four and six o'clock p.m. a beautiful shower accompanied by thunder and lightning, then a rainbow.

During the day Mr. Richardson came into Camp and said the Camp had damaged him $20, by the horses eating his trees, but the land was not his, he only had a claim; there was no land in all this region of country that had ever been brought into market.

Thursday, March 19—Very little corn or fodder of any kind to be had at this place. The most of our travel this day was over a beautiful Prairie, and it seemed as though the very few inhabitants could not satisfy themselves without fencing their farms across the public road, so as to push travelers into all the mud holes possible.

Brother Kimball and I called on brother Isaac Chase soon after we started in the morning, and found him convalescent and he went on with the Camp. Dr. Alphonzo Young and family being sick tarried with some of the brethren near Richardson's Point; Dr. Brailey also stopped at the same place to cure a man for a yoke of oxen.

With great reluctance the Widow Evans *permitted* us to use some of the fallen timber (on the public domain) when there was more in sight than she would use during her life time.

Friday, March 20—Evans' Encampment. Wind continued brisk and cool, pleasant weather.

The Camp struck tents at an early hour, taking a westerly course for three miles, when we came up to O. Pratt, John Taylor and Captains Averett and Roundy's encampment and took in thirty bushels of corn collected by the Pioneers; continued our route seven miles further and came to a long and deep mudhole, on the bank of Fox river, where the brethren had to double teams, and spent several hours in getting through. Many of the last teams went around the head of the slough; brother Kimball, Richards and I stayed and helped till all the teams got through, then I walked back one and a quarter miles to see the situation of the teams, and counsel the brethren. I then passed on and crossed Fox river on a bridge, thence over a very hilly, rough and muddy country, about two miles, and came on to the old Mormon trail, which we followed about one mile, then turning a little to the right encamped in the edge of the timber, mostly hickory, in Davis County. The Band encamped back one mile from the river. One of my heavy wagons being broken, stayed at the river Camp; began to pitch tents at 2 p.m., while others did not arrive until after dark.

Saturday, March 21—Messenger returned to Bishop Miller's Camp, with leave for them to remove to Shoal Creek. I rode back to Fox river to see if all was well with my team that broke down last evening; bros. Grant and Hanks rode three of my horses to trade for oxen. Most of the Camp went out about 9 o'clock. I returned at noon and started with my company about 1 p.m., traveled twelve miles and camped on a hill within five miles of the Chariton in Appanoose

Country, Iowa, at a place called Coffman's settlement where not a house, barn, hut or wigwam or anything else was to be seen, except hills, grass, bushes and trees.

I remarked today that Bishop Miller seeks to go ahead and separate himself from his brethren, but he cannot prosper in so doing, he will yet run against a snag, and call on me and the Camp for help.

Sunday, March 22—Camp started at an early hour, after passing three miles over the hills and Prairie, and two miles over the lowland, arrived at the ford on Chariton river, which is about four rods wide and two feet deep, with a stony bottom, steep banks on either side, which made it necessary to let the wagons down into the river, with ropes and to assist the teams up the opposite bank in the same manner, a new road was cut down at two points at the same time; the brethren were very diligent and the teams all passed over in three or four hours with very little damage, except breaking a tongue out of one of my heavy wagons.

Afternoon, several of the brethren forgetting it was the Sabbath went out on a hunting excursion with very little success, notwithstanding there was plenty of Deer, Turkeys, Ducks, Elk, etc. in the vicinity.

About 5 p.m. bros. John Young and Evan M. Greene arrived in Camp from Nauvoo, bringing a large package of letters and newspapers.

I said I wanted a new leaf turned over, and if there was not, a scourge would come upon the Camp; we must give more attention to keeping the Sabbath, and quit shooting and trading, and not pass it off carelessly as any other day, for I know it is wrong; we will tarry here tomorrow; let the Captains of Companies select a few good hunters, let them meet on the campground before day, and organize, and go and bring us in some deer, turkeys, etc., for we want some fresh meat; and let no man go who is not sent; let others be engaged in getting grain, others in browsing the cattle and feeding the horses; others in burning coal, some in chopping wood, some fishing, etc. When we get to Miller's encampment, seven miles ahead, we will organize, and if Bishop Miller moves again before our arrival he will be disfellowshipped from the Camp, unless he repents.

Monday, March 23—Chariton encampment. Wind South, considerable rain during the night.

The hunters met and dispersed to their hunting grounds.

I was frequently in the Post Office during the day, attending to a variety of business, wrote a letter acknowledging the receipt of a plate of honey which came from a tree found by M. Johnson.

The hunters returned in the afternoon with but little game; the day was so damp and so many went without counsel, that it was more of a fright than a kill to the poor animals. Burrier Griffin presented me with a turkey which weighed twenty-nine pounds before it was dressed. Brother J. D. Lee came in with thirteen squirrels and gave the Historian two.

About 4 p.m., the ground was whitened with hail the size of peas.

Bishop Miller moved on four miles to the middle fork of Shoal Creek. Elders

P. P. Pratt and George A. Smith moved up the hill from Shoal Creek, about half a mile; it rained hard, and was a day of extreme suffering for man and beast.

Tuesday, March 24—Chariton. Wind north, slight showers during the forenoon.

This morning, Henry Russell and George Allen started with a four horse team to bring grain to Camp, but found the Chariton river so high they could not cross; consequently, the Camp was obliged to do without corn except what little they had brought with them, which was not enough to supply the teams; the horses, oxen and cows were taken on to the flat to browse, the day was cool, chilly, damp and very uncomfortable, the sky was clouded, the earth very wet.

Five deer were brought into Camp this day.

Evening, in Council with Elders Kimball, Richards and others in the Post Office; the conversation was mostly about arranging certain loads so that some of the brethren might return to Nauvoo; making arrangements to get corn for the Camp and have a company go a fishing in the morning.

A Mr. Devlin was reported in Camp, and had been some days; he was believed to be the man who stole a horse in Missouri.

Wednesday, March 25—Wind Northwest, accompanied by snow which continued falling until 2 p.m.

Howard Egan went into the country this morning to buy corn, and Henry Russell and others went out with teams to fetch it; a load of flour and pork belonging to the Church was distributed in Camp this a.m.

I was in the Post Office writing from 10 a.m. until 1 p.m.; the day was very unpleasant, but little business was done except browsing the teams and chopping wood, for fires; about 5 p.m. the clouds broke away considerably and the sun shone.

The teams returned to Camp about dusk with thirty bushels of corn. Howard Egan engaged a considerable amount of corn at 20¢ per bushel, payable in feathers. Thomas L. Williams coming up to the man soon after, and learning his bargain with Egan, told him he would give him 25¢ and pay him the cash; this is one of the many difficulties which are liable to arise in a large Camp where there is not a perfect organization and the agents of the different divisions do not understand each others movements.

Thursday, March 26—Wind brisk in the North West, sky mostly clear.

About 8 a.m., the Captains of hundreds, fifties, and tens were called together in front of my tent; I gave them a lecture concerning the folly of one brother's overbidding another in purchasing corn, etc. I said I wished I could see the man that followed Egan yesterday and overbid him, that I might kick him out of this Camp; meeting was adjourned to meet at 10 o'clock at Captain Scott's tent.

I was with them at that hour, and sent Howard Egan to purchase corn for the Camp,—inquired of the brethren if they were all punctual to attend to prayers with their different families and tents; said, that I hoped the Lord would forgive our sins, as we forgave each other's—proposed sending the Pioneers on to Grand river to take jobs, etc.; had conversation on various subjects; Council closed about 12 noon.

Friday, March 27—I told Captain Stout that his guard was of little use to the Camp, and that some of them would sit by the fire and sleep and let the cattle eat pickles out of the bus, and crackers out of the sacks.

About 10, Elders H. C. Kimball, John Taylor and myself, and others left headquarters on the Chariton in carriages and on horse back; and after passing through one mud hole only, which was about six miles in length, arrived at Capt. Elisha Averett's tent.

I charged the Captains particularly to instruct their respective divisions, to be very careful about setting the Prairie or woods on fire, especially in a dry time, lest they bring trouble upon the Camp; to prohibit all discharge of fire arms in the Camp and to keep their guns and pistols out of sight.

Saturday, March 28—Chariton river, Wind Northwest. Cold and cloudy.

About 8 a.m. I went into the Post Office and signed a letter to Captain Daniel C. Davis, of Montrose, requesting him to send on the family of Josiah Arnold to Camp. Spoke highly of the Council of yesterday, and had conversation with Captain Hosea Stout concerning the guard; Captain Stout said, that he had done the best he knew how, and so had the Guard—that I had never told him what to do and what he did he had to guess at. I told him that was the way for him to do, and when he got wrong then it was for me to put him right.

A boy, by the name of Edmund Whiting, shot an otter at the bank of the river, he afterwards discovered that the Otter was caught in a trap, he took off the skin and carried it to Camp, leaving the trap on the bank; in the course of the day the trapper who lived a short distance off, came into Camp and stated that he had eight traps set in the neighborhood, and had lost six of them, intimating that the Camp had stolen them, but this was not believed. In the evening the Council heard what the boy had done with the Otter skin, and called him into the Post office with the skin, when he related all his doings concerning the matter.

The Council were satisfied that he meant no harm, and instructed him to go early in the morning and bring the trap, and take it and the skin to the trapper in company with Stephen Markham.

I instructed bro. Markham to say to the man that if one of his traps were found in the Camp within one thousand miles of that place it should be sent back to him with the man that took it.

Captain Elisha Averett, with his company of Pioneers, built a bridge, sixty feet long over Shoal Creek.

Captain Averett came in from P. P. Pratt's encampment on Shoal Creek and said that one of O. Pratt's men went a hunting before breakfast on Friday morning and has not been heard from since; the Camp were hunting after him today.

Monday, March 30—Edward P. Duzette and family arrived at Chariton river, this afternoon; in letting his wagon down the bank, the boat broke away, the wagon plunged into the river and upset, but he succeeded in saving most of his goods, although they were thoroughly wet, except his cooking utensils which were left in the river.

Stephen Markham reported, that he could not find Edmund Whiting, the boy that shot the otter in the trap, and that he had returned the skin to Mr. Davis the trapper, who was satisfied with the actions of the Officer of the Camp and that two traps had been found in a hollow log, supposed to have been lost, and are ready for Mr. Davis, who says he has two more yet missing.

I was at the Post Office about 8 this evening, and on hearing the report ordered the Captains to cause their wagons to be searched early in the morning for the traps yet missing. Previous to this I said if any man in this Camp was found stealing, he forfeited all his property.

The hunter of the first fifty killed one deer and one turkey.

Tuesday, March 31—Chariton River, Camp Of Israel.

Sky clear, weather pleasant, wind south-easterly, severe frost during the past night; the health of the Camp much improved and fast recovering from the severe colds occasioned by the late storms.

About 2 p.m., O. P. Rockwell arrived from Nauvoo, bringing with him one hundred and forty letters, papers, and packages, one letter from W. W. Phelps to W. Richards and Council, one from O. Hyde for me and one from Mr. Matlock, Editor of the "Hancock Eagle."

The hunters of the first fifty brought in two deer, and two turkeys.

The Camp during the month of March have traveled about one hundred miles; the roads have been nearly impassable most of the time. The storms, cold and wind caused considerable suffering. Our teams were light. Our animals had scanty supplies of grain which we procured from the settlers in exchange for our labor, building houses and splitting rails. Nearly one hundred wagons returned to Nauvoo, having brought out provisions and forage. Notwithstanding the exposure, general good health prevailed in Camp, and more unity and good feelings than could have been expected under the circumstances.

Wednesday, April 1—Camp of Israel, Chariton river, clear and frosty.

The first and fourth fifties commenced moving about 9 a.m. The historian and I were among the last that left the ground. After traveling six miles we crossed the bridge over the east fork of Shoal creek, built by Captain Averett's company of pioneers, where we found Benjamin F. Johnson and company. We passed on about one mile and camped on a rise in the prairie. The fourth company was in the edge of the timber, about thirty rods east, where Geo. A. Smith, with a part of the third fifty, was encamped. Some of the teams of the second company had gone into the country for corn and had not yet returned. John D. Lee brought in a fine wild turkey which weighed thirty lbs. Early this morning the Camp was searched for the two lost traps belonging to Mr. Davis, one was found in a hollow tree, a quarter of a mile from camp.

Captain Averett's company of pioneers built two bridges over Locust Creek, seventy and twenty feet long respectively.

Thursday, April 2—Four fine turkeys were brought into camp by the hunters of the first fifty. Sixty-five bushels of corn were bought at twenty cents for bushel and brought into camp. A draft of sixteen men was made from the first fifty to complete a contract of rail making, and other companies were selected to take the teams to the creek bottom to browse.

146

Friday, April 3At sunrise all the first fifty were under way. After traveling five miles, crossing the west fork of Shoal creek, on the pioneer bridge, came up with a part of the second company. A letter was received from H. G. Sherwood, dated from Grand river, informing us that we could get some jobs of work about thirty miles from Miller's Camp, and some corn, though it was scarce, on the road at 37½ cents per bushel, but off the road 25 cents. Roads good and dry. Jobs of work and trade for oxen, etc. bid fair at Weldon fork, Grand river. From Weldon fork Judge Miller recommends the northern route; because of more settlements, smaller prairies, less bitterness and prejudice among the people and corn is only 15¢ per bushel.

Some of the company tarried at this point for breakfast, others passed on to bishop Miller's encampment, the distance of two miles, where, at 10 a.m. was a slight shower of rain and hail accompanied with thunder. About 11 a.m. company began to move on. At noon a steady rain commenced and continued most of the afternoon. My family carriage and a few wagons arrived at a hickory grove about one mile east of Locust creek, at 2:30 p.m. distant twelve miles from Miller's encampment or twenty miles from Shoal creek. The other wagons continued on until after dark, excepting my heavy wagon which halted seven miles back, and Dr. Richards' four wagons some three or four miles back, all of which stayed on the prairie over night, leaving the Dr. without tent or food except as he was kindly fed by his neighbors; his family sat in the carriage during the night. He lay on the floor of my omnibus. Part of the second and third tens, first fifty, the artillery and part of the guard went on to the creek and camped. Others companies tarried at Miller's encampment.

The evening was dark and rainy, wind high, the camp very uncomfortable, yet without a murmur.

Saturday, April 4—Hickory Grove encampment, incessant rain through the past night, Dr. Richards' wagon came in this forenoon with double teams; my wagon was brought by eight yoke of oxen; travelling exceedingly difficult, very little corn in camp and none to be had in the neighborhood.

About 11 a.m., the wind changed to the northwest, occasional showers through the day. I rode down to the creek in search of a dryer camp ground, returned after dinner and decided to stay where we were. I was also engaged in the fore part of the day in cutting wood and fixing about my tent. In the evening the clouds broke away and the moon shone.

Monday, April 6—Rained all day. About 6 a.m the wagons commenced to move with doubled teams, about noon the ground was cleared except Dr. Richards' tent, carriage and two wagons; the Dr. was unable to remove until afternoon when the water in the creek had risen so high that it was impassable.

The companies passed over the east and middle forks of Locust creek and encamped on the west bank, about three miles distant. The forks of Locust creek at this place are one mile apart.

The artillery company built another bridge over a slough at the east fork.

We herded our teams as there was no corn in Camp. It thundered and lightninged at intervals all day, with a strong north-westerly wind which prostrated a tree, twelve inches in diameter, across brother Tanner's wagon, in which were three persons who escaped unhurt. The forest was so dense on Locust Creek that the first and fifth companies and artillery experienced but little damage from the storm. The tents of the second and fourth companies were mostly blown down. I was in the rain all day, arranging the wagons, pitching tents, chopping wood until all were comfortable. Dr. Richards' tent pins were sometimes flying in the air. Dr. working in his shirt sleeves until he was wet to the skin, sometimes lying flat on the ground holding down the tent, while the pins were being driven.

Tuesday, April 7—Locust Creek encampment. Middle branch, morning clear, ground frozen and covered with a light snow. The creek had risen six feet during the night, making an island on which the first fifty found their cattle, which could not be got off without swimming.

Sister Stewart wife of Rufus Putman Stewart was delivered of a son, the mother having walked two miles through the dark last evening and crossed the creek on a log, after her labor pains commenced, to get into a vacant house where she would be shielded from the storm.

Wednesday, April 8—Morning clear and frosty. About 6 a.m. brother Wm. Coray started for Nauvoo after his family, taking with him a mail of twenty letters. 8 a.m. accompanied by G. D. Grant and John Scott, I rode out to the west fork of Locust Creek to examine the road. Returned to Camp about 1:30 p.m. and reported the road unfavorable for travelling, the bank on the opposite side was wet, several hands from the first fifty were engaged in cutting down the bank, and crosslogging the road at the foot of the hill.

Dr. Richards and those that were with him left Hickory Grove and arrived in Camp at noon, a deer and turkey were brought into Camp.

A company of artillery engaged to make three thousand rails at fifty cents per hundred and board, payable in a good milch cow at ten dollars and the remainder in bacon at five cents per pound.

Friday, April 10—Morning lowery, occasional showers. During the night the creek had risen about five feet and was still rising. At 10 a.m. the male members of the camp met at Captain Stout's tent when I suggested the propriety of sending as many wagons as the teams can conveniently draw through the mud, and all the men that can be spared from camp, and a part of the families to Weldon fork of Grand river, where they can get jobs of work, and grain to feed our teams, and recruit them, while we are waiting for the roads to get better and the grass to grow. I also recommended sending Orson Pratt and some of the contracting commissaries up Grand river to select a location for a settlement, and while we were weather and water-bound we could clear and fence one hundred acres, and break them up, and leave such families as were not prepared to proceed farther at present, and when they have raised a crop, let them leave it, and pass on to the Missouri river, where they can winter their stock without grain, then when a company comes on from Nauvoo they will have a resting place, and they can feed from that place to do them through to the Missouri river, and so continue on for years to come until the land is brought into market.

I recommended to the captains of companies to select a steady, fatherly man in each ten to act as teacher and see that prayers are offered in their season in all the tents.

I walked to the creek where some men were pinning down the puncheons on the bridge. At this juncture the men were driven into their tents by a sudden gust of wind from the Southwest, which terminated in rain.

Sunday, April 12—Morning clear, ground frozen. I met in general council at H. C. Kimball's encampment. Present H. C. Kimball, P. P. Pratt, O. Pratt, Geo. A. Smith, J. Taylor, A. Lyman, Samuel Bent, Bishops Whitney and Miller, C. C. Rich and about thirty brethren of the Camp.

I told them that I was satisfied that we were taking a course that would prove to be salvation, not only to this camp, but to the saints that were still behind. I did not think there had ever been a body of people since the days of Enoch, placed under the same unpleasant circumstances that this people have been, where there was so little grumbling, and I was satisfied that the Lord was pleased with the majority of the Camp of Israel. But there had been some things done which were wrong. There were among us those who were passing counterfeit money, and had done it all the time since we left Nauvoo. And there were men among us who would steal, some pleaded our suffering from persecution and said they were justified in stealing from our enemies because they had robbed us, but such a course tends to destroy the Kingdom of God.

I proposed that we proceed to the New purchase on Grand river, Iowa, and fence in a field of two miles square, build about twenty log cabins, plough some land and put in spring crops, and thus spend our time till the weather settles. Select men and families to take care of our improvements and the rest proceed westward.

We will also send men back from Grand river to look out a new and better road, to pilot the next company so they may avoid the creeks, bad roads and settlements through which we have passed. Then those who follow can tarry on Grand river or go on to the Missouri bottoms and other places, where there will be plenty of feed for their cattle, and tarry through the winter, and come on another season as soon as they can make their way through.

Friday, April 17—Rolling prairie encampment. 8 a.m. camp started for Medicine Creek, ten miles, passed through Bishop Miller's camp about 2 p.m. Late in the evening two of bro. Boswick's children were buried; their death was caused by measles. There are many cases of measles and mumps.

Saturday, April 18—Pleasant point encampment. Morning pleasant. I wrote to the council of the camp, captains of hundreds, fifties, etc. to meet in council this morning at 10, to select men to go and sell property, and to send men to labor. Also select men that can outfit themselves for the mountains, and they can get ready immediate. The rest of the company go to Grand river where they can locate themselves for the season, and the borrowed teams that are going back to Nauvoo—go on to help the families on to the location. These are the whispering of the Spirit to me. Council met accordingly. Present H. C. Kimball, P. P. Pratt, W. Richards, Bishops Whitney and Miller and others in all about fifty-three. I stated that unless the hands of the Twelve could be untied it would be impossible for them to go over the mountains. The teams that had been returned by the church had been smuggled by individuals for their own use. It is for this council to say who shall go over the mountains. On motion of Cap. Markham it was decided that the presidency should select the men that should go. I said every one that could outfit might go. Council decided that the captains of tens should make an inventory of all the property belonging to the companies that it might be known who could outfit. I suggested there should be a commissary over each ten and deal out half a pound of flour to each person, every twenty-four hours, and that no person be allowed to start with less than one hundred-fifty pounds of breadstuff, one cow to every two persons, ten pounds of salt and half a bushel of seed wheat to every five persons, and other seeds. That we overhaul our goods and send out traders immediately to the Missouri river.

Council directed an inventory of the public property to be taken this afternoon.

Sunday, April 19—Morning pleasant. The saints assembled in the grove north of the encampment. Singing by Elders Pitt and Kay on the exodus of the saints. Prayer by bishop Miller. I said I was thankful for this meeting, a privilege that we had not had since we started, owing to the inclemency of the weather. I never felt a sweeter spirit than that which I have enjoyed since we started. I have seen things I did not like, but I could not get angry, when I saw any of this people taking a course that would finally destroy them it caused me to rise in the strength of the Lord and admonish them using the authority of the priesthood. We would call out those who were to cross the mountains and we would take the public teams and load them with church property and no longer suffer our hands and feet to be fettered as they had been by men smuggling the public teams. We would help the saints on the Grand river, and locate those who cannot outfit to over the mountains this season, and let them put in crops, and erect taverns and resting places, from one point to another, even to the Missouri river, where they can winter their stock without much grain. Elder Taylor preached.

I said that many who could not walk a mile when we started, would, before we got to our journey's end, walk twenty miles in a day. There is Dr. Richards, who has to be poulticed all over to keep life in him, before we get to the pass in the mountains, he will skip and run like a boy, with a gun on his shoulder, after deer, elk, and buffaloes. Geo. A. Smith who could scarcely ride on horseback when we started can now skip into the wagon like a boy. Elder Kimball, Elder Geo. A. Smith and Bishops Whitney and Miller bore testimony to the truth of my remarks.

Monday, April 20—After the last mail from Nauvoo was received, I was continually teased by men, saying, "May I go back to Nauvoo for my family," I counselled the brethren to let their families remain where they were, and go and make farms and raise something for them to eat when they do come.

I almost felt to curse the man that would not hearken to counsel, but would tease and beg continually to be permitted to go back, before he had accomplished the object for which we had started, which was to find a resting place for the saints.

Tuesday, April 21—The first and sixth companies and some others left pleasant point and travelled nine miles to camp creek, and began to form camp on the south side of the creek, when the grass caught fire near the magazine, by the greatest exertions the flames were subdued. The Camp then built a bridge and moved to the other side of the creek. I rode on to look out a route for the next day, returned at night. About sunset Captain Stout's wife was delivered of a son. Two bears were brought into camp by the first and sixth companies. Occasional showers throughout the day.

Wednesday, April 22—Camp Creek; 9 a.m. Orin P. Rockwell started for Nauvoo with about forty letters. I rode ten miles to Pleasant Grove and selected a campground. My horse was bitten on the nose by a rattlesnake. I cut the snake into pieces and applied them to the wound. They drew out the poison, leaving the horse uninjured.

Two deer, four turkeys, and one woodchuck were brought into camp by the hunters of the sixth company.

Thursday, April 23—In the evening there was a thunder shower, followed by a rainbow. The hunters brought into camp two bears, four turkeys and a bee tree.

Friday, April 24—Muddy Creek, the first fifty built a bridge over the creek, and then passed on five miles to a grove on the west bank of the east branch of Grand river and camped. 2:30 p.m. H. G. Sherwood and I rode up the branch and selected a location for a settlement. We returned about dark and found the brethren had been planting, digging a well, and preparing wood for a coal pit.

The grass was about eight inches high, and the trees leaved out.

Saturday, April 25—Camp of Israel, Garden Grove, 10 a.m. four hunters came in bringing a turkey; two of them, J. D. Lee and Levi Stewart had been absent since Thursday morning. All they had eaten while gone was one squirrel and two half grown owls which they found dead.

Sunday, April 26—Rainy. The saints assembled, sang a hymn, I prayed, Elder John Taylor preached. 3 p.m. Saints again assembled, about three hundred and twenty-five persons present, opened with singing, and prayer by Orson Pratt; I preached.

I related the following anecdote, "A young widow who wished to rise in life, hired the servants of a rich widower, and kept them all day counting and recounting a few coppers. Making them covenant to tell their master that she had had them counting money all the time, which caused him to think the widow was rich. Soon after the widower visited and married her, and supplied her with the same means to keep house with as he had his former wife, by economy she saved half her allowance, his table was better furnished and the servants fed better than formerly.

"One day being short of means, he asked his wife to lend him some. She gave him one hundred dollars. Soon after she gave him five hundred more. He then asked her how much money she had at their marriage; she replied, 'Only a few coppers' and then explained the artifice she had used, and told him how she got the money she had lent to him. He was more pleased with her economy than if she had been rich.

"We intend to organize this evening so that every man can go to work to plant, build, dig, etc.

"I know that if this people will be united and will hearken to counsel, the Lord will give them every desire of their hearts. The earth is the Lord's and the fulness thereof and he intends that the saints shall possess it as soon as they are able to bear prosperity."

Elder Kimball concurred with the previous speakers, said the provisions of the camp were nearly exhausted, and that it would take years to cross the mountains at the rate we had been travelling.

I said, "The Spirit of the Lord and keys of the priesthood hold power over all animated beings. When father Adam transgressed the law he did not fall at once from the presence of the Lord but spake face to face with him a long time afterwards. Men continued to sin and degenerate from generation to generation until they had got so far from the Lord that a veil of darkness sprang up between them so that men could no longer speak with the Lord, save it were through a Prophet. During this time the earth and all creation groaned in sin, and enmity increased, and the lives of men and beasts decreased. For this cause the Son of God descended below all things that he might reach every man and that he might return to the Father and have power over all things.

"In this dispensation the keys that were committed to father Adam will be restored, and we are to return into the favor and presence of the Lord. If we cease hostility, with the serpents and lay aside all enmity and treat all animals kindly, being humble and faithful with long suffering and forbearance no man need ever have a horse or a cow bitten by a snake. The serpents would soon become perfectly harmless, so that they could be handled without danger, children could play with them without receiving harm."

Shadrach Roundy arrived in Camp three and a half days out from Nauvoo bringing a mail of twenty-eight letters, among them one from Elder O. Hyde, informing me that a wealthy Catholic bachelor wished to purchase the Temple and thereby immortalize his name, he would probably give two hundred thousand dollars for it. If he buys the Temple he will also buy other property but not otherwise.

Bro. Hyde offered to lease it to him, but he would not lease.

Bro. Hyde was afraid the Temple would fall into the hands of our enemies as borrowed means were being called for, and numerous obligations were rolling in upon the trustees without means to liquidate them, and asked if it would not be better to sell the Temple at Nauvoo, also the Temple and Church property at Kirtland, and with the proceeds assist the Saints to emigrate westward.

At 8 p.m., myself, H. C. Kimball, P. P. Pratt, J. Taylor, W. Richards, and fifteen others met in council at the post office. Three hundred and fifty-nine laboring men were reported on hand, besides trading commissaries and herdsmen. One hundred men were selected to make rails under the superintendence of C. C. Rich, James Pace, Lewis D. Wilson and Stephen Markham. Ten under

James Allred were appointed to build fence. Forty-eight under father John Smith to build houses. Twelve under Jacob Peart to dig wells. Ten under A. P. Rockwood to build bridges. The remainder to be employed in clearing land, ploughing and planting under Daniel Spencer.

A letter from J. O. Heywood to H. C. Kimball was read. Stating that his house had been sold and thirty-five yoke of oxen received on payment; Elder Roundy stated that Joseph Young had sold his house and lot for Six Hundred and Fifty dollars, and that the anti-Mormons of Nauvoo had secretly held a meeting in opposition to mobocracy but had not closed their business when he left.

I received a letter from Elders Geo. A. Smith and Amasa M. Lyman announcing that thirteen wagons were encamped at Point Pleasant unable to come up at present. They felt willing that the Temple should be sold to assist the poor if the council thought it best.

Monday, April 27—The council decided that the Trustees might sell the Temples at Nauvoo and Kirtland and all other property of the Church and help the poor saints to move westward. The Council considered that the Temple would be of no benefit to the saints if they could not possess their private dwellings, and the time should come that they should return and redeem their inheritances they could redeem the Temple also, that a sale would secure it from unjust claims, mobs, fire and so forth, more effectually than for the Church to retain it in their hands.

Bishop Whitney had some doubts as to the propriety of selling the Temple.

I related a dream I had the night previous which is as follows: I saw myself employed in the service of an aged man, a Lord, Superintending the affairs of his dominions (assisted by the council); I directed some important steps to be taken, which I considered necessary, notwithstanding the Lord had not instructed me to do so. By and by he came to me smiling, his hair was as white as the purest wool. I told him what I had done, and asked him if I had done right. Pausing a moment, he turned to me with a smile on his countenance and said, "You have done well. I intend to buy a large store filled with all kinds of commodities all of which shall, be under your control as you understand the affairs of my government and will do my people good." Whether Bishop Whitney's doubts were removed or not after hearing the dream he voted to sell the Temple. The Council wrote Elder Hyde their decision.

Rained constantly all day.

Tuesday, April 28—Rained all night. I was ill in bed till 8 a.m. At 9 had a council in my tent with Elders Kimball and J. D. Lee, and decided that the trading commissaries tarry in camp until the storm abates or until the camp arrives at the next place of settlement when they will be nearer the inhabitants on the Des Moines river than they now are to the Missourians who, we hear, are preparing to fight the saints.

Rained all day.

Wednesday, April 29—Rained all night, and all day. I was quite unwell.

Harriet, wife of Wilber J. Earl, was delivered of a son.

Thursday, April 30—Rainy. Camp nearly destitute of breadstuff. Creeks so high that teams cannot cross nor mills grind.

The Temple at Nauvoo was dedicated this evening. Elders Orson Hyde, Wilford Woodruff, John, Joseph and Phineas H. Young, J. M. Bernhisel, J. L. Heywood, and several others were present. Elder Joseph Young offered up the dedicatory prayer, dedicating the Temple, and all that pertained thereto to the Lord, as an offering to Him as an evidence of the willingness of His people, to fulfill His commandments, and build His Holy house, even at the risk of their lives, and the sacrifice of their labor and earthly goods. He prayed for the Twelve and all the authorities of the Church, and for the workmen that had wrought upon the Temple in the midst of persecution, want and suffering, and for the deliverance of the poor; that the Lord would direct the brethren of the Camp of Israel, open the way before them and lead them to a place of His own appointment for the gathering of all the Saints that God would avenge the blood of His servants, the prophets and of the saints who had been slain for the testimony of the truth and mete out to our enemies the same measure which they have meted out to us.

Friday, May 1—The Temple at Nauvoo was publicly dedicated by Elder Orson Hyde; Elders W. Woodruff, A. W. Babbitt, and Joseph A. Stratton were present and took part in the services. Fee for admission one dollar, to pay the hands employed on the Temple.

Saturday, May 2—Evening, Elder Richards and I conferred with Captain Elijah Averett who reported that the feelings of the Missourians were softened towards us, that he and bro. Elisha Averett and their company of about thirty men had received about one hundred dollars worth of grain and bacon in exchange for clearing land and building two barns. Samuel Thomas died of consumption.

Sunday, May 3—The Saints met; Elder Orson Spencer preached. I also addressed the assembly, referring to the travels of the brethren from place to place, and how they would continue to be led about and wasted away, unless they would be united and feel after each other's cares and bear each other's burdens; and said that there were many who had been benefitted by the teams and provisions of the poor families yet back; we should plant for such, that upon their arrival here they should have something to come to. It were better to sell some beds, silks, dresses or a wagon for provisions to sustain us a few weeks while we are putting in grain, than sacrifice one-half of what we have to support ourselves with next winter. The word of the Lord is, for this people to plant at this place, go ahead and plant again. Joseph Smith said that where the keys of the Kingdom were, there would be the place to gather.

Wherever the Twelve and Council are, there will the keys be, and the place of Gathering. When the removal westward was in contemplation at Nauvoo, had the brethren submitted to our counsel and brought their teams and means and authorized me to do as the Spirit and wisdom of the Lord directed with them, then we could have outfitted a company of men that were not encumbered with large families and sent them over the mountains to put in crops and build houses, and the residue could have gathered, beginning with the Priesthood, and the gathering continued from year to year, building and planting at the same time. Were matters so conducted, none would be found crying for bread, or none destitute of clothing, but all would be provided for as designed by the Almighty. But instead of taking this course, the Saints have crowded on us all the while, and have completely tied our hands by importuning and saying do not leave us behind, wherever you go we want to go and be with you, and thus our hands and feet have been bound which has caused our delay to the present time; and now hundreds at Nauvoo are continually praying and importuning with the Lord that they may overtake us, and be with us, and just so it is with the Saints here. They are afraid to let us go on and leave them behind; forgetting that they had covenanted to help the poor away at the sacrifice of all their Property.

No one can prosper who thus neglects compliance with this obligation, not only so but I know that the same cause caused Joseph to lose his life, and unless this people are more united in spirit and cease to pray against Counsel, it will bring me down to my grave. I am reduced in flesh so that my coat that would scarcely meet around me last Winter now laps over twelve inches. It is with much ado that I can keep from lying down and sleeping to wait the resurrection.

Come, brethren, will you harken to counsel, if you will manifest it by raising the right hand. Every hand was up and every heart responded to the call.

In the morning let every man go to work under his respective Captain taking up his cross (his ax, maul and wedge), and let us fence the fields and plant them, and when this is accomplished we will go on to the next location.

Rain fell in torrents for two hours.

Monday, May 4—William G. Young at headquarters on his return from Missouri, leaving his wagon back five miles on the Prairie on account of the mud.

The water was so high the mills could not grind short of a week's dry weather; he reported that the traders of the third, fourth, and sixth companies were in the neighborhood of Miller's Mill and they had articles sufficient to trade for all the cows, provisions, etc. they wanted.

I expressed my satisfaction at the number of traders out and proposed deferring trading much until we get to our next location.

I labored through the day on the bridge.

The brethren commenced fencing at the north west corner of the farm. Three bears were brought into Camp. This is the first day of the last nine that it has not rained at Garden Grove.

Tuesday, May 5—I shouldered my axe and engaged in chopping and raising the bridge till about eleven.

Pleasant day; about ten p.m. a heavy shower of rain.

Wednesday, May 6—Counseling the brethren and fitting up my wagons for the mountains. The Historian inditing history.

The brethren generally very diligent fencing the farm.

Afternoon, a violent storm of wind blew down many trees that were girdled in and about camp; one tree fell on a mule, and another on a cow; almost every man, woman and child were engaged in holding down the tents.

A large tree fell within five inches of Parley P. Pratt's wagon without touching it. Capt. C. C. Rich's family narrowly escaped. In ten or fifteen minutes the wind changed to the southwest, attended with a heavy thunder shower and some hail when the storm abated. I went round my company, and found that no serious injury was sustained.

Thursday, May 7—My horse was bitten by a rattlesnake. Bro. Hendricks horse died, which was probably bitten the evening before. Many horses have been bitten in Camp, two have died. Several of Elder Kimball's animals have been bitten; he has doctored little, but has prayed for them and they have recovered.

Friday, May 8—Bro. Andrew Cahoon arrived with a mail of thirty-three letters.

He reported that Orin P. Rockwell had been arrested for shooting Frank Worrel in obedience to Sheriff Backenstos' orders last fall, and was in Quincy jail.

The fence around the south field was completed.

Saturday, May 9—Clear, warm and pleasant.

The brethren commenced building houses on the East and West sides of the south field; four were put up on the west side under the direction of Capt. Stephen Markham.

This is the third day we have had at this encampment without rain.

Bro. Lewis returning from Missouri was bitten by a rattlesnake on his great toe, it bled freely, he bound tobacco leaf on it and walked into camp.

Hyrum, son of Hosea and Louisa Stout, died, aged about two years.

Sunday, May 10—Warm.

About four hundred saints were addressed by Elder Jedediah M. Grant on the first principles of the Gospel. Elder P. P. Pratt followed him.

Afternoon, Sacrament was administered by Elders Samuel Bent and Aaron Johnson. I said that this was the first Sabbath since we left Nauvoo that we had not been interrupted by rain or storm. I moved that inasmuch as those who are to leave this place and return to Nauvoo for their families have fenced the lots, built, the bridges, houses, etc. that they should have the right of possession. I remarked that any person who chose might go and locate by himself, but those who did should not come here to beg. Such would dry up and wither like a dead branch. Those who came to this place from Nauvoo should have equal privileges with those here. Elder Samuel Bent was appointed president at this location.

I advised that if a man would not till his land, it should be taken from him, and if he would not gather his crops, let Father Bent put them into his own store house. Ezra T. Benson and David Fulmer were appointed councellors to Samuel Bent.

Voted that all who remain and will not work on the Garden Grove farm shall be cast out as idlers.

Tuesday, May 12—Very pleasant and warm.

While I was standing with Prest. Kimball at his tent, an outcry was heard from Peter Haws' Camp; we repaired thither and found that Haws and Thomas Williams and two others had a quarrel about some property, etc. that Haws had let Williams have some bogus money on shares and Williams had not paid him his share of the profits. I reproved them for dealing in base coin and told Haws he could not govern himself, his family, or a company; and unless he repented and forsook such dishonesty, the hand of the Lord would be against him and all those who partook of such corruption.

Elder Samuel Bent received his letter of authority to preside over Garden Grove settlement, to divide out the land fenced by the advanced companies, to see that no man has the use of land which he does not till, to tithe the saints for the benefit of the poor and sick, and to see that the crops are secured and nothing lost.

William Edwards died at three a.m. of billious fever; he had been sick for ten weeks.

Wednesday, May 13—Cloudy, warm day with slight rain.

Elder Richards and I started for the next location west.

After traveling about eight miles on the divide in a west north-west direction, bros. Richards and Rockwood stopped on the right at a hickory grove where some brethren were camped, which they called Hickory Thunder, for before they could pitch a tent there was thunder, lightning and rain in abundance.

Amelia Pierson, who was sick and had ridden all the afternoon, was obliged to continue sitting in the carriage, much exhausted, with Dr. Richards. During the whole shower, Dr. Richards went from carriage to wagon and wagon to carriage to fasten the covers, and protect his family from the rain and wind till eleven. Wet to the skin and remained wet all night. Many others were in like predicament.

The water fell one inch per hour for two and a half hours.

Monday, May 18—Pleasant. At sunrise about thirty men were detached from the various companies by Cap. Rockwood and built a bridge.

Accompanied by Elders H. C. Kimball, Geo. A. Smith, Captains Rockwood and Sherwood, I went on to look a road, instructing the Camp to wait till we returned, but as soon as the bridge was done, the Camp went on without a pilot and took a very crooked route, till about noon when Captain Rockwood returned and stopped the Camp at a creek where they built a bridge, and waited till we returned and reported Parley P. Pratt's trail within about two miles, and soon after Bro. Lorenzo Snow arrived from Bro. Pratt's Camp and reported it encamped on Grand river about five miles. The whole camp moved on and arrived at Middlefork of Grand River, which Parley called Mount Pisgah, from five to seven p.m., having traveled about thirteen miles. After passing the bridge built at noon and ascending the hill there is a mass of grey granate, which has the appearance of an ancient alter, the parts having been separated by fire and fallen in various directions. This is a curiosity in a country where there is no rock. We are in the country of the Pottawatomie Indians.

Tuesday, May 19—Cloudy day.

The Major and the officers of his company, in Nauvoo, during May reported weekly in the papers, the number of persons and wagons that left the city.

Major Warren's position was, certainly, in some respects, an unenviable one; he was a government officer, bound to obey orders. He was expected to see that the treaty between the "Mormons" and the Anti-Mormons and Governor was duly observed according to "the understanding of the Executive and the State at large" and that was, the entire removal of the "Mormons" by the first day of May. And it was therefore, while in the discharge of his duty, that he said, April 16th, for the peace of the inhabitants, and honor of the state, public expectation must be gratified. Individually, he evinced the feelings of humanity, in pleading for time in behalf of the oppressed, and in pronouncing the conduct of some of the anti-Mormons as bad as the savages.

He felt that his position was a conspicuous and responsible one; but that position, while it compelled him to enforce the assumed conditions of the treaty, also gave him an opportunity, by a stretch of power, to grant some lenity to the oppressed "Mormons." Thus while with one hand he pushed the saints from their possessions across the river, to save their lives, with the other he kept at bay the savage fiends who thirsted for blood, and who would fain have washed their hands in the blood of innocence and feasted their eyes on the smoking ruins of their property.

Two Pottawatomie Indians came into Camp and got a stray horse which the brethren had taken upon the Prairie.

I received a letter from Wm. Felshaw soliciting aid to help him to move out of Nauvoo, many brethren have written from Nauvoo making the same request; I expressed my sympathy for their situation by sending all the teams and wagons back that I could control.

I received a letter from Bro. J. W. Binley announcing that he had taken several jobs of building and that to facilitate him in procuring contracts, he had drank and caroused with the Gentiles.

To this the council replied;

"Close your contracts and take no more new ones at present, but hasten to this place and assist us in getting in a crop. We would also say that if it is absolutely necessary for Saints to lay aside the principle of morality and act like the devil in order to deal with them to advantage it will be better to lay aside your saints-ship and become a devil in reality without acting the hypocrite and stay and associate with them."

"If we take a firm, independent, straight, forward course, honoring our religion, Priesthood and our God, and let them know we are a praying People, they would respect us, and the Lord will work to our advantage.

Wednesday, May 20—Captains H. G. Sherwood, Hazen Kimball and G. S. Clark left camp for the Pottawatomie village to confer with their chiefs.

After much conversation on the traveling of the Camp under the increasing difficulties, Elder H. C. Kimball said that to proceed farther as we were situated, we could not reach our destination. George A. Smith offered his teams to me and he would tarry behind, if circumstances required it. I offered to stay, or leave my family and go.

Elder Kimball moved the Twelve stay here and let those who are ready go on, seconded by Dr. Richards. I moved that the Twelve and such others as they may select go on over the mountains. Carried. The Council decided that all the saints at Garden Grove who wish, have the privilege of removing to this place; and that a general council of all the brethren be called in the morning at nine, and the business of this days council be laid before them and ascertain their minds.

I suggested the propriety of those who were ready, going on with some Pioneers and opening a way to Council Bluffs.

Rain continued.

Thursday, May 21—Mount Pisgah; some rain during the night, and a heavy rain this morning till 9:30 when clear sky began to appear.

Council of the Camp assembled in front of my tent. Present Elders H. C. Kimball, Geo. A. Smith, P. P. and O. Pratt, A. Lyman, W. Richards, and all the brethren. Prest. Kimball stated the time had come for the brethren to decide whether the twelve go on or stay and let others go on, that I and others had to double teams all the way from the farm hither and we could do so no longer; that he would rather go back into the vineyard and preach, convert the people, and raise means than proceed in this manner; that the Twelve brought out provisions for a year but they had fed it to the brethren who came out without supplies. The people have stripped the Twelve, and he wanted it understood that unless the people let the Twelve go and find a place of gathering, the Church will be scattered.

A motion was made that the brethren outfit the Twelve for the mountains. A part voted in favor, and a part did not vote either way.

Elder Kimball, Richards and I voted the Twelve stay and outfit the brethren.

I spoke confirming bro. Kimball's statements, and the gathering of Israel. The Church was told publicly at Nauvoo that those authorities of the Church against whom all the artillery of the enemy was aimed, should be removed, but we had to stop on Sugar Creek three weeks to get teams to drag out Bishop Whitney and Wm. Clayton, with the public property, they had in charge, such as Mill Irons, saws, guns, etc., while there were fifty teams lying at Sugar Creek loaded with families that neither God, man nor the devil cared about their going.

Eight hundred men reported themselves without a fortnight's provisions.

That I had a year's provisions for my family but had fed it all out and now if the brethren will continue to tie our hands so that we cannot find a resting place, our enemies will inquire, where is Zion, Don't know, and where is your Gospel, You have none!

Bishop Whitney and Wm. Clayton and the artillery and public stores have not teams to go on. Neither has Dr. Richards, the Historian, and the Lord's house must be established in the tops of the mountains, where the people may gather, the saints receive their endowments, and the Lord hide Israel while his indignation shall pass by. I said the brethren had better not all settle together, as timber was scattered and a few families might locate together.

Friday, May 22—Elder Kimball and I counselled with Prest. Huntington about a location for a farm.

Two p.m. the saints assembled. I requested those who intended to go westward and could not outfit, to separate themselves from the congregation, which the majority did. It was voted that all who remained form together in one large field and that all who would not should be disfellowshipped. I told the saints that all who should start not fully supplied must suffer the consequences and must not expect assistance from others.

It was voted that those who were intending to go on should, while they tarry, assist those who were to remain in building, ploughing, planting, etc.

Sunday, May 24—A.M. rainy. P.M. cloudy.

At noon the horn sounded for the saints to assemble, but few came out.

I addressed them and told the people the time had come when I should command them what to do inasmuch as they were not willing to harken to counsel.

Saturday, May 30—Morning pleasant. I met with H. C. Kimball, P. P. and O. Pratt, John Taylor, Geo. A. Smith, A. Lyman, W. Richards, Father John Smith, Wm. Clayton, Wm. Huntington, Ezra T. Benson, Charles C. Rich, Daniel and Orson Spencer, and N. K. Whitney. We proceeded in carriages and on horseback on the prairie three miles north, formed a square with two tents, all kneeled and prayed.

I was mouth. A. P. Rockwood and Wm. Kimball watched the teams and tents without.

Elder Kimball prayed for the general prosperity of the Church; and prayed again for O. Hyde, W. Woodruff and O. P. Rockwell—Geo. A. Smith mouth.

We returned with renewed assurance that the Lord was with us and were comforted.

Sunday, May 31—Camp met. Elder Geo. A. Smith addressed the meeting until I arrived, when on motion the meeting was resolved into a special conference.

I urged the importance of the brethren working together for the general good, and the responsibility of all equally to preach the Gospel and save the saints in this time of scarcity and trouble.

Ninety-nine hundredths of the means raised by the Sectarians for evangelizing the world are spent in fighting each other; and the Latter-day Saints have never been united as they should be.

It has been reported the past week to new comers and news has been sent back that the Twelve command the people and are going to take everything from them. I shall command when God requires it of me.

I want to know whether those that have recently arrived here will be united and work for the general good, and not desire to separate themselves.

There are some who are always doing good; others will do as Brother Brigham or the Twelve say, but never step forward and say, here is all I possess, take it and dispose of it for the good of the cause.

Elder Geo. A. Smith moved that those who are going on help build a fence around the field, when many voted.

I advised that all the brethren help build a fence around a farm of Five hundred or a thousand acres, and plough all they can at the same time, and explained the general principles in the letter of instructions to President Huntington.

Exhorted the saints to live up to all of their privileges, for the saints have to become so pure that their bodies will be changed in a moment as Jesus was, and not rest in the grave one hundred or a thousand years.

I informed the brethren that the Presidency of Mount Pisgah would divide the lots when the land was fenced. It should be divided up into five, ten and twenty acre lots and the brethren cast lots for land. Those brethren who are going on will carry all the provisions they can. We calculated to carry upwards of two hundred pounds to a person, none should go with less than two hundred pounds.

About one half of the assembly voted that they would remain at this point and go to work.

I exhorted all who stayed to abide the counsel of the Presidency, to be upright and united, and when a horse or tools were wanted, ask for it, and never take anything not their own without liberty, and be certain when you get done using it to return it immediately. There has been too much liberty taken with property; it is not right.

Monday, June 1—At Mount Pisgah.

It rained last evening and until nine this morning.

Friday, June 5—Travelled fourteen miles and camped on the prairie near a Shoal Creek, having forded what we supposed to be the west branch of Grand river, and found the Indian trail to Council Bluffs.

Saturday, June 6—Eleven oxen were missing this morning, but were found seven miles ahead.

Sunday, June 7—About eleven a.m., Elder Kimball called the meeting to order inside of the circle, where a temporary stand was erected; there were eight Indians present. He spoke of the ancient saints and their tribulatons and journeys, referred to our traveling and tenting by the way as they did; said, Many were too selfish, but when the saints would seek each other's interests they would prosper.

I followed Elder Kimball and counselled none to start without ample supplies for we would probably be more strict about provisions when we reached the Missouri river.

I rejoiced in the nobleness of soul evinced by many of the brethren who were going forward, who unhesitatingly left the farms they had commenced; when we reached the Bluffs it would probably be one continual train from Nauvoo thence.

I told the saints they were hedging up their own way by the course they were pursuing; some say, I am poor, I have done all I could for the church; now, for Heaven's sake, don't leave me. I want to go with the Church, and every man that could start, is on the way; their faith is, that the Twelve might not get far ahead of them, and the Devil help them.

I can safely prophesy that we will not cross the mountains this season, and that is what many of the brethren wish, they would rather go to hell than be left behind.

I instructed the Sisters to keep themselves and tents clean, and not to dictate those over them, it was their duty to raise all the children they could lawfully, and rear them up in the name of the Lord, watching over them and keeping them from playing with ungodly children, or from falling into danger, or exposing themselves to sickness; and when they have raised them up to deliver them over to their father's charge. Instead of meddling with their husband's business, they should be careful of his feelings, and seek his interest, and men should be kind and affectionate to their wives, not abusing or exposing them to hardships.

Monday, June 8—At eight a.m. the Camp started, passed Pottawatomie Indian Town, crossed a branch of Nishnabotna River on a flood-wood bridge built by Gen. Geo. Miller and Pioneers, who had gone in advance to locate roads and build bridges, and forded another branch. Saw many Indians who were very friendly.

Traveled fourteen miles to a creek which we crossed.

After starting this morning, and while in sight of the Pottawatomie Village, we were met by a brave, who informed us we must pay duty for passing through their village and for the grass our Stock would destroy; he was no doubt instigated by our enemies; but on our informing the Indians that instead of injuring them, we would do them good, by making bridges, etc., they readily consented to let us pass.

I instructed the captains of tens to move out in order and help their companies over the creeks and see that the guns and pistols in their companies were all cleaned and conveniently placed.

Beautiful day.

Thursday, June 11—About two p.m., James W. Cummings arrived from his visit to Emmett's company, accompanied by Bro. Potter; he said Emmett had taken seven horses, some jewelry and with a young squaw left the company; it was supposed he had gone to St. Peters,—that Emmett's company were at the fort thirty miles below the bluffs, and John L. Butler with them.

Friday, June 12—At nine a.m., bro. Wm. Porter was dispatched to Emmett's company with a letter from the council, recommending them to outfit themselves for the mountains and to stay where they are, until they hear from us again.

Traveled nine miles and encamped on the east bank of a small stream, and waited to build a bridge.

The banks of the creek were very miry, some forty or fifty cattle had to be pulled out of the mire which prevented building the bridge.

Saturday, June 13—Built a bridge this morning. Traveled ten miles and camped on the hill near Mosquito creek to build another Bridge.

Miller's, Spencer's and Parley's companies encamped near the creek; many bushels of wild strawberries were gathered; Elder Richards and I fished from five to six p.m.

Sunday, June 14—At eleven, the camp started and crossed Mosquito Creek on the bridge built by Bishop Miller.

Encamped at five p.m.; all the companies came together and we formed a hollow square on the bank of the Missouri river.

At eight p.m., the Horn sounded and a general meeting convened.

Bishop Miller explained to the brethren the order of the camp; said that according to the laws of the United States, the Church had no right to trade with the Indians; that no man would be permitted to come in through our lines after night without liberty, and that men would be appointed from the company to herd the stock; and when the herd is gathered we should not do as some have done heretofore, that is bring their own stock, for herdsmen are required to bring up every creature.

The brethren voted to submit to the order of the camp, and that those who would not, should be disfellowshiped; also that no man go a trading unless authorized.

Monday, June 15—Missouri River Encampment. Slight clouds, wind south-east.

A general rally after the stock which were brought together on the prairie. It was reported that the Indians had killed three but there was only one missing.

Elder Richards and I, with the committee, visited the Indian agent for the Pottawatomies and traders, and priced their goods which they were willing to sell us at fifty percent lower than to the natives. We purchased several articles and returned about three p.m.

At eight p.m. the camp met.

I repeated the instructions given last evening pertaining to trading, and observed that misunderstandings arose from persons being absentminded and not paying attention to what is said.

I explained the object of the meeting, which was to take into consideration the policy of removing the camp back to the bluffs where we could get good spring water and be away from the Omaha Indians.

We decided that Capt. Miller's company continue their operations on the boat, and that Frederick Hesler direct the hands; also that Capt. Miller keep up the fishery.

I advised the brethren to be wise and say little.

Thursday, June 18—About noon, the council rode to the creek in company with Pieme La Clair, the great chief of the Pottawatomies, partly of French origin; he spoke good English.

He understood the situation of the Saints, was very friendly, social and obliging.

After parting with him we went north half a mile and picked strawberries.

Elders Kimball, Richards and I chatted on the prairie, between five and seven p.m. Geo. A. Smith and his Father arrived with about one hundred wagons.

Friday, June 19—Camp of Israel, at Mosquito Creek. Very warm and pleasant.

At nine a.m., Messrs. Sarpy and Gyren, Indian traders, arrived in Camp and called at the post office whither Elders Kimball, P. P. Pratt, J. Taylor, George A. Smith, W. Richards, Bishop Miller and I repaired.

We had a long conversation about the road, country, and climate to and about the Rocky Mountains.

About 1 p.m., I went and picked strawberries, till five.

Saturday, June 20—Mosquito Creek. About ten a.m., Elders H. C. Kimball, O. Hyde, P. P. Pratt, O. Pratt, J. Taylor, W. Richards and I with our families, the Band, and many others from the Camp, started for the Indian agency at trading point, and about noon stopped at Major Mitchell's, the United States Indian Agent of the Pottawatomie's; many Indians and others were assembled. Halfday and Hoby, two chiefs, were introduced to the Presidency and band. After a few tunes the Presidency, Ladies and band dined with Major Mitchell, Twelve at a table, six tables; thereafter music and dancing and a few songs by John Kay till about half-past six when the party started for the Camp, and arrived about half-past eight; all parties appeared highly delighted with the repasts and amusements of the day, and the best of feelings were manifested by the citizens and Indians towards the saints.

Sunday, June 21—I attended meeting in a small grove on a branch which runs west, emptying into Mosquito creek.

I called for six counter hewers for building boats, eight volunteered; for four carpenters, eight volunteered; eight choppers, nine volunteered; Twelve spadesmen, twelve volunteered; six yoke of oxen to haul the gunnels for the ferry boat, and twelve yoke to haul the logs to the Indian saw mill and two wagons to haul the plank from the mill to the boat, which is being built on the river, above the agency, as fast as they are sawed.

I told the brethren not to ride another man's horse without leave; that one hundred mounted men, wagons with provisions, etc., for them are to be raised to guard the camp, and any man who sleeps on guard will be punished.

I acknowledged the hand of the Lord in bringing us from Nauvoo.

Amos Fielding counted nine hundred and two wagons in three days as he was returning to Nauvoo.

I called on all who were willing to do as I commanded to hold up their right hands; hands up generally.

It is a law of the Camp that all dogs shall be chained during the night, or from sundown till seven next morning; and if any dog is found worrying sheep it may be shot without trial.

A piece of bogus money was palmed off upon the Pottawatomies who took an ox from the next company and killed it; I said, they did right.

Thursday, June 25—Cloudy and foggy, occasional showers till two p.m., when the clouds began to break and so continued till about five, when it commenced raining and continued till dark.

I rode to trading point, in company with Charles Bird. Mr. Sarpy informed me that Major Mitchell had written to the commander of the troops at the fort, that the Mormons were conniving with the Indians and had committed some depridations at Pottawatomie town, and wanted the Dragoons to come up and keep the peace and prevent their uniting with the Indians to fight the United States.

Friday, June 26—Mosquito Creek.

Weather clear and pleasant, wind northwest.

I met in council on the Prairie north of Headquarters, at eleven a.m., with Elders Heber C. Kimball, Orson Hyde, Parley P. Pratt, Orson Pratt, John Taylor, Geo. A. Smith, Amasa Lyman, Willard Richards, Newel K. Whitney, Albert P. Rockwood, John Smith, George D. Grant, and Levi Richards.

Conversation ensued in relation to Mitchell's writing to the fort, for troops to take the Mormon ladies and drive off the leaders, as reported by Sarpy.

Voted that Orson Hyde and Newel K. Whitney go to Major Mitchell's and inquire if he has written to Fort Kearney for troops; and if so learn the cause, and give him information of the true state of affairs, and get him to write a letter to counteract his former letter.

Council adjourned to Major Hunt's camp, two miles north, where we dined, except Elders Hyde and Whitney, who retired to visit Major Mitchell.

After dinner, Major Hunt went with the council to Headquarters, where Elders P. P. Pratt, H. C. Kimball, Geo. A. Smith, and I went to the boat where we met brothers Hyde and Whitney, who informed us that Major Mitchell said he had not written any letter to Fort Kearney, except one, which he wrote two months ago, about Emmett's company; that since his acquaintance with the Mormons his feelings had materially changed, that he had found them gentlemen, and wished them well, and he would do all in his power to do them good; and he would write to Fort Kearney if the committee wished it, but it was of no use as the officers had taken no notice of his letters, and the officers wanted the Mormons to go forward to this destination.

Saturday, June 27—The apostacy of Elder Page was taken into consideration, when it was motioned by George A. Smith and seconded by John Taylor, that John E. Page be cut off from the Quorum of the Twelve apostles, carried unanimously.

Sunday, June 28—I addressed the assembly on the situation of the Church, the gathering of Israel, and the building up of the kingdom of God.

I said all things are controlled to the perfecting of the Saints, and the overthrow of the wicked, and that although an evil deed may be over-ruled for good, yet a good deed may bring a greater good.

At four, I met with Father Smith, H. C. Kimball, O. Pratt, Geo. A. Smith and W. Richards in council, at the post office, and heard a sketch read from the St. Louis, New Era, that whipping, driving and threatening prevailed in Hancock County, Illinois, on the eleventh inst.

I proposed sending a company from this to Bear River Valley in the Great Basin, without families forthwith.

Elder Geo. A. Smith called the sheep owners forward; fifteen present, who voted to put their sheep together and herd them, to protect them from the wolves.

I instructed the newly arrived brethren to report themselves and be enrolled in a company as one would be selected to go over the mountains and put in seed; for I was aware, that all that men and hell could invent to hedge up the way of the camp, would be hatched up.

I moved that we all go over the mountains, leaving our families, which was sustained by unanimous vote.

I asked, who would volunteer to leave their families and go over the mountains. Scores voted.

I said, if the Church is blown to the four winds and never gathered again, remember I have told you how, when and where to gather, and if you do not go now, remember and bear me witness in the day of judgement.

When God tells a man what to do, he admits of no argument, and I want no arguments, and if they will go I will warrant them safety in so doing.

At eight, council met and conversed on many points relative to the mountain mission.

Monday, June 29—I heard that U. S. officers were on their way from Garden Grove to enlist soldiers for Santa Fe.

At nine, I met in Council with Elders H. C. Kimball, O. Pratt, Geo. A. Smith, A. Lyman, W. Richards, N. K. Whitney and John Scott.

A letter was received from Elder Wilford Woodruff announcing Capt. James Allen's visit to Mount Pisgah, to raise volunteers.

I counselled all the Twelve to be at the river immediately, and help Col. Scott over to night, with the heavy wagon, and be ready to help others tomorrow.

Tuesday, June 30—Evening, brother Thomas Grover arrived at Headquarters, and informed the council that Capt. Allen of the U. S. Army had arrived on the hill, and wanted volunteers; the Captain had agreed to meet in council in the morning at ten.

I met with bros. Kimball and Richards in bro. O. Pratt's tent. Decided it was best to meet Captain Allen in the morning and raise the men wanted.

Wednesday, July 1—Pleasant weather.

Forenoon, Elders H. C. Kimball, W. Richards, O. Pratt, and I rode to Elder Taylor's camp at Mosquito creek where we met Orson Hyde, Geo. A. Smith, John Taylor, John Smith, Levi Richards, and Capt. James Allen accompanied with two others from Fort Leavenworth.

The Captain presented a letter of introduction from Wm. Huntington and Council at Mt. Pisgah, directed to Wm. Clayton, Clerk of the Camp.

Forty five minutes after eleven, adjourned to the wagon stand where I introduced Captain Allen, who addressed the people.

He said, he was sent by Col. S. W. Kearney through the benevolence of James K. Polk, President of the U. S., to enlist Five hundred of our men—that there were hundred of thousands of volunteers ready in the states.

He read his orders from Col. Kearney and the circular which he issued at Mount Pisgah and explained.

Noon, I addressed the assembly; wished them to make a distinction between this action of the general government, and our former oppressions in

Missouri and Illinois. I said, the question might be asked, Is it prudent for us to enlist to defend our country? If we answer in the affirmative, all are ready to go.

Suppose we were admitted into the Union as a State and the government did not call on us, we would feel ourselves neglected. Let the Mormons be the first men to set their feet on the soil of California. Capt. Allen has assumed the responsibility of saying that we may locate at Grand Island, until we can prosecute our journey. This is the first offer we have ever had from the government to benefit us.

I proposed that the five hundred volunteers be mustered, and I would do my best to see all their families brought forward, as far as my influence extended, and feed them when I had anything to eat myself.

Twenty minutes after twelve, p.m., Capt. Allen said, he would write to President Polk to give us leave to stay on the route where it was necessary—the soldiers daily rations would be eighteen ounces of bread and twenty ounces of beef, or twelve of bacon, and they would be paid every two months.

Elder H. C. Kimball moved that five hundred men be raised in conformity with the requisition from government, seconded by W. Richards and carried unanimously.

I walked out as recruiting Sergeant, with my clerk, W. Richards, and took several names as volunteers.

The Twelve and Capt. Allen repaired to Mr. Taylor's tent. I asked the Capt., if an officer enlisting men on Indian lands had not a right to say to their families, 'you can stay till your husbands return.' Capt. Allen replied, that he was a representative of President Polk and could act till he notified the President, who might ratify his engagements, or indemnify for damage: The President might give permisson to travel through the Indian country, and stop whenever and wherever circumstances required.

Half an hour past one, Capt. Allen left, and the Twelve continued to converse on the favorable prospects before us.

It was voted that Prest. H. C. Kimball and I should go to Mount Pisgah to raise volunteers. I said, I would start soon, and I desired the companies to be organized, so that we could ascertain who could go to make a camp at Grand Island, and who must remain after raising the troops; the Twelve to go on westward with their families.

Thursday, July 2—I finished crossing my teams, and in the evening returned to J. D. Lee's encampment on the East side of the river. Elders Kimball and Richards visited the river about noon, found they could not cross, returned to their encampment, and dug a well about ten feet deep, plenty of good water.

Friday, July 3—Elders Heber C. Kimball, Willard Richards and I started at nine a.m., in my carriage for Mount Pisgah: brothers Joseph S. Scofield, James H. Glines, Thomas S. Williams and George W. Langley accompanied us on horseback.

About five, we passed several small companies travelling, total one hundred and eight wagons. We encamped and staid with Ebenezer Brown and John I. Barnard having travelled about thirty four miles: very cheerful on our ride.

We conversed with the brethren about enlisting near midnight.

Nancy B., wife of John Freeman, was delivered of a daughter at six p.m., which was named Rosaline Beal, reported by Patty Sessions, midwife.

Sunday, July 5—Clear and calm morning.

Oquakee, White Hawk Chief, and other Indians encamped near us last night, and were hungry; I told a brother to give them a fat cow and I would give him one on his arrival at the bluffs: the Indians were highly pleased.

Tuesday, July 7—Mount Pisgah. Clear and pleasant, south wind.

I addressed the brethren on the subject of raising a batalion to march to California, and was followed by Elders J. C. Little and H. C. Kimball.

John M. Highbee, Daniel Tyler, Robert Pixton and sixty three others volunteered.

We counted and reported two hundred and five wagons at Mount Pisgah, which with these on the road and at head quarters make a total of Eighteen hundred and five wagons.

Wednesday, July 8—Pleasant and warm.

Elders Kimball, Richards & I visited the saints at Mount Pisgah this forenoon.

Dr. Richards administered to sister Moss, who had been bitten by a rattlesnake.

I spent the evening with Dr. Richards, Gen. Rich, and Elder Little.

Friday, July 10—Cloudy morning.

We started at half-past four a.m., rode half a mile and breakfasted with Samuel and Daniel Russell.

Ten minutes after six, we started and after nine, baited our teams on the prairie, during a thunder shower. About one p.m., found Pooroocks and son and the braves of the Misqaukies, who wanted the Mormon chiefs to wait till they could send for Powsheek, who had something to say. We consented to stay, and their messenger started; a heavy rain commenced—dined with Jacob Baum about five.

About seven, Powsheek arrived and went into Dr. Geo. W. Coulson's tent, with his chiefs and braves, followed by Elders Kimball, Richards, myself, our escort, and others.

Powsheek wanted to see the Mormon chief, and to know where he came from, and where the Mormons were going; he said, his people were going off with the Pottawatomies—that Kokuk had sold their land—enquired about the war with Mexico; and said, he was friendly, and would like to go with us, but unless he crossed the Missouri river and located on the land appointed, he would not get his annuity from the government.

Powsheek and his Indians visited several of the Mormon camps, on his way to Council Bluff Agency and danced and received feasts and provisions.

Saturday, July 11—Cloudy morning.

Cyrus H. Wheelock let the Musqaukoe Indians have a two year old heifer, by my order.

The Musqaukoe are the Fox band of the Sac and Fox Indians.

At seven a.m., we went into Council in Powsheek's tent, which was on the East side of the creek.

Powsheek asked, where we would winter and where we would cross the Missouri. It was reported that somebody had stolen from the Mormons. Powsheek said, if he found anything he would return it; he wanted the Mormon chief to tell him something. I told him to come over the mountains and see us when we got located, and bring his men to hunt for us, and we would make them blankets, guns, powder, cloth, etc.

Powsheek said he would like to go. I told him I would send a messenger in two or three years, or as soon as I could, to bring them to us; he said, white men watch where he goes and don't want him to go far, but would go when we sent, and would send his son, Red face. I asked Red face if he would like to go with us, he replied, "when we sent for him." I said, when they came to see us, I would tell them a great many things. Cap. Wolf (an Indian brave) said he liked what the Mormons said.

Powsheek spoke of Joseph Smith, the prophet, who had been murdered and with whom he had been acquainted; said, the Prophet was a great and good man.

Council closed about half-past seven.

As the Presidency passed out of the tent Baquejappa, a Pottawatomie chief, called us aside, and presented a paper, counselling the Indians not to sell their lands, given them by John Dunham, and two sheets of hieroglyphics, from the book of Abraham.

We started at ten minutes after eight, rode till twenty two minutes after ten, when we stopped at the west branch of the Nodaway, with Ezra Chase; resumed our journey at half past eleven and arrived at Pottawatomie Indian village forty five minutes after one p.m.

A Pottawatomie Captain presented two sheets of the book of Abraham, the world, etc; also a letter from their "Father," Joseph, dated 1843, and map of their land by Phelps; we bated at twenty seven minutes after three, and arrived at Nishnebotana at eight, and put up with brother Savage.

I slept in my carriage, many mosquitoes, little rest. Thirty three miles from general encampment. Wind north west.

Monday, July 13—Camp of Israel, near Mosquito Creek.

Cloudy morning, at eight a.m., rain commenced, heavy shower till ten, then pleasant.

The brethren began to assemble according to appointment; Col. Thomas L. Kane and Captain James Allen were present about eleven.

Major Hunt called out the first company of volunteers.

I met with Col. Kane in Elder Woodruff's carriage, and conversed about the state of the nations. I told Col. Kane the time would come when the Saints would support the government of the U.S. or it would crumble to atoms.

Wednesday, July 15—Cloudy. It rained some.

At nine a.m., Council assembled in Elder Taylor's tent, and conversed on various subjects.

I proposed to cross the river and visit my family, accompanied by Elders

Kimball and Richards; the others of the Twelve to get the soldiers together and instruct them how to behave, etc., on their expedition; they should wear their temple garments, and prove the best soldiers in the U.S. service.

Lots were cast between Elders O. Hyde, P. P. Pratt, and J. Taylor, which two should go to England; the lot fell on Elders Hyde and Taylor to go.

I suggested that the soldiers might tarry and go to work, where they would be disbanded; and said, the next temple would be built in the Rocky mountains, and I should like the Twelve and the old brethren to live in the mountains, where the Temple will be erected, and where the brethren will have to repair to get their endowments.

I said I could prophesy that the time would come when some one of the Twelve or a High Priest would come up and say, can we not build a Temple at Van Couvers Island, or in California. It is not wisdom to unite all our forces to build one house in the mountains.

Captains Hunt and Hunter called on the Council and received instruction to ascertain how much wages each soldier would be paid at Fort Leavenworth.

Thursday, July 16—At nine a.m., Elders H. C. Kimball, O. Hyde, W. Richards, and I met the brethren near the cold Spring.

Elder Kimball gave the brethren the privilege of going into the army, over the mountains, to Grand Island, or back over the river to winter.

A number voted to go over the mountains, some to go to the Island. Volunteers were called for to repair the ferry road.

About noon, Elders Kimball, Hyde, Richards and I walked out on the prairie and consulted about the English mission, and the Church affairs in England.

Half-past one, p.m., I started for the river in Elder Kimball's carriage, crossed the river at half-past two, and proceeded to the bluff. About half a mile east, met most of the volunteers ready to be delivered into Captn. Allen's care; arrived at Bro. O. Pratt's tent, on the flats near the bank of the Missouri river.

Two Indians came with a letter from Major R. B. Mitchell, Indian sub-agent, to have the Mormons find six stray horses. Council replied to Mitchell, assuring him that they had no knowledge of them, but they would advertise the horses in their public meetings.

Voted unanimously that Ezra Taft Benson be ordained an Apostle.

The Twelve knelt before the Lord and prayed, I was mouth, then arose and laid hands on Ezra T. Benson, and ordained him an apostle in the Church of Jesus Christ of Latter-day Saints, with all the keys and power and blessings pertaining to the apostleship, and to take the crown of him who has fallen from the Quorum of the Twelve (John E. Page).

Elder E. Woodruff recorded that "this was an interesting day in the Camp of Israel. Four companies of the volunteers were brought together in a hollow square by their Captains, and interestingly addressed by several of the Quorum of the Twelve. At the close of the meeting they marched in double file from Redemption Hill across the Missouri river bottom to the ferry, seven miles."

Friday, July 17—Pleasant morning. Camp of Israel, Council Bluffs.

I instructed Bishop Whitney to gather up all the Church cattle and let Father Lott take them up the river to winter.

Forty or fifty volunteers were called for to fill the fifth company of the battalion. I remarked, that hundreds will eternally regret that they did not go, when they had a chance, and retired.

Half-past eleven, meeting re-assembled, Elder Kimball called for volunteers to work on the road over the river, and a contribution for brother Yolkum, who was shot in Missouri by the mob.

I went to meeting and proposed that brethren be selected to take care of the families who were left by the soldiers.

I asked the volunteers to leave their wages for the benefit of their families and directed the Bishops to keep a correct account of all moneys and other property received by them, and how disposed of, at the risk of being brought before the Council and reproved.

A concert was appointed at one p.m. tomorrow, for Captain Allen and the troops.

Saturday, July 18—I instructed the captains to be fathers to their companies, and manage their affairs by the power and influence of their priesthood, then they would have power to preserve their lives and the lives of their companies and escape difficulties. I told them I would not be afraid to pledge my right hand that every man will return alive, if they will perform their duties faithfully without murmuring and go in the name of the Lord, be humble and pray every morning and evening in their tents. A private soldier is as honorable as an officer, if he behaves as well. No one is distinguished as being better flesh and blood than another. Honor the calling of every man in his place. All the officers, but three, have been in the Temple. Let no man be without his under garment and always wear a coat or vest; keep neat and clean, teach chastity, gentility and civility; swearing must not be admitted, insult no man; have no contentious conversation with the Missourians, Mexicans, or any class of people; do not preach, only where people desire to hear, and then by wise men, impose not your principles on any people; take your bibles and books of Mormon; burn up (playing) cards if you have any.

Let the officers regulate all the dances, if you come home and can say the Captains have managed all the dancing, etc., it will all be right; to dance with the world cannot be admitted; all things are lawful, but not expedient; never trespass on the rights of others; when the Father has proved that a man will be his friend under all circumstances, he will give to that man abundantly, and withhold no good thing from him. Should the battalion engage with the enemy and be successful, treat prisoners with the greatest civility, and never take life, if it can be avoided.

I spoke of President Polk's feelings towards us, as a people,—assured the brethren that they would have no fighting to do; told them, we should go into the Great Basin, which is the place to build Temples; and where our strongholds should be against mobs. The Constitution of the United States is good. The battalion will probably be disbanded about eight hundred miles from the place where we shall locate.

Bishop N. K. Whitney, Daniel Spencer and Jonathan H. Hale were proposed as agents to go to Fort Leavenworth and receive the pay of the soldiers for their families.

After much conversation and explanation, we adjourned, and returned to Camp about sunset; bro. Kimball and I retired to Ezra Chase's and bro. Richards and Little to bro. Boss' tent.

Sunday, July 19—At nine a.m., Elders Kimball, Richards and I borrowed horses and went across the river to our families.

Half-past one p.m., I attended public meeting, Elders Kimball and Hyde present.

I spoke at some length in relation to starting a company over the mountains, getting hands to repair the river road, tend the ferry, and have herdsmen to keep the cattle out of the Indian's corn.

About sunset, brothers Kimball, Richards and I started in my carriage, and arrived at Elders Taylor and Woodruff's tents on the bluff, near Musketoe Creek, about eleven p.m., where exertions had been made to raise twenty or thirty more volunteers to complete the five hundred for Col. Allen.

Monday, July 20—Missouri river, East side.

At eight a.m., Elders Kimball, Lyman and I started across the Musketoe on to the bluffs to raise volunteers, and returned at half-past nine.

Elder Woodruff put up his new patent iron wheat mill to experiment on grinding wheat and corn.

The weather was excessively hot, little air stirring.

The Band gave a concert, on the bluff near headquarters, and spent the afternoon dancing.

Friday, July 24—Missouri river, west bank.

Four p.m., Council dressed and prayed; laid hands on Elders O. Hyde, P. P. Pratt, and J. Taylor and set them apart for their mission to England, and E. T. Benson for his mission to the States; O. Hyde prayed in the Quorum. We conversed about the privileges of the Elders travelling, and on the laws of marriage.

I gave the brethren some instruction.

Tuesday, July 28—Omaha nation.

At nine a.m., the chief and some of the warriors of the Ottoes came to the Spring to see the Mormon chief and get a beef. I shook hands with them and directed a beef to be given them: tears started in the chief's eyes.

The Council adjusted a difficulty between Wm. H. Martindale and his wife.

Two p.m., a thunder shower commenced from the West and continued one hour; it rained till midnight. The water ran six inches deep through the tents, no wagon was exempt from water, and goods and provisions were more or less damaged; no one in camp remembered such a succession of heavy thunder and lightning, and rain in so short a space. An ox was killed by lightning.

Thursday, July 30—After supper a tremendous storm of wind, thunder and rain commenced. Elder Taylor lowered two of his tents, and the third, prepared to lodge Elders Richards and Little, blew down and covered them while the water fell in torrents. They soon repaired to brother Wilcox' tent, which had blown down and left his wife Wealthy Merrill, exposed to the storm, who, although delivered of a daughter the Sunday previous, fled to her father's (Phinehas Richards) tent, where Elders Richards and Little staid and watched with the family the remainder of the night.

I occasionally name a few of the incidents consequent upon the storms, as specimens of the many.

Saturday, August 1—After dinner, Elder Kimball and I rode with our ladies in carriages to the Omaha village, on the west bank of the Missouri, and returned about half-past five p.m., bringing some green corn, purchased at one cent per ear.

Afternoon, cloudy, strong south wind.

The Ottoes brought roasting ears into camp to sell; supposing them to have been stolen from the Omaha's corn fields, I counseled the saints not to purchase.

Monday, August 3—Omaha nation. Weather warm and pleasant.

Forenoon, I was quite unwell. One of my oxen fell in the creek and broke his neck. It was immediately bled, dressed and distributed to the Camp.

Tuesday, August 4—Four p.m., with most of my encampment I started up the river to find winter quarters. Travelled nine miles and encamped on a prairie ridge near the timber.

Wednesday, August 5—I rode out with the brethren of the Twelve and others to view the timber and find an encampment; the camp travelled a few miles.

Friday, August 7—At half-past eight a.m., I met with Elders H. C. Kimball, W. Richards, W. Woodruff and others to consult on a location.

Luman H. Calkins reported that he had followed the Indian trail up the river about twelve miles; found some patches of scrubby timber, but none suitable for building.

I asked the brethren if we should stop here, or look farther, and whether we should settle together or every man for himself.

C. P. Lott, Reynolds Cahoon and others spoke in favor of following the counsel of the Twelve.

I proposed that the brethren on this side of the river settle together, and organize in city form; and said, I could draw my logs for houses five miles, and build my bed room in a hay stack, if necessary. We will build a house for council and praying, and another for a schoolhouse; if the brethren wish to hear preaching they must stay at headquarters. We should be organized as one family, in order, and be in a compact body, build in a systematic order and keep clean, and build pounds for our cattle. If a few settle alone they will be liable to be robbed by war parties of Indians. If the brethren conclude to stop here, we will choose a committee to settle families and manage town affairs. I am willing to stop here.

President Heber C. Kimball concurred in my observations, and said, he would go five miles and get his house logs, if there was not sufficient timber in the little groves nearer. He motioned that we appoint Twelve men to superintend the settling of the camp, and all matters relating to the town corporation.

Voted that the brethren on the West side of the Missouri settle together.

Voted that the Council locate the camp on the top of some bluff near a spring, cut our hay and let not a stick be cut for timber till hay is gathered.

I advised the brethren to be careful and not infringe on each other when cutting the grass; and that as the Omahas like to be consulted about settling on their lands, we would see the chiefs when they come home; told the brethren not to disturb an Indian grave, because the Indians frequently deposited their dead in the branches of trees, wrapt in buffalo robes and blankets leaving with them arrows, pipes and other trinkets, which they considered sacred and we should not remove them and our children should be taught to let them alone.

I informed the Col. (Kane) we intended settling in the Great Basin or Bear river valley, and those who went round by water would settle at San Francisco. We would be glad to raise the American flag; we love the constitution of our country, but are opposed to mobocracy; and will not live under such oppression as we have done. We are willing to have the banner of the U. S. constitution float over us. If the government of the U. S. are disposed to do us good; we can do them as much good as they can us.

Col. Kane said, Gov. Boggs had been working against us in Washington; and asked whether we should like a territorial government. I replied we should, and that many of our English emigrants would probably settle at Vancouver's Island.

The Col. said that Lord Aberdeen informed Mr. McLane that the British government designed to colonize Vancouver's Island. I said, we would be willing to carry the mail across the continent and build block houses wherever the United States might wish.

I preached the Gospel in plaines to the Colonel and expressed my warm feelings for him, and that portion of mankind who did not believe in persecuting their fellows because of their religion. He asked whether we believed in conversing with the Lord bodily. I replied, no, but in vision, by the spirit; we live for a glorious resurrection, Joseph was engaged in this work ten years before he confessed he was a prophet.

Prest. Cutler, by request, reported that himself and others, had searched diligently for the most suitable place for winter quarters and decided that the neighboring grove, northeast, is altogether the most suitable; the council concurred.

I said, that this Council which we have organized would act as a city and a high council and decide matters of difference between the members of the church. Some had already transgressed and should be brought to justice—that I was not so much afraid of going into the wilderness alone, as to let offenders go unpunished.

Elder Kimball and I laid hands on Col. John Scott, who was sick.

Sunday, August 9—Pleasant day.

Half-past ten a.m., the saints at the place prepared last evening for meeting, where sufficient seats had been collected to accommodate three hundred.

Meeting opened by singing and prayer.

Elders W. Woodruff, L. D. Young and Lorin Farr preached.

I remarked, that I had not expected to see the Rocky mountains this year; but whenever the Lord commanded me to go, I intended to start, if I left all and went alone, but I thought the Lord would let me take the people with me, and when I found the place for the Temple I would work hard until it was built.

Monday, August 10—The Council instructed the Marshal to request the brethren when cutting poles to cut them near the ground, that turnips may be sown.

I said, I was aware of the feelings of the people in regard to working in associations, still I deemed it best to work together because of the scarcity of tools, which would necessarily leave many idle; and when we can be united in all things so that each will seek the interest and welfare of his brother, then the Lord will take up his abode with us.

Tuesday, August 11—Very pleasant morning, strong east wind.

At eight a.m., I began to move my family on to the new camping ground, where the camp is expected to stay till after haying.

Elder P. P. Pratt arrived from Fort Leavenworth, with a special message from the battalion to N. K. Whitney, for council, signed by O. Hyde, and a package of $5,860, being a portion of the allowance for clothing of the battalion, which was paid to them at the rate of Three dollars and fifty cents per month. The money was found to be correct.

Council voted that the brethren be advised to sow turnips as soon as they have built their fences.

I referred to a man who had passed Fifteen dollars bogus gold, below the settlement, and gone on west in Miller's company, for whom I had sent to return immediately, and pay the man whom he defrauded and satisfy him for his trouble, repent, and make satisfaction to the Church; or, he should pay four fold, if it took the last farthing he possessed, and be cast out from among us and that is the law to Israel, "and you may write it."

Wednesday, August 12—South wind till near noon, when it changed to the north.

Seven a.m., Dr. Richards met the brethren between the two camps and called off between two and three hundred letters; then returned to his wagon and made out the mail for council point, one hundred and eleven letters, and thirteen for the eastern mail and delivered the same to William Miller, who had come from the opposite side of the river and brought a letter from Daniel Spencer, saying his wife and child, and his brother Hiram Spencer were dead, and asking Council how to distribute the property.

Bro. Richards and I wrote him a word of consolation and invited him to move over the river, to take care of the widow and orphans, and when he should arrive, we would give him further instructions; also, informed him of his appointment to receive and disburse funds for the Mormon battalion; and sent by Wm. Miller.

I proposed that each company prepare a yard for cattle, build a necessary, keep their yard clean, draw wood, cut it short and burn it in chimneys made of turf, and have the road outside of the encampment; keep hay in the cattle yard and keep up a sightwatch.

Brothers Richards, Lee and I walked south on the green and saw the young people dance about half an hour, then returned home.

Thursday, August 13—I desired the Council to take into consideration the propriety of sending Bishop Whitney to St. Louis, for the purpose of laying in supplies for the Camp, as there were many women in Camp whose husbands in the army, had sent them money, and we have them to take care of, and all we can help them to save, we save to ourselves for we would have to pay it out of our own pockets. If they lay out their money here they will pay three prices for what they get. Flour is worth three dollars a hundred, and we can get wheat for twenty-five cents per bushel; the grinding of which would justify us in getting a small set of mill stones and irons to move by two, three or four horse power, and with out labor added to our means, make a great saving of money, and I want this council and the High Council over the river to take into consideration the propriety of this thing, and also of getting two sets of burr stones and mill fixtures to carry with us over the mountains.

Saturday, August 15—About eight o'clock, a general turn out on horses, mules and on foot to gather all the stray cattle: returned to the yards with them about noon: I joined in the drive on horseback.

Afternoon, the strays were gathered from the prairie and the cattle assorted. Some hay was cut and put in the yards.

I nominated A. P. Rockwood, Jed. M. Grant, and Charles R. Bird as a committee to visit the Omahas who had returned from their hunt.

I remarked that it was my impression that the Committee should not enter into any specific agreement, but endeavor to create a friendly feeling, and have a meeting at a future time; and that we should not invite the Indians to our camp, we could go and see them. We want the privilege of staying on their land this winter, cutting timber, building houses, perhaps leaving some families and crops—suggest that we might do them good, repairing their guns, and learning them how, and teaching their children, and if they want pay for occupancy of their lands we will pay them; they should not touch our property, and we will not their's. I would not be disappointed if we made a strong foot-hold at the bluffs, and more or less tarry for some time to come; and that I would rather go to the Mountains, than anywhere else to live on account of health.

Elder Woodruff reported a man had thrown down his fence, and let out his cattle, just for the sake of getting a nearer path. I suggested that all such persons be notified to appear before the Council on Monday next.

Reynolds Cahoon, Committee on sowing turnips, called for twenty-five men and boys and eight yokes of oxen to commence to plow up land for a turnip field.

Sunday, August 16—Meeting opened and addressed by Elder O. Pratt, who showed that the Saints were at present, privileged to live under their own laws—that the reason why the Twelve had changed their counsel so often was, because the people did not abide the best counsel, which was given by the spirit of God. The best counsel was for the Church to fit out a company to go with the Twelve over the mountains, but as they were dilatory and failed to do this, the Twelve would not forsake them, but give the next best advice so that no one has a right to find fault with the council for changing their advice from time to time. It is unbelief that causes all our whining. The Council are determined to carry out those principles which are made manifest to them by the whisperings of the holy spirit, if it takes the last shirt from their backs. There has been some fault-finding by those who have recently arrived in camp, because they want to cut their own hay and put in their own turnip patch, but we must be one, and feel a general interest for the whole, and when any one is told by the foreman to pick up a basket of chips and tumbled them out again, then pick them up again and find no fault, but should the foreman do wrong let the council judge and not the people.

I said, I had a short discourse to preach to the sisters whose husbands, brothers, etc. have gone into the army. I wished every family left here to feel their dependence on their brethren who have looked to them and took care of their cattle, etc. Elders Orson Hyde, P. P. Pratt and John Taylor were led to Fort Leavenworth at the very time the soldiers were receiving pay for their clothing, and prevailed upon them to send a part of their money to their families, consigned to N. K. Whitney, J. H. Hale and D. Spencer, and I saw several whining and crying, the very day bro. Parley arrived, and before the money was counted, and some have written to their husbands to send no more money to the Church, for they could not get what they had sent.

The names of all who have written, such news to their husbands, will be written in the history to be read in future days.

The sisters can have their money if they wish and do what they please with it; but such a course will release us from all the obligations we are under by our pledge to look to them. We will send N. K. Whitney to St. Louis to get such things as we want to carry over the mountains, at wholesale prices, and I recommended to the sisters to let their agents retain their money to buy sugar, shoes, coffee, etc. at St. Louis, and wheat in Missouri for twenty-five cents per bushel, and save all we can.

I exhibited two Missouri bank bills and wished to know if any wanted their money, after they understand the designs of the council, if so, they shall have it and I will feel released from all the obligations I am under to see that they are taken care of.

I asked if the congregation counseled the sisters to let their money lay in the hands of Bishop Whitney, to be laid out by him to the best advantage for their families; all who did so were requested to manifest it by uplifted hands, the congregation generally raised their hands, an opposite vote was called for, but none voted.

I gave notice that those who wanted to send to St. Louis better make out their bills and send them in soon; there is a feeling of distrust among the Saints about honest deal, and if any man says we deal dishonestly, he lies, and he knows he lies before God. For two years, while the Twelve have been building they have paid, when they have borrowed, as they have agreed to. A man apostatized and returned to Nauvoo and said Elder Kimball had stolen all his beans; Elder Kimball put two bushels of beans in his wagon for him to haul and afterwards went and distributed them to the poor, and the man apostatized.

I informed the brethren that the council had estimated the expense of two sets of four feet burr stones with the fixtures, which would cost about eight hundred dollars, weight about five tons, and the iron might be carried on the wagons that carry the stones; I wished the brethren to form a company to buy all the necessary materials and carry them on and build a good mill in the mountains; I did not want them to put a dollar into the Trustees hands, nor into the hands of any of the Twelve. We will trust in the invisible hand of a kind providence, as we always have done. I called on all who were in favor of buying the stones, irons, etc., for a grist mill on the plan proposed either by a single individual or a company, to signify it by saying, aye; all said aye. I prophesied that if the brethren would follow counsel five years would not roll away before there would not be a poor man in the Church of Jesus Christ of Latter-day Saints.

7:45, Orin P. Rockwell arrived in Camp with a mail of thirty-nine letters and many papers. About eight, in company with several of the Council and O. P. Rockwell, I called to see Wm. Clayton, who had been sick about eleven days, found him in great distress, laid hands upon and prayed for him, and he felt better. The brethren sat down and read a letter from John M. Bernhisel informing us that Emma Smith had sold the lot on which the Nauvoo house stands. We conversed until near ten, then returned home.

Monday, August 17—Cutler's Park, Omaha nation. Pleasant morning.

Nine a.m., I called at the post office with many of the brethren and read newspapers until eleven, when Elders W. Woodruff, Geo. A. Smith, W. Richards and I called on Wm. Clayton and found him better. Visited Bishop Whitney, and the Bowery, and counselled bro. Marble not to go with his wife to Mount Pisgah; I would counsel no man to go back.

Dr. S. S. Sprague reported one hundred cases of sickness in camp, mostly fever.

Wednesday, August 19—Camp of Israel. Clear morning.

From nine to eleven a.m., Elder Heber C. Kimball and I met in Cap. Rockwood's tent, and heard Orin P. Rockwell give an account of his arrest, imprisonment and liberation.

Dr. Richards wrote a letter to Captain Jefferson Hunt, and the officers and soldiers of the battalion, counseling them to live by faith, using such herbs and mild food, as were at their command, and *let Surgeons medicine alone*; informing them of the arrangements made to send to St. Louis for goods; and counseling them to be prudent and economical, that they might be made a blessing to their families and the poor, as they were placed in circumstances which enabled them to control more means than all the rest of the saints in the wilderness; also, sent them the general news.

Thursday, August 20—I remarked that if a man was willing that his property should be disposed of in any way as the Lord directed, the Lord was willing he should be made a bishop.

In relation to the families of the Battalion we have taken them into our charge as we take charge of our own families, not to be their servants.

I proposed that we hire some of the Omaha Indians to watch our cattle this winter; also, that some of our boys should be sent to Pottawatomie town to live this winter to learn the Indian language; and if the Omahas will guard our cattle, we will make them a cornfield, and teach them to work, to recompense them for our staying on their lands.

The subject of employing the Omaha Indians to herd our cattle was referred to the High Council of this place.

I proposed that the Committee agitate the subject with the chiefs and half breeds and see if a chief can be hired to select a company to watch our cattle.

Friday, August 21—Camp of Israel, Cutler's Park.

Between twelve and two a.m., Dr. Richards made up a package of forty-six letters for the Mormon battalion, and was called up about eight a.m., to close the Fort Leavenworth mail of sixty letters.

About eleven, Dr. Richards called on Col. Kane, found him better, conversed with him about hiring the Indians to herd cattle, and writing to President Polk. He concurred and desired to present the subject to the President.

The Council wrote to the High and Municipal Council requesting them to take such measures as wisdom directs to prevent the too frequent repetition of evening parties and dances, injurious to health and the quietness of the sick.

Monday, August 24—Near Musketoe Creek.

Forenoon, Elders Heber C. Kimball, Orson Pratt, Wilford Woodruff, Geo. A. Smith and I visited at Henry W. Miller's, who had purchased the improvements of an Indian chief (subsequently called Kanesville). Dr. Richards and Amasa Lyman arrived at noon, when we dined upon green corn, cucumbers, suckatash, etc. After dinner all ate heartily of water and mushmelons.

Tuesday, August 25—Bro. C. Kennedy said the Omahas had returned from their hunt,—that bros. A. P. Rockwood, J. M. Grant and Charles Bird had been to see them; they were friendly and wanted a council, and Thursday had been proposed as the time.

Wednesday, August 26—The High Council of Cutler's park met. The manner of treating the Indians was under consideration: Elders Rockwood and Grant were appointed a Committee to draft resolutions concerning the burying of the dead.

Thursday, August 27—One p.m., I met in Council, at bro. Samuel Russell's tent, with Elders Heber C. Kimball, Orson Pratt, Wilford Woodruff, Willard Richards and the High Council.

Voted that all dogs be tied outside of the yard from sunset to sunrise.

The propriety of disposing of our old oxen was discussed by the council. Bro. L. D. Young said, it had been proposed that all old oxen be gathered, fattened and butchered, as fast as they are wanted, and be distributed, giving the hide and tallow to the owner and meat at intervals as he might wish, saving all the young cattle. I proposed that the council recommend the brethren in camp to fatten their old cattle, and have men appointed to buy, butcher and sell them, and find out by Bishop Whitney what can be had for hides delivered at this point, or the sub-Indian Agency below, next spring.

Voted that Lorenzo D. Young, Alpheus Cutler and Cornelius P. Lott, be said beef Committee.

Half-past five p.m., Council was informed that the Omaha chiefs had arrived, and voted to adjourn till tomorrow morning at 8:30 at headquarters.

Friday, August 28—Cutler's Park.

Half-past nine a.m., I met with the High Council of the Camp, in a double tent, with the principal Omaha chiefs and braves and about eighty of the Omahas, and after shaking hands, smoked the pipe of peace. Big Elk the principal chief and Logan Fontenelle, the interpreter, was present.

Several of the Otoes staid near camp last night.

I told the Omahas we were on our journey to California and the United States had called on us for soldiers, and left us without teamsters, and with their permission we would like to winter here. I said,

> "We can do you good. We will repair your guns, make a farm for you, and aid you in any other way that our talents and circumstances will permit us. We would also like to get some of your honorable man to watch our cattle. We will assist you for any favors you may see fit to confer upon us. Can you furnish some one who will watch our cattle and keep them safe? Have you any objections to our getting timber, building houses, and staying here until Spring or longer? The government is willing if you are. Would you like to have some of our mechanics stay with you and make and repair guns? Do you feel disposed to be on amicable terms with us? Are you willing we should sow wheat here this fall and plant corn next year? I will be glad to hear you express yourselves freely in answer to all of these questions.
>
> We are your friends and friends to all mankind. We wish to do you good, and will give you food if you need it. We are acting in accordance with the instructions of the government, and we wish you to give us a writing statement what you are willing to do, and if you wish we will prepare to have schools kept among you. If we make a field for you, you will raise more grain, with less trouble than at present.
>
> The Otoes have stolen corn from you and traded it to our people; but when we learned this we ceased trading with them.
>
> We are willing to pay for all the corn our cattle eat and keep all things right."

The Clerk read Captain Allen's permit to the Mormons to stay at the bluffs. Big Elk said,

> "I am an old man and will have to call you all sons. I am willing you should stop in my country, but I am afraid of my great father at Washington.

I would like to know what the Otoes say, if they claim this land, you can stay where you please, if they do not. I am willing you should stay. One half of the Otoes are willing the Omahas should have these lands. The Puncahs belonged to the Omahas. I hope you will not kill our game. I will notify my young men not to trouble your cattle. If you cut down all our trees I will be the only tree left.

We have been oppressed by other tribes, because we were weak. We have been like the hungry dog which runs through camp in search of something to eat and meets with enemies on every side. We have been oppressed for ten years, at many times we could have defended ourselves, but our great Father told us not to fight with any tribe unless they came to our villages to destroy us.

We heard you were a good people; we are glad to have you come and keep a store where we can buy things cheap. You can stay with us while we hold these lands, but we expect to sell as our Grandfather will buy: we will likely remove northward.

While you are among us as brethren, we will be brethren to you. I like, my son, what you have said very well; it could be said no better by anybody."

Monday, August 31—Cutler's Park.
Pleasant morning.
About eight a.m., I rode on horseback to Elder J. M. Grant's tent to see Col. Kane, and sent for Dr. Richards who had gone over to Elder Kimball's encampment. I laid before Col. Kane our talk with the Omahas relative to our staying on their lands, and concerning the affairs of the government of the U.S., and the actions of great ones at Washington, and said, that if I was compelled by the action of the U.S. I would leave my wife and children to be murdered by them and flee to the mountains and never stop till I had satisfaction; that if they would treat us as they ought, we would fight for them, and do them good, but we never would consent to be governed again by unjust judges or governors, let the consequences be what they might—that we had more influence with the Indians than all other nations on the earth, and if we were compelled we would use it; but if they will permit us, we will use it to their advantage, fight for them and do them good.

Thursday, September 3—Elder Orson Pratt reported that in connection with the brethren appointed, he had visited the Otoes on the north bank of the Platte, and told them we wished to tarry on this land over two years, and that we wanted to take no part in the difficulties between them and the Omahas, and desired to know definitely whether we might stay in peace. They evaded the question three times, but said they would visit another chief and return in three days with an answer, and dance for us.

Elder Pratt said the Omahas were afraid we would burn all their timber, but he informed them, we used stoves and burned but little wood; and that the houses, fences and improvements we made, would remain for the benefit of the owners of the soil. Big Elk could not allow his young men to herd, unless we could let them have as many young men to take care of their families.

Elder Pratt referred them to the book of Mormon, etc. They said, they were going to fight the Sioux, and would return in a few days and dance.

Elder Kimball recommended the brethren to cut hay on the bottom. It was decided to send the oxen not needed, the dry cows and calves northward to be herded among the pea vines.

Saturday, September 5—Cutler's Park.

Elders H. C. Kimball, O. Pratt, W. Woodruff, J. M. Grant and others went in search of a location for a ferry.

They went down the river five miles, saw many elderberries, grapes, hops, two deer and shot a turkey. They took a leather (Cather)? boat with them in which the company numbering seven crossed the river, and met Isaac Morley, Geo. W. Harris, Phinehas Richards and others, a committee from Council point on the same business; they saw about two hundred Brant in the river—picked about two bushels of grapes—built a bridge across a creek and returned.

Reports were read from 11 divisions of the first company concerning their labor; they had made and hauled 657 tons of hay.

Bishop Whitney reported a difficulty between Stephen Markham and Mrs. Moesser which was referred to Alpheus Cutler for settlement.

Voted that Charles Bird, herdsman, call on the owners of the sheep through their foreman for help to herd, and if any one neglects to pay his proportion of the expense that it be paid with his sheep, and that C. Bird and C. P. Lott use their discretion in controlling the bucks.

Sunday, September 6—Cutler's Park.

I recommended that a small settlement be made above Council Bluffs to serve as a guard for our cattle and build cabins where it might suit the Omahas.

Daniel Barnham, Pelatiah Brown and Jackson Clothier received thirty lashes each, administered by the Marshal with a hickory switch, upon the bare back, for illicit intercourse with females.

Tuesday, September 8—Cutler's Park.

As Col. Kane was about to leave this morning, Elder Richards and I called on him. He expressed the warmest satisfaction in relation to his treatment while in the camp of Israel, and his strong determination to do us good: he started about nine a..m.

The herds started for the pea vines this morning.

I met with Elders Heber C. Kimball, Orson Pratt, Willard Richards and the High Council, at 7 p.m.

The Council were informed that persons who had labored for pay on the East side of the river, were trying to place themselves in the third division of first company, to fill the places of some who had left that division.

I said, I was opposed to such persons claiming any share of the hay, without paying for it.

Voted that J. M. Grant visit the Omaha chiefs and invited them to come up and advise with the committee in relation to where we should build.

Voted that the Marshal make enquiry through the foreman of each division and learn how many teams can be obtained to go to Nauvoo and bring the poor who wish to come.

Wednesday, September 9—I received a letter from Jacob Gates, dated at Pawnee Village, 2nd inst., stating that fourteen families in Miller's company, after much persuasion had volunteered to stay at that point, over whom he had been appointed to preside—that they had moved into the houses at the mission and were comfortable—that the Pawnees returned from hunting six or eight days after the brethren left them, and most of the Indians appeared friendly, though some were displeased because considerable of their corn had been destroyed by bro. Miller's company as they passed along; the brethren however had held a council with the Indians, and agreed to lay them in some corn, which they expect to get from the Missionaries; this seemed to satisfy the Indians, and they expressed a willingness that the brethren should stay and promised to use them well. Their thievish propensities, however, were so often manifested, that some of the brethren were almost disheartened, and a few were leaving. Bro. Gates intended to remain until he was driven away or counseled to remove. He asked for counsel whether his company should sow fall grain and whether any of them had better accompany the Pawnees on their fall and winter hunt; the company had commenced haying and preparing for winter.

At seven p.m., I met with Elders H. C. Kimball, W. Richards, A. Lyman and the High Council.

Twelve teams were reported by the Marshal ready to go to Nauvoo for the poor.

I proposed to raise teams by donation to bring the poor out, and then give them the teams, and offered three yoke of cattle as my donation.

I said my feelings were at present to stay here and locate our families for a year or two; meanwhile, fit out companies to go over the mountains with seed grain, mills, etc., to sow, build and prepare for our families that we need not carry provisions for them over the mountains, and wished the committee to have this in view in settling this camp, and select healthy locations. There were teams enough in the Church to do all that is needed in gathering Israel and establishing ourselves in the mountains.

Elder W. Richards read a letter from Joseph Herring requesting counsel about getting his sister from the Cherokees. Voted to send a team for her.

Elder Gate's letter was read; the Council considered the situation of the few families left at Pawnee among the Indians rather precarious and directed that a messenger be sent thither with counsel.

Prest. Cutler stated that individuals had been cutting timber for the nuts.

Voted that the Marshal instruct the foreman of divisions to stop the cutting of timber except for fuel and fencing.

Friday, September 11—Cutler's Park.

About half-past ten a.m., Elders Heber C. Kimball, Orson Pratt, Willard Richards, Wilford Woodruff, Geo. A. Smith, Amasa Lyman and I walked northwards and selected the site for Winter Quarters, and returned to Camp.

Saturday, September 12—Cutler's Park.

The Marshal was instructed to see that sufficient lumber was sawed to make coffins, and that the foreman of each division send two men to help John Tanner to repair the miry roads.

William Kay had his dog killed last evening about sunset. I told the Council it would not do to let dogs kill dogs, it would bring trouble upon the Camp. I promised the brethren they would see the time when they would be thankful to have a good dog in the Indian country, if dogs must be killed let it be by order. Voted that there be no shooting allowed in or about Camp after sunset.

I said, in the name of Israel's God, if every man would do right, and when he has done what he knows is right, then stops till he knows what next, there never would be a jar in the camp. And I defy the man to come forward that ever led so large a people in such difficult and trying circumstances, in so much peace, as I have led this people during this campaign, with the help of God and my brethren.

Some boys have been whipped in camp, and it is right. I did not know of it till after it was done. If we allow young men to come in here and set up their own plans, three years will not roll round before we will have cutting of throats here.

I protested against any man's stealing, who claims to belong to this kingdom, and continued to exhort the brethren to good works until about eight p.m.

I remarked in relation to unruly cattle that if a four rail fence would stop all the cattle in town but one animal, it should be appraised, paid for, and sent to the slaughter house. Dogs should be kept by their owners in their own yard, out of stranger's paths, and turned loose in the night to watch the house, stables, etc. No man has a right to keep a dog to tip over his neighbor's milk pans.

Monday, September 14—Wealthy Lovisa, daughter of Franklin D. and Jane Richards, died.

Aura Anetta, wife of James W. Cummings, was delivered of a son, which was named after his father.

Tuesday, September 15—Cutler's Park.

About nine a.m., I rode out on the bluff accompanied by Dr. Richards and my family, and surveyed a burying ground and returned about eleven. As we returned twelve wagons passed out of camp with from two to five yokes of oxen each, going after the poor.

I met at seven p.m., with Elders Heber C. Kimball, Orson Pratt, Willard Richards, Amasa Lyman and the High Council.

Voted that the burying ground selected, on the hill west of Winter Quarters, be adopted. Several were buried near Cutler's Park.

Bro. Edward Hunter having offered some seed rye, Council voted that it be received and sown, also some fall wheat on the bottoms.

Wednesday, September 16—Cutler's Park.

Samuel Russell was selected to keep a tent of entertainment for strangers. Alanson Eldridge was appointed to superintend the stocking of ploughs.

Thursday, September 17—Cutler's Park.

At seven p.m., the High Council assembled. Bros. H. C. Kimball, W. Richards, O. Pratt and I attended.

John Tanner, herdsman, sent in a Journal of labor for last week which was read and accepted.

Voted that no stock be taken from the herdsmen without an order.

Voted that the Sexton have $1.50 for digging a grave and burying a corpse.

Friday, September 18—I met with the Twelve and the High Council. We discussed the propriety of laying our city nearer the Missouri river; some preferred the table lands and some the bottoms.

I desired the camp to locate together for protection and safety from Indians and mobs.

Monday, September 21—Cutler's Park.

Pleasant weather, still and warm.

Several of the Twelve continued surveying at the new location.

Bro. W. Richards and I left a notification at the three companies constituting the Camp, for all the men to turn out, and see that their guns were in order, and retire to rest under arms. I sent two spies northward and two southward in consequence of a rumor reaching camp that an armed body of men were on their way to Camp.

Tuesday, September 22—Cutler's Park.

Pleasant morning, south wind.

About nine, the brethren of the camp assembled between the different companies of the encampment. I informed them we had came together to organize and take care of ourselves in this savage country and prepare for going over the mountains. I asked if we should take the old officers in the Nauvoo Legion or choose new ones. Voted unanimously to take the old officers. The names of officers were called out and they were requested to form companies of twenty-five each and make out their rolls.

The officers were instructed to fill up their companies with officers, tell their men when and where to meet again and to have their arms in readiness. The Colonel formed a hollow square and I instructed the brethren as to removing to the flats, and expressed the utmost satisfaction with the appearance of the Regiment.

It was voted unanimously that I should be commander in-chief of the Legion and that Col. Rockwood should be my aid de camp. Four yokes of oxen were called for to take a cannon to Ponca; Willard Snow, Zerah Pulsipher, Nahum Bigelow and Jacob Woolsey volunteered to furnish the oxen.

I wrote a military order directing that all discharging of fire arms about camp by night or day unless by special permission should cease, and that caps be removed from percussion locks, and tow cloth or some other suitable substance be substituted for powder in the pans of flint locks for the safety of the people.

The Council concluded to build a water mill, and appointed me to superintend it, they consenting to assist me by every possible means.

Voted that the excavations for back houses be dug eight feet deep and on the back end of each lot.

Wednesday, September 23—The Camp began to move on to the new location for Winter Quarters, the city was laid out in blocks of twenty rods by forty, each lot four rods by ten. I assisted the brethren to build a yard large enough to hold all the cows of the division.

Sunday, September 27—Winter Quarters.

Pleasant weather, wind south.

At two p.m., the saints assembled on a rise of land on the west side of Main Street.

Elder Orson Pratt opened the meeting by prayer, and made a few good remarks.

Bro. Daniel H. Wells by request, gave an account of the battle of Nauvoo, and was followed by bro. Wm. L. Cutler.

I said, I was pleased to see the brethren who have come with the news. Bro. Cutler has been in camp before. Bro. Wells has been in our society for several years and I have had considerable acquaintance with him and am more than ever satisfied with his course. We have prayed for our brethren continually. I have felt sensible there was a good deal of suffering among the saints in Nauvoo, and there has been amongst us, but the Lord God who has fed us all the day long, has his care still over us and when the saints are chastened enough it will cease. I have never believed the Lord would suffer a general massacre of this people by a mob. If ten thousand men were to come against us, and no other way was open for our deliverance, the earth would swallow them up.

Dr. Richards urged the necessity of and good that might result from gathering and using hops.

Thursday, October 1—Winter Quarters, Omaha nation.

Weather pleasant.

Dr. Richards and I started on horseback up Turkey Creek, and viewed the mill site. We visited my brothers John, Phineas, and Joseph, and dined at Bro. Phineas'.

The Dr. and I visited and laid hands on the sick. We prayed for my bro. John.

Friday, October 2—Winter Quarters.

Weather pleasant, wind south and brisk.

At ten, I heard the relation of a family difficulty by the parties.

At noon, accompanied by my wife, Dr. Richards and Col. Rockwood, I rode out to see the brickyard; returned at one, having seen an excellent bed of clay and pound stone in the river to stone wells.

A load of onions were offered in camp at $1.50 per bushel.

Saturday, October 3—Winter Quarters.

Weather variable, and wind northwest.

John Hill and Asahel Lathrop arrived; having left their families on the rush bottoms about seventy miles above on the Missouri river, with seven other families and three single men. They had left Bishop Geo. Miller at Ponca and moved down to their present location to get better feed for their cattle. For the last six days they had lived on two squirrels, one goose and a turtle. They said there were plenty of rushes where their families were.

The stand, used to preach from at Cutler's Park, was brought to Winter Quarters.

Sunday, October 4—Winter Quarters.

Frost last night.

Meeting at the Stand.

Elder Orson Pratt preached on the first principles of the Gospel.

During intermission, Elders Pratt, Lyman and Woodruff divided the city into thirteen wards and appointed a bishop over each; they ordained six Bishops.

Afternoon, the saints assembled again.

I spoke of wintering our cattle on the rush bottoms; and of sending teams to meet bro. Whitney, and declaimed against paying triple prices to pedlers for goods.

Volunteers were called for to help build a bridge. Many lost and strayed animals and articles were advertised.

Monday, October 5—Winter Quarters.

Warm day, south wind.

I visited the sick. Finished stoning my well, which was thirty-two feet deep.

Tuesday, October 6—About sunset, A. W. Babbitt and William Picket arrived at Winter Quarters.

The Mill dam commenced.

I met with Elders Heber C. Kimball and Geo. A. Smith at the post office, when Babbitt delivered forty-four letters which were taken out of the post office and paid for by C. Kennedy, and twenty-two letters from the Nauvoo post office to be paid for or returned, likewise one file of the Hancock Eagle and about one hundred late papers from various parts of the union.

We chatted on a great variety of subjects. Babbitt said, the mob had got possession of Nauvoo; they had got most of the brethren's guns; had defaced the Temple; only one store open; many of the poor brethren had gone to Burlington, St. Louis, etc.

He reported that the Trustees had cancelled obligations to the amount of $60,000, and that about $25,000, was yet due; and that they could sell the Church property for $125,000. He said, he wanted nothing for his services.

Elder N. K. Whitney reported, by letter, his arrival near Montrose, where he met with many of the brethren and sisters who had been driven from Nauvoo, who were in very destitute circumstances. He had procured some flour at Bonaparte for their present relief, and administered to them such counsel as was beneficial and necessary. He was unable to do any business in Nauvoo, owing to the unsettled state of affairs there.

Bishop Whitney also wrote to Elder Kimball that he considered fifty wagons would be ample to remove those driven from Nauvoo, who were helpless and destitute.

Wednesday, October 7—Winter Quarters.

Elders Heber C. Kimball, Orson Pratt, Willard Richards, Amasa Lyman and I started for the old chimneys at the herdground; A. W. Babbitt and William Picket accompanied us.

We found a majority of the High Council in session, in relation to herd affairs.

Voted that the herdsmen's labors be received as satisfactory.

I directed that every man leave the herd ground that does not herd regularly under Father Tanner.

Voted that as soon as the tents can be had every herdsman have cloth for a frock and pantaloons.

I counseled the brethren to gather out the spare cattle and take them to the rushes.

Visited the mill site returning home.

Bro. Asahel Dewey was buried this evening.

I spent the evening with several of the Twelve at the post office. Counseled bro. Babbitt to sell the Church property at Nauvoo without delay, if he could at wholesale, and could get $125,000; and do as he pleased with the property of the Church at Kirtland.

Friday, October 9—Winter Quarters.

Cloudy and cool weather.

Elders Kimball, Woodruff, Pratt, Lyman, Richards, Geo. A. Smith and I at the post office from nine till twelve.

A. W. Babbitt started, taking a mail of fourteen letters for Nauvoo and twenty-five for intermediate points.

The poor camp on the bank of the Mississippi opposite Nauvoo, was organized. Flocks of Quails lit about their encampment and flew around their tents and wagons. Many caught them with their hands.

The Camp journalist recorded, "That the brethren and sisters praised God that what was showered down upon the children of Israel was manifested to them in their persecution."

Saturday, October 10—Winter Quarters.

Cloudy, south wind.

Elders Kimball, Richards and I laid hands on Eliza Ann Pierson: she was very sick.

Elder Kimball and I rode south to see the beef cattle. Most of the Camp left for the herd early. The cattle were gathered, but many were missing, the company remained all night at the herd ground.

Sunday, October 11—Winter Quarters.

Wind south. Rain commenced about ten and continued till one p.m. During which time the herd arrived in the town. The cattle were so uneasy they could not be kept on the prairie.

After the rain the brethren selected their cattle.

Tuesday, October 13—Winter Quarters.

Elder W. Woodruff and I, with the relatives attended the funeral of Eliza Ann Pierson, Dr. Richards' niece.

A son, named Isaac Cutler, was born to Heber C. and Emily C. Kimball.

Wednesday, October 14—Winter Quarters.

Cloudy, wind south, it rained some.

Elder Heber C. Kimball completed the body of his log house; I laid the foundation of mine.

Thursday, October 15—Winter Quarters.

It was reported that the Indians were killing two or three oxen per day. Many cattle have strayed.

About four p.m., Elder W. Woodruff was brought home badly hurt by the falling of a tree which he was chopping. His breast bone and three ribs on his left side were broken, he was very severely bruised.

Elders Kimball and Richards and I called and administered to him; we promised him in the name of the Lord that he should live.

Friday, October 16—Winter Quarters.

Cold, cloudy day.

Sister Joan Campbell was delivered of a dead male child; soon after delivery she had a chill and in about an hour was a corpse. When the mob attacked Nauvoo she was in very good health, but consequent upon the expulsion and living on the slough opposite Nauvoo, exposed to the rain and storms, at a time when she was least able to bear it, she was seized with the chills and fever, with which she was afflicted until her untimely delivery and death. The Camp journalist recorded, "This is the effect of persecution by the Illinois Mob."

Saturday, October 17—Winter Quarters.

Cold day.

Engaged with Elders H. C. Kimball and W. Richards preparing to send our cattle to the rushes for the winter.

Council wrote to Logan Fontenelle, Omaha interpreter, that they wished a conference with him and the chiefs of the nation to explain matters, that the Indians might have a right understanding, and cease their stealing, etc.

Sister Joan Campbell and babe were buried in one coffin, followed by one mourner—her husband, Robert L.

Sunday, October 18—Winter Quarters.

Hard frost last night. Warm day, wind south.

I attended meeting at the stand. Elders H. C. Kimball, W. Richards, O. Pratt, G. A. Smith and A. Lyman, the High Council and a few saints, present.

I complained of the brethren not resting on Sunday and of their negligence in not attending meeting. I referred to the killing of our cattle by the Omahas, and counselled the brethren not to feed them, nor to let them into their tents; for they would steal with one hand while you give them a loaf of bread in the other. Cautioned the brethren against selling their dogs, and told them to refrain from shooting Indians, if they did catch them skinning their oxen. If we are driven to it we can build a fence around our tents. I have sent to the Interpreter for an interview and will tell the Indians they cannot be allowed in camp. The Indians will not be converted this winter.

About noon, Logan Fonenelle, the interpreter, and Mr. James Case arrived at the stand. I told Logan that any information as to how to prevent the Indians from stealing would be thankfully received. He said, we must catch and whip them and the chiefs would approve of it.

Prest. Alpheus Cutler called on the Bishops to guard their wards, seven of whom were present, who agreed to do so.

I counseled the brethren again to camp closely together.

The assembly voted to gather and form a ring with tents and wagons, compactly.

I proferred $200 for wintering one hundred herd of cattle, those lost by miring or straying will be the herdsmen's loss, those by disease, mine.

We wish men to take the cattle of the sisters whose husbands are in the battalion and also those of the sick.

A. P. Rockwood spoke in favor of a general search for cattle; five volunteered for a two day's tour.

Monday, October 19—Winter Quarters.

Wind, N.W., clear and cold.

About noon, Prest. Kimball started about one hundred and thirty head of cattle to the rush bottoms. I sent one hundred and ten head.

Evening, Elders Kimball, Richards and I laid hands on Joseph Young's wife, who was sick.

We agreed to send the Church cattle North in the morning.

Tuesday, October 20—Winter Quarters.

Warm day, wind north.

The Church cattle and others were started for the rushes, accompanied by herdsmen.

About eleven a.m., the Prairie south commenced to burn, and about four p.m. Elders Kimball and Richards raised help, which they sent and extinguished the fire. Two stacks of hay were burned.

Wednesday, October 21—Winter Quarters.

Warm day, northwest wind.

About nine a.m., I called on Dr. Sprague, who was going to St. Louis for medicine and paid him Thirty dollars, Elder Kimball gave him ten, and Dr. Richards fifteen, to buy medicine for us.

Three Otoe Indians came into office and reported their chief and twenty Indians on the way to visit us; they wanted a cow.

Thursday, October 22—Winter Quarters.

I went with Elders Kimball and Richards to the beef market and met several of the Otoe Indians and gave them a beef.

William W. Major, portrait painter, arrived.

About eight, Elders Kimball, O. Pratt, and I called at the post office, and walked to bro. Benbow's. We laid hands on Sister Benbow and prayed for her. She gave us a cake which she had made in Nauvoo.

Friday, October 23—Winter Quarters.

Warm and pleasant day.

At sunrise, the brethren met at the stand. I gave directions as to the cattle drive. One hundred volunteered to hunt cattle on the north.

Elder Kimball and I rode north on horseback. Returned at one p.m., and found Big Elk, and twenty Omahas, who had encamped beside my new house. Many droves of cattle brought in during the afternoon.

Fifty extra men were appointed to guard the camp this morning. The Council voted that the ferry boat be removed to this place.

Saturday, October 24—Winter Quarters.

At one p.m., I met with several of the Twelve and Big Elk with about twenty of his braves and Logan Fontenelle.

Big Elk said, he understood there was bad feelings between the Omahas and our people and he came to settle them. The Omahas saw things done which they did not like and perhaps the Omahas had done things we did not like. He enquired how many oxen and sheep had been killed. I informed him about fifty oxen and many sheep.

Big Elk thought that we were soldiers enough to defend ourselves and our property, and considered the destruction of his game, timber and land of more value than the cattle taken. He said, he had some bad young men, he was old and could not restrain them, said we promised in last summer's counsel to go north and fix ourselves in a fort, so that the Indians could not get in, but our people were scattered and we were to blame. His young men could not help stealing when our cattle were all about, and they would steal if they were admitted into our camp; his young men did not like white people, and they did not like him; he told them we would do them good, and they call him a liar.

The Omahas would have been gone on a hunt but for sickness, the half of them had died in his village in a month. His young men felt bad when we crossed the river. When we cut their timber, we left them like the trunk of a tree,— without leaves or limbs.

I told the Indians we were their friends, we had no bad feelings to them. If it was their wish we could keep their young men out of our villages, and we would do it—that we expected and had been ready to draw their corn—that we would give them some tobacco, powder and lead; and that if our cattle could be allowed to run on the bottoms, without molestation, we could devote more time to building a fort or stockade for our safety and the preservation of our cattle.

Big Elk said they had cached their corn in the village to keep it from the Otoes. He knew the white people were quick tempered, his people were slow; he should counsel them till he went into his grave; he came to settle the difficulty and beg. He said, we had cut a deal of timber, he wanted us to use it. He would not ask for powder and lead, if he had means to buy it.

I talked of hiring a piece of land from them.

The Historian, Dr. Richards, was crowded off the ground, and was unable to take further minutes.

I addressed the Council and Bishops, said, I had pledged myself that the families of the brethren in the battalion should be taken care of. I wished the brethren to help me in doing so.

I want the Bishops to see to the people and number them, find how many can go to making willow baskets; if houses are wanted, have them built, and if the

Bishops need help they can appoint counselors.

I gave a synopsis of the Council with the Indians; and said, we had better picket our city; and that this council would have to decide on the property of deceased persons.

Sunday, October 25—Winter Quarters.

Warm day, south wind, cloudy.

About noon, I attended meeting at the stand, several of the Twelve, and many of the Saints present.

Elder Heber C. Kimball preached on economy.

I proposed picketing the city. Agreed to commence on Monday week.

I offered to furnish wheat at one third and corn at one half to those who would haul it here, or I would haul it if others purchased.

I remarked that the wicked are a rod in the hands of the Almighty to scourge the Saints, and our stopping here would prove a great blessing to this people. Father James Case has been ten years in this country and he never knew October to pass away without a snow storm. We live in wagons and tents.

Dr. Adison Everett wants the sisters to go to making willow baskets, and supply the Western market. Spin up their wool, knit stockings and get deer and elk skins and make leggins for the men.

I spoke about the Sabbath. Revelation required us to worship God one day in seven, and when we have traveled on the Sabbath, since we left Nauvoo, we have been sure to stop two or three days during the week. It is wisdom to rest on the Sabbath and partake of the Sacrament.

George Miller arrived from Ponca. He informed us his camp was at the junction of the Running Water and Missouri rivers, 153 miles distant. The Camp were in good health, there had been six deaths. Their situation good for keeping stock, on the rushes of the island of Running Water. They had brought down forty wagons for provisions. They had sent a party to examine the road to the North pass. Their Camp were in good spirits, their farming land better than this, there was some oak, ash and walnut on the Running Water. Indians friendly.

Brother Lewis said, the Indians had killed some of their cattle, but those who killed them were whipped severely by their own people. The Indian chief told bro. Miller, it made him sick to see his men kill the cattle.

Brother Miller said they had not agreed to defend the Poncas from the Sioux.

Sunday, November 1—Winter Quarters.

Mild, warm day; south wind.

The saints met at the stand. Elder B. L. Clapp preached.

A call was made for teams to go to St. Joseph for the heavy goods left there by Bishop Whitney; twenty-one teams were volunteered.

I submitted a draft by Orson Pratt, for a tabernacle.

The location of the mill site having been removed down stream, men were called for to dig on the lengthening of the race.

Major Harvey, Superintendent of Indian affairs, Mr. Mitchell, sub-Agent, and Mr. Miller visited me. Harvey said he had letters from Washington, in which the Indian department had expressed their expectation that we would leave the Pottawatomie lands in the Spring; and he would like to have us over there this winter. He complained at our burning wood on the Omaha lands, and wished to know our reasons for stopping here. I informed him that while on our journey westward we were met by Captn. Allen with a requisition from the President of the U.S., through the War department, for a battalion for the Mexican War, with which we complied by sending our most efficient men, and which left us unable to move their families—that we were in the service of the U.S., and that we intended to leave our families here in the Spring and prosecute our journey over the mountains and put in a crop; and that we should not move from either side of the river. Capt. Allen had said it would be impolitic for us to attempt to go on under our circumstances, and that the Government had not power to remove us this winter.

Wednesday, November 4—Warm and pleasant day.

At six p.m., Elders Kimball and Richards called on me. I had just received Fifty-two Dollars and sixty Cents of ferriage money which was charged to me. I loaned Elders Kimball and Richards ten dollars each.

The prairie on fire westward, it continued to burn until it reached the top of the bluffs near the city, when it was stopped.

The Trustees at Nauvoo wrote to me under date of Oct. 20th, that Reubin Miller had returned to the Church by baptism on the 19th; also, that the keys of the Temple had been delivered up by the mob to Bro. Paine, in their behalf.

Friday, November 6—Cloudy morning, after a rainy night. Forenoon, showery.

Geo. D. Grant and others returned from the rush bottoms, and reported they had been two hundred and fifty miles up the river.

Marshal Eldridge reported that Bro. Beers had abused his family and turned his wife out of tent last evening in the rain.

Saturday, November 7—Very pleasant, warm day.

Many Omahas in the city.

Sunday, November 8—Pleasant, warm day.

I attended meeting, Elders Joseph Young and Heber C. Kimball preached. I related the interview with Major Harvey, and proposed that the Sisters keep their gold rings and silk dresses, and go to work and manufacture willow baskets, and that the Seventies make wash boards and tables, with which we would carry on a trade with the Missourians for grain and the commodities we needed.

Dismissed at 1:30 p.m., and at 3:30 the Presidents of the Seventies met with me in my new house, with doors but no windows, and chimneys built of brick obtained from the ruins of an old fort at Council Bluffs, but no floor.

I spoke to the Presidents and related a dream which I had concerning the Rocky Mountains. Brother Joseph proposed to the Seventies to dig the mill race on Saturday, and also to give one tenth, if need be, to sustain the poor in their respective Quorums and that each quorum provide for their own poor. Seventies adjourned.

The Bishops were requested to ascertain the amount of seed in Camp.

Monday, November 9—Some rain, thunder and lightning.

I called on Dr. Richards and related a dream which I had last night of harvesting oats, wheat, etc.

Thursday, November 12—I met with twenty-six members of the General council. I requested the brethren to be free and speak their minds; and said, that I did foreknow that we should go in safety over the mountains, notwithstanding all the opposition and obstacles government officials and others might interpose.

Elder Woodruff's son, Joseph, died, aged one year and about four months.

Sunday, November 15—Wind south; chilly and cloudy day.

About ten a.m., Elder Kimball and I called at the post office, thence accompanied by Dr. Richards went to the South of the city and saw Bishop George Miller who was just starting for Ponca and gave him some counsel—told him we had nothing against him, but did not like his absenting himself from our Councils and company.

We returned to my house where we found Big Elk, with letter from Logan Fontenelle, in which Big Elk expresses his gratitude for the powder and lead sent him, and that he returns two horses sent in from Camp by his son, and that there were several horses on the Papilon, which were so wild that the Indians could not catch them. His letter also states that he was *very hungry!*

I told him that his people continued to kill our cattle which was a heavy tax upon us. He replied, that his bad young men would do so, although they had been chastised for their conduct.

Thursday, November 19—Cold day.

Mr. Smith, Catholic priest and missionary to the Black Feet Indians, called on me. I procured for him a newspaper containing a report of a traveller concerning the Munchie or White Indians.

Friday, November 20—Elder Kimball and I called on Dr. Richards and found him sick.

Saturday, November 21—Bros. John D. Lee and Howard Egan returned from their mission to the battalion, acompanied by bros. Samuel Gully and Roswell Stevens. They brought a mail of 282 letters and 72 packages, and some funds from the battalion—first payment in government drafts.

Sunday, November 22—Cool day.

I took the battalion letters to the stand which were brought by bros. Lee and Egan and Elder O. Pratt called them off; he was appointed deputy postmaster during Dr. Richards' sickness.

Monday, November 23—Cold day.

Dr. Richards received a beef from the Council to assist him in building his house.

I met with several of the Twelve and the High Council; explained to the High Council their duties to attend to temporal as well as spiritual things, and help to bear off the burthens of the Church—to take care of the poor and appoint Bishops to do the same, and also to call Bishops to an account from time to time and devise ways and means for the poor to sustain themselves by their own labor instead of calling on the rich to hand out what they have. I informed them that my plans were laid to pay every dollar for the building of the mill, and that it would do good for years to come.

Tuesday, November 24—Cool day, wind northwest.

Dr. Richards some better, he called upon me accompanied by Geo. A. Smith; we spent most of the day together. Mr. Justin Groselande, a trader for the American fur company, and Mr. Cardinal also called upon me. Mr. G. said he was called Frederic among the Crows, where he had been the principal trader for some years. He was a native of Switzerland, educated in France, and had been among the different Indian tribes sixteen years, and spoke most of their languages this side the mountains. He was at liberty next season and would pilot the camp over the mountains for Two hundred dollars and Mr. Cardinal would go along and hunt for Two hundred dollars more. Mr. G. gave an interesting account of the sources of the Yellowstone and sketched with pencil a map of the country west of the Missouri and north of Ponca above the Yellowstone. Elder Kimball joined us in the evening.

Wednesday, November 25—Elder O. Pratt and I attended the High Council.

They voted that the city be divided into smaller wards; also that every laboring man be tithed each tenth day to be applied for the benefit of the poor, or pay an equivalent to his Bishop.

Sunday, November 29—Clear and cool day.

Meeting at the stand; Elder E. T. Benson preached.

Sister Benbow was buried; bro. Benbow was unable, through sickness, to follow her to the grave.

Monday, November 30—Mild day, wind south.

Evening I attended the High Council; they decided a difficulty between William Beers and his wife.

Dr. Richards gave notice that he would have a bee, and invited the Twelve and High Council to help him to cover his Octagon house on Thursday.

Thursday, December 3—I ordained Joseph Knight, Jr., a bishop and set him apart to officiate on the East side of the river near the ferry.

The brethren turned out liberally and covered Dr. Richards' (Octagon) house with straw, then put on about forty-five loads of earth, which in shape made it resemble a new England potato heap.

Wednesday, December 9—Very cold day.

About three a.m., the report of six guns was heard in camp in rapid succession followed by a terrible outcry of Indians and the barking of dogs. Big Head, an Omaha Chief, with his family and relatives had encamped in their lodges a little north of Winter Quarters, and were fired upon while in sleep; Big Head and two others were severely wounded. The Indians came into camp immediately and were attended by Drs. Cannon, Sprague and Levi Richards.

I wrote an account of the occurrence to Maj. Miller and informed him that a band of Iowas had been seen on the East side of the river by whom it was supposed the outrage had been committed.

Friday, December 11—A severe frost last night.

Elder Kimball slept in his new house last night, which was a story and a half high built of logs, hewed inside, containing two rooms on each floor, about sixteen feet square each, covered with oak shingles, with chimney in the middle.

Saturday, December 12—Major Miller and Logan Fontenelle called upon Dr. Richards. Fontenelle stated that the soil at the head of the Yellowstone river was sandy or clayey, not suitable for raising grain; and that the road to the mountains via the Platte river was preferable to the road up the running water.

At one p.m., I met in Council with the Twelve and other brethren, also Major Miller, Fontenelle, Big Elk, Big Head, Mary and eight other Omahas. Council decided it was best for the Indians to move down the river, and we concluded to build them a house.

About seven p.m., a frenchman, named La Fras, came into camp and informed us, through the Interpreter, that about one hundred Sioux had killed about forty Omahas last night, sixty miles north, about eight escaped. I wrote to La Fras' father-in-law, Mr. Sarpy, and informed him of the massacre.

Sunday, December 13—Pleasant day, wind southeast.

About noon, the saints assembled at the stand, Father Cornelius P. Lott preached. I made a few remarks pertaining to the complaints of the battalion sisters about receiving so little money, and informed them that their *dear* husbands had only sent about five thousand dollars from Leavenworth where they had received Twenty-two thousand dollars; the most of which they should have sent to their families; and that when the council had sent after them to Santa Fe, they had only sent Four thousand dollars back.

I exhorted the High Council to faithfulness in their duties, told them to have a list of the Bishops read over and see that they attend meeting and if they did not magnify their calling drop them, for it would not do for this people to go into the wilderness and forget their God. Remarked, that if I had been intent on getting riches I never should have had the knowledge God has bestowed upon me, some one else would have stood in my place—the Bishops should know what every man in camp does, when the Bishops or High Councillors don't do their duty, they should be reported and dealt with.

The Bishops were requested to meet once a week with the High Council, and I instructed the Council to watch over the Bishops with a fatherly care and see that they organize and watch over their wards, have weekly meetings therein; also see that those under their charge have work and that none suffer through want, also instruct their wards to establish schools.

I desired the Twelve, the High Council, and twenty-two Bishops should each bring a log twenty-five feet long that we might build a Council house near my house. Council adjourned.

The Twelve remained about an hour after; when bro. Luke Johnson stated that all but one who were engaged in mobbing, tarring and feathering Joseph and Sidney in the town of Hiram, Portage County, New York, in 1832, had come to some untimely end, and the survivor, Carnot Mason, had been severely afflicted. Carnot was the person who dragged Joseph out of the house by his hair. Dr. Denison prepared the vial for Joseph, supposed to be aqua fortis.

Monday, December 14—Snow on the ground, wind east.

I rode six miles south accompanied by Elder E. T. Benson, and others, and selected a site on which to build the house for the Omahas. Major Miller did not meet us. Dr. Richards walked on the ice over the Missouri and visited bro. Neff, who was sick.

Tuesday, December 15—A slight snow fell this afternoon.

The Council directed the Historian to issue a form to the bishops, that their reports might be made uniformly.

Elder Kimball said he dreamed that he and I were traveling along and felt well; we flew some distance and lit upon a plain, in traveling over which we perceived groups of snakes: we jumped lively from place to place to get past them, they did not molest us.

Elder Kimball counseled the Bishops to get up a reformation and teach the people to cease their complaining and seek diligently after the Holy Ghost, that the Twelve might not be driven from their midst.

I desired the Bishops to report the organizations of their wards, their business, number of men, women and children, how many sick, tithing paid, etc., with the totals, that their reports can be seen at a glance. There are twenty-two bishops here, their reports should all be read in forty-four minutes. If men who have been in the Church thirteen years cannot do business with dispatch and correctly, the Council must teach them.

The Council requested me to give them instructions. I told them that unless this people would humble themselves and cease their wickedness, God would not give them much more teaching nor would it be long until the Priesthood would be hunted by those who now call themselves saints. I told the brethren if the people would do as I said they would be saved. I asked my Heavenly Father what he had for me to do, and when he dictated I performed accordingly, and I left the issue with Him believing that it would come out all right. As to the complaints about the goods, I said I was ready to render an account; I asked if I were to blame because goods were high in St. Louis or because the freight up the Missouri rose from seventy-five cents to two dollars and twenty-five cents per hundred. I said I did not want such complaining, and asked why the battalion brethren who sent Five Thousand Dollars from Leavenworth to the Camp of Israel, did not send Sixteen Thousand Dollars.

Thursday, December 17—I received a letter from Joseph Holbrook, Ponca, with an account of an attempted exploration made by him and bros. Mathews and Emmet of a route to Laramie from the Ponca camp; accompanied by a small sketch of the route traveled, rivers, etc. They reported favorably concerning the route, but said they were compelled after traveling one hundred miles to return, the feed on the route having been eaten out by the numerous herds of buffalo.

Dr. Richards spoke of the bushels of papers now in his possession not filed and of the need of a place to gather and arrange for future history; and said a man should have his mind free and unburthened by care who writes a history for time and eternity.

Elder Woodruff said, the subject alluded to by the Doctor, was of benefit to the whole Church and kingdom of God. When he heard Joseph preach he could not rest until he wrote it,—felt we were living in the most important era of the world, and the people ought to keep a strict eye upon the Historian—felt deeply interested in the books out of which he was to be judged. He rejoiced that the Church had a ready writer and said he felt the Doctor should go to work and save the Church history.

Friday, December 18—The remnant of the massacred band of Omahas passed through the Camp of Israel (Winter Quarters); the others in Camp proceeded South with them.

Saturday, December 19—I reported the lower story of the flouring mill completed. G. A. Smith had been putting dirt on the roof of his house. Orson Pratt studying the polarization of light. Elder Kimball had built thirteen cabins with the help of those living with him and had also built about as many more by hired help.

Voted that the Church cattle be sold to pay the Church debts and help bro. Richards.

I asked the Quorum what their feelings were towards me; when all present expressed the best of feelings and their approval of my course.

Sunday, December 20—About one p.m., the bell rang and the Saints assembled at the stand. I preached on the condition of the Camp of Israel—showed there was complaining and iniquity—that some indulged in laboring on the Sabbath, in taking the name of God in vain and damning their brethren, while others stole wood and hay, used profane and unbecoming language and refused to pay tithing or to assist the poor.

I instructed the Bishops to hold meetings where the Saints might assemble, confess their sins, pray with and for each other, humble themselves before the Lord and commence a reformation that all might exercise themselves in the principles of righteousness; and, if those who had received the Holy Priesthood did not abide their covenants and walk uprightly before the Lord and their brethren, that those who did would be taken away from their midst, and the wicked would be smitten with famine, pestilence and the sword, and would be scattered and perish on the prairies. I said I would prefer traveling over the mountains with the Twelve only than to be accompanied with the wicked and those who continued to commit iniquity; and warned those who lied and stole and followed Israel that they would have their heads cut off, for that was the law of God and it should be executed.

I told those who expected to journey with us that they should help the poor whether they belonged to the Church or not; and said, if the Saints would reform and act upon the knowledge revealed to them, flood gates of knowledge would be opened to them and they would be filled with light and intelligence, but if they did not the gates of knowledge were closed against them and would remain so.

Tuesday, December 22—Winter Quarters. Mild winter day, wind south.

Evening, the Twelve met at my house. Reuben Miller's letter to Trustees at

Nauvoo was read. I remarked that I considered contending with Strangism, was like setting up barleycorns to see them fall over.

Thursday, December 24—(Winter Quarters). Very mild weather.

Dr. Richards covered his office with straw and dirt. It joins his Octagon house or Potato heap.

At six p.m., I met with the Twelve and municipal High Council.

Voted that the Bishops report the number and kinds of houses erected in their wards, with dimensions. Samuel Williams was ordained a high priest.

Voted that three-fourths of one percent be assessed on the property in the city. (Winter Quarters). Orson Pratt was appointed Treasurer.

Voted that all ardent spirits that are now or shall hereafter be brought into this Camp, be taken to the Bishops for them to sell, the profits to be appropriated to the support of the poor; the owners of the liquor to be remunerated for the same.

Voted that all persons who have ardent Spirits for sale, be notified of the vote of the Council, and if they refuse to obey the resolution that they forfeit all such stock on hand.

Voted that bro. Higbee be instructed not to ferry over another barrel of whiskey without license from the Council.

Friday, December 25—Mild day. Christmas.

Col. John Scott discharged the cannon thrice at sunrise.

I wrote to Mr. Fontenelle, Indian interpreter, as to some articles abstracted by the Indians from Camp, also expressng a wish that Major Miller would inform us where he wished the house built for the Indians, as we had gone South at the time appointed but he had failed to meet us.

Monday, December 28—Weather mild.

This afternoon a stranger walked into my house and abruptly seated himself upon my table without speaking; he soon jumped up and went out, conversed with some person a few minutes, then returned to my house, and asked to speak with me alone; I replied, "I am here, speak on." He demanded his wife and two children, said they had been taken from Nauvoo by the Mormons; I enquired whether he knew the individual who had taken them, he mentioned and implicated four or five persons whose names he called, all of whom were unknown in Camp. I asked him, if he were in the mob at Nauvoo, he replied, he was sick at that time. I asked him if he could identify the person he accused, he thought he could and walked out of doors, where were about thirty persons, amongst who was Major Miller from the point. I invited Major Miller to supper. The stranger retired and soon crossed the river.

The brethren continued their labors on the Council House.

Geo. A. Smith moved into his house.

Tuesday, December 29—Light snow fell, wind south.

At thirty minutes past two p.m., I met in Council in Elder Kimball's house with Elders Heber C. Kimball, Orson Pratt, Willard Richards, Amasa Lyman, Geo. A. Smith, N. K. Whitney, Peter Haws, Albert P. Rockwood, E. T. Benson,

Joseph Young, Geo. D. Grant and were shortly after joined by Wilford Woodruff and P. H. Young.

We conversed on the organization of the Camp of Israel and our contemplated journey, concerning which several important questions were asked and discussed. I considered the Pioneers should find a location to put in crops this season, and described the order of building in forts, for safety.

After a short recess, I reassembled with the brethren named, also J. D. Parker and O. P. Rockwell.

About seven p.m., brothers Smithies, Hutchins, Duzette and Clayton joined us and played on their instruments and the brethren danced.

Dr. Richards measured forty-three inches round the breast, I measured forty-one inches.

At nine o'clock, all in the house united in singing several hymns; afterwards, the followed me in prayer. I felt to thank the Lord for the privilege of praising Him in the song and dance. I spoke in tongues and conversed with Elder Kimball in an unknown tongue.

I proposed to form a company of fifty of my own family, and find out how many men could go as Pioneers, how many families could go, etc. I also proposed that a field be ploughed here for those who stay, and to move some of the small houses on a line for fence, etc.

Thursday, December 31—Evening, I met with the Twelve and the Municipal High Council.

Several Bishops made reports of houses, etc., in their wards.

The buildings of the city were generally of logs averaging from twelve to eighteen feet long, a few of which were split; the floors were laid with puncheon (legs split about three inches thick and hewed on one side). The timber used for floors was principally lynn and cottonwood; a great many roofs were made by splitting oak timbers into boards called shakes, six inches wide about three feet long and half an inch thick, which were kept to their places by weight poles, a few were nailed on; many roofs were made with willows, straw and earth about a foot thick while a few others had puncheon. Many of the cabins had no floors. A few persons who could not procure logs made dugouts on the side hills, cutting out a fireplace at the upper end, the ridge pole of the roof was supported by two uprights in the centre, such were generally roofed with willows straw and earth. The most of the chimneys were built of prairie sods, and the doors made of shakes pinned together, wooden hinges and finished with a string latch. The log houses were daubed inside with clay; a few rather more aristocratic cabins had fireplaces made of clayu pounded in for jams and back. A few persons had stoves.

The building of these houses was prosecuted with unremiting energy, at any hour of the evening the sound of the ax or the saw relieved the stillness of the night.

There has been considerable difficulty to get flour and meal in sufficient quantities to feed the Camp; a little grain has been ground at Week's mill (twenty-five miles distance, built by government for the Pottawatomies), the balance by the mills in Missouri, upwards of one hundred and fifty miles distant, which made very coarse flour and meal. The inhabitants of Winter Quarters have had to grind wheat and corn by coffee and hand mills, which in many instances only cut the grain, others pounded it was a pestle suspended to a spring pole and sifted out the finer for bread, the coarse for hominy. Some eat their wheat boiled, others boiled their corn in lye and made hominy while some boiled corn in the ear until it was sufficiently soft to be grated, many pieces of old tin were converted into graters for this purpose. Much anxiety is manifested for the completion of the mill.

1847

Friday, January 1—New Year's day was ushered in at Winter Quarters, subsequently known as Florence, Nebraska, by the firing of cannon. About an inch of snow fell; wind northwest, very cold.

I was at home. Dr. Richards and I consecrated a bottle of oil.

The anti-Mormons at Nauvoo, Ill., gave a grand military and civic Ball in the Mansion House. Gen. Brockman and his military colleagues who had distinguished themselves(!) on the occasion of the expulsion of the sick and helpless remnant of the Saints from Nauvoo, in September last, were managers.

Wednesday, January 6—Severe frost, the coldest day of the season; Thermometer 2 degrees below zero.

Thursday, January 7—Thermometer 8 degrees below zero; coldest day this winter.

Cynthia, wife of Geo. P. Dykes, was delivered of a daughter. She was formerly James Durfee's wife; this is her tenth daughter and twentieth child.

Friday, January 8—My wife, Loisa Beeman, was safely delivered of a son. Adeline, wife of Gilbert Belknap, was also delivered of a son; and Melissa, wife of Geo. B. Wallace, of a daughter.

I wrote to Levi Stewart and the herdsmen of Israel on both sides of the Missouri river in relation to two Indian horses, found by herdsmen near the late battle ground between the Sioux and Omahas, belonging to one of the Omahas, who says he has not killed any of our cattle. I exhorted the brethren to refrain from any such conduct and manifest to the natives of the forest that we actuated by more noble principles than they; and hoped that if such animals were in the possession of any of the brethren they would be immediately forwarded.

Saturday, January 9—I went to the Octagon. I married Elizabeth Hendricks to Isaac Grundy. Evening, took a walk with Elders Kimball, Woodruff and other conversing upon a variety of subjects.

Sunday, January 10—Thermometer 13 degrees below zero. The brethren of the Twelve Apostles preached in the various wards.

I told the brethren I dreamed of seeing Joseph, the Prophet, last night and conversing with him, that Mother Smith was present and very deeply engaged reading a Pamphlet, when Joseph with a great deal of dignity turned his head towards his mother partly looking over his shoulder, said, 'Have you got the word of God there?' Mother Smith replied, 'There is truth here.' Joseph replied, 'That may be, but I think you will be sick of that pretty soon.' Joseph appeared to feel extremely well, was sociable and laughed heartily. Conversed freely about the best manner of organizing companies for emigration, etc.

Tuesday, January 12—I visited at bro. A. O. Smoot's. The ice on the river very strong; large quantities of wood being drawn over the river.

Thursday, January 14—I commenced to give the Word and Will of God concerning the emigration of the Saints and those who journey with them.

At seven, the Twelve met at Elder Benson's. I continued to dictate the Word and Will of the Lord. Council adjourned at ten p.m., when I retired with Dr. Richards to the Octagon and finished writing the same.

Friday, January 15—The Twelve Apostles met at Elder E. T. Benson's. It was decided that the Word and Will of the Lord should be laid before the Councils of the Church.

Evening, I went to the Octagon (Dr. R's office) with Wm. G. and Ute Perkins, who conversed with me on the principles of adoption and the Levitical priesthood. I told them that no son of Levi has yet been found in these last days to minister at the altar.

Saturday, January 16—I counseled the brethren to get timber and season it to be ready for wagon timber one year hence.

Elder Willard Richards read "The Word and Will of the Lord." (See Doctrine & Covenants, Section 136).

Reynolds Cahoon moved that the communication be received as the Word and Will of God; Seconded by Isaac Morley.

Alanson Eldridge approved of the same: it was plain to his understanding.

Isaac Morley approved of it.

Reynolds Cahoon said it was the voice of righteousness.

Winslow Farr said it reminded him of the first reading of the Book of Mormon; he was perfectly satisfied and knew it was from the Lord.

Cornelius P. Lott was perfectly satisfied.

Daniel Russell said it was true; felt as he did after the first Mormon sermon that he heard.

Ezra Chase was perfectly satisfied.

Geo. W. Harris was so well satisfied that he wanted all to say, Amen, at once.

Thomas Grover felt that it was the voice of the Spirit. The vote passed unanimously.

H. T. Eldredge felt to receive it as the Word and Will of the Lord and that its execution would prove our salvation.

Hosea Stout said if there is anything in Mormonism that is the voice of the Lord to this people, so is the Word and Will of the Lord. He meant to live up to it. Council adjourned.

I proposed that Elders E. T. Benson, Erastus Snow, Orson Pratt, W. Woodruff, A. Lyman, and Geo. A. Smith call brethren to their assistance to help them organize their respective companies. I remarked that a body pure enough to receive a pure spirit and so that an evil spirit can have no influence over it, was susceptible of angelic converse at any time. I said some men were afraid they would lose some glory if they were sealed to one of the Twelve, and did not stand alone and have others sealed to them. A Saint's kingdom consisted of his own posterity, and to be sealed to one of the Twelve did not diminish him, but only connected him according to the law of God by that perfect chain and order of Heaven, that will bind the righteous from Adam to the last Saint. Adam will claim us all, as members of his kingdom, we being his children.

Sunday, January 17—I met in Council with several of the Twelve, many of the Seventies and High Priests. Dr. Richards read "The Word and Will of the Lord" and all present voted unanimously to receive it.

I addressed the Assembly showing that the church had been led by Revelation just as much since the death of Joseph Smith as before, and that he was as great and good a man, and as great a Prophet as ever lived upon the earth, Jesus excepted. Joseph received his apostleship from Peter and his brethren, and the present apostles received their apostleship from Joseph the first apostle, and Oliver Cowdery, the second Apostle.

The Twelve met with the Municipal High Council. The conduct of the Sexton pertaining to charges was canvassed. I cautioned the brethren against selling whiskey to the Indians and said if any did so they ought to be handed over to the Indian Agent to be dealt with according to the laws of the United States.

Monday, January 18—Cold day. Themometer 20 degrees below Zero.

At six p.m., I preached at the Council House to many of my company, whose names were read over. I warned all who intended to proceed to the mountains that iniquity would not be tolerated in the Camp of Israel. I did not want any to join my company unless they would obey the Word and Will of the Lord, live in honesty and assist to build up the kingdom of God.

Each company should take an equal proportion of Widows and Orphans. I had not cattle sufficient to go to the mountains next spring, but I had no more doubts nor fears of going to the mountains, and felt as much security as if I possessed the treasures of the East.

When Joseph and Hyrum and others were in prison I said I knew that they would be delivered safely out of the hands of the Missourians. I know that every man who puts forth his means to build up this kingdom will receive a hundred fold.

Joseph Herring, by birth a Seneca Indian, was cut off the Church by the Twelve.

Tuesday, January 19—Elder H. C. Kimball organized a Company to journey westward.

Saturday, January 23—In the evening I attended the Council of Seventies and made arrangements for several dances and festivals in the new Council room. I told the brethren and sisters I would show them how to go forth in the dance in an acceptable manner before the Lord. I then knelt down and prayed to God in behalf of the meeting imploring His blessings to rest upon those present and dedicating the meeting and house to the Lord. At the sound of the music I led forth in the dance accompanied by Elders H. C. Kimball, W. Woodruff, and Joseph Young; the dance went off with much satisfaction.

Sunday, January 24—Dull, heavy day. I attended the Municipal High Council in the evening and requested the Bishops to see that the Houses in their wards are not left in a situation to catch fire through negligence. If anyone suffers, all the community suffers loss, and remarked that it would be wisdom to see that all the straw roofed houses were covered with dirt.

A vote was taken that all the Powder in Winter Quarters be delivered up to the Captain of Police for safe keeping.

Monday, January 25—I informed the people that in the Government of this Church, in business transactions, every man should have a voice in the matter, as if the whole responsibility were on his shoulders. It belonged to the people to appoint captains of hundreds and fifties. When we emerge into national existence do you suppose all the officers will be appointed by one man!

The Captains of companies were instructed to take names and fill up their companies; the captains of tens to ascertain what property their ten possessed, so that the widows and women whose husbands were in the army might be taken along, so far as there was means to take them.

After this organization if effected the Council will make a calculation who shall go; then a new organization will be entered into to find who can go as Pioneers, and who can follow them. The houses will be moved into line so as to form a stockade to protect those who remain at this point for another year. These we will help to make gardens before we start.

Tuesday, January 26—The Seventies had a picnic dancing party at the Council House; bro. Benson and I attended.

Wednesday, January 27—Elders Kimball, Benson and I met with the Presidents and Captains of the emigrating Companies and assisted them to organize. We blessed W. B. Richards and Sister Hinman's daughter. Attended party in the evening.

Thursday, January 28—Three inches of snow fell.

The Twelve and Seventies spent the day in the Council House, singing, praying, dancing and making merry before the Lord.

Friday, January 29—Elder Geo. A. Smith returned to Winter Quarters this afternoon and reported that Elder Lyman and he had held eight meetings at various places between the point and bro. A. H. Perkins', generally known as the Macedonia Camp. They had found the brethren in a cold and indifferent state, when compared with the brethren in Winter Quarters.

Elders Kimball, Woodruff, Smith and Benson and I called on Dr. Richards who was sick in bed.

Sunday, January 31—I was sick in bed.

Monday, February 1—The Twelve met in Council in the evening. I felt some better, but was confined to my room. Dr. Richards called on me and reported that rumors were afloat that some of our people had robbed the Omahas that were massacred by the Sioux.

Tuesday, February 2—About eleven a.m., Elders Kimball, Richards and Woodruff called on me; my health improving. Letters were read to Major Miller and others written by the Council to allay any excitement that might arise in relation to robbing the dead Indians.

Wednesday, February 3—I had a family party in the Council House in the afternoon and evening. My health improved.

Friday, February 5—About three p.m., Father John Smith sent an invitation to the Twelve to attend the Silver Gray Picnic. The Twelve went immediately and found the House well filled with fathers in Israel and their wives. I told them that this meeting was for the purpose of showing to the world that this people can be made what God designed them. Nothing will infringe more upon the traditions of some men than to dance. Infidels dance, also the wicked, the vain, foolish, giddy and those that know not God. There is no harm in dancing. The Lord said he wanted His saints to praise Him in all things. It was enjoined on Miriam and the daughters of Israel to dance and celebrate the name of the Almighty, and to praise Him on the destruction of Pharaoh and his host.

For some weeks past I could not wake up at any time of the night but I heard the axes at work. Some were building for the destitute and the widow; and now my feelings are, dance all night, if you desire to do so, for there is no harm in it. The prayer of the wicked is an abomination in the sight of God, but it is not sin for a saint to pray; where there is no evil intended there is no sin. I enjoin upon the Bishops that they gather the widow, the poor and the fatherless together and remember them in the festivities of Israel.

Patriarch John Smith made some comforting remarks and exhorted the brethren and sisters to dance, sing, and enjoy themselves the best way they could.

The center of the floor was then cleared for the dance when the "Silver Grays" and spectacled dames enjoyed themselves in the dance; it was indeed an interesting and novel sight, to behold the old men and women, some nearly an hundred years old, dancing like ancient Israel.

Tuesday, February 9—The Bishops had a picnic party at the Council House. With Elders H. C. Kimball, W. Richards and Bishop N. K. Whitney I attended a blessing meeting at Elder Kimballs, when seven of his sons and daughters were blessed; Dr. Richards wrote the blessings.

Wednesday, February 10—The Twelve met in Council.

Ebenezer C. Richardson, Geo. Peacock, and D. Shockley arrived from the herd-ground North bringing some horses and a letter from A. A. Lathrop and John Lowry of Jan. 16, stating that the Sioux chief, Eagle, was in their vicinity with a portion of three bands of Indians. They had stolen several horses and killed about thirty cattle and horses. The chief wanted a council. A feast was prepared, after which Eagle returned four horses for the four stolen, but some of the Indians stole them again. Eagle said, he intended to make a finish of the Omahas when Spring came, but he wished the brethren to let the Pottawatomie chiefs know that they wanted to be at peace with them. Our herdsmen moved their horses fifteen or twenty miles, but the Indians discovered them and had stolen nine head, when the brethren concluded to send the remainder to Winter Quarters; they were destitute of bread stuff and also medicine for their sick.

Friday, February 12—I met with the Captains in the first division and gave an account of the loss of horses and cattle in Lathrop's herd on the Rush bottoms of the Missouri river where were 1200 head of our cattle. I preached against selfishness and covetousness; and advised that twenty more men be sent to aid the herdsmen, to prevent the Indians from stealing cattle.

Sunday, February 14—Elder W. Richards sick, Elders W. Woodruff and Geo. A. Smith called on him, then attended meeting in Bishop Hunter's ward.

I met with the High Council and advised the Bishops to make a feast for the poor. I also counselled those who lived in sod houses to pack up their goods that they might not be detroyed by the rains which doubtless would soon fall.

Tuesday, February 16—The Bishops met in the Council House and made arrangements to feast and entertain the poor. It was ascertained that there were 117 poor adults and it was decided to take the first eight wards one day, the second eight wards the next day, and the third eight wards on the third day.

Shortly after noon, I met with sixty-six of my family including my adopted children; there were also present Elders H. C. Kimball, O. Pratt, W. Richards, Geo. A. Smith, E. T. Benson, and A. Lyman of the Twelve Apostles. I preached upon the doctrines of selfishness, sealing, and family relations. Elders Kimball and O. Pratt spoke and questions were asked pertaining to the endowment.

Wednesday, February 17—About two p.m., The Twelve attended a meeting of my adopted children. Bros. Kimball and O. Pratt preached; after which the party dined. Four tables were covered with eatables, in succession. Elders Richards and Woodruff preached; the former called on me and read six letters from Pueblo; I was in bed unwell. After listening to addresses from bros. Geo. A. Smith and Amasa Lyman my family engaged in the dance.

This afternoon, Capt. Tarlton Lewis and company returned. They had obtained information that the Sioux chief had sent his men on their spring hunt. The Indians had quarreled over the thirteen stolen horses and shot twelve of them.

Friday, February 19—I was considerably better today. The brethren of the Twelve called on me this evening; Bro. Hathaway came in, to whom I addressed myself emphatically on the necessity of saints being *honest* and upright in all their transactions.

Tuesday, February 23—I met with the brethren of the Twelve in the Historian's office. Conversation ensued relative to emigration westward. I related the following dream; While sick and asleep about noonday of the 17th inst., I dreamed that I went to (see) Joseph. He looked perfectly natural, sitting with his feet on the lower round of his chair. I took hold of his right hand and after which Eagle returned four horses for the four stolen, but some of the Indians stole them again. Eagle said, he intended to make a finish of the Omahas when Spring came, but he wished the brethren to let the Pottawatomie chiefs know that they wanted to be at peace with them. Our herdsmen moved their horses fifteen or twenty miles, but the Indians discovered them and had stolen nine head, when the brethren concluded to send the remainder to Winter Quarters; they were destitute of bread stuff and also medicine for their sick.

Friday, February 12—I met with the Captains in the first division and gave an account of the loss of horses and cattle in Lathrop's herd on the Rush bottoms of the Missouri river where were 1200 head of our cattle. I preached against self-ishness and covetousness; and advised that twenty more men be sent to aid the herdsmen, to prevent the Indians from stealing cattle.

Sunday, February 14—Elder W. Richards sick, Elders W. Woodruff and Geo. A. Smith called on him, then attended meeting in Bishop Hunter's ward.

I met with the High Council and advised the Bishops to make a feast for the poor. I also counselled those who lived in sod houses to pack up their goods that they might not be destroyed by the rains which doubtless would soon fall.

Tuesday, February 16—The Bishops met in the Council House and made arrangements to feast and entertain the poor. It was ascertained that there were 117 poor adults and it was decided to take the first eight wards one day, the second eight wards the next day, and the third eight wards on the third day.

Shortly after noon, I met with sixty-six of my family including my adopted children; there were also present Elders H. C. Kimball, O. Pratt, W. Richards, Geo. A. Smith, E. T. Benson, and A. Lyman of the Twelve Apostles. I preached upon the doctrines of selfishness, sealing, and family relations. Elders Kimball and O. Pratt spoke and questions were asked pertaining to the endowment.

Wednesday, February 17—About two p.m., The Twelve attended a meeting of my adopted children. Bros. Kimball and O. Pratt preached; after which the party dined. Four tables were covered with eatables, in succession. Elders Richards and Woodruff preached; the former-called on me and read six letters from Pueblo; I was in bed unwell. After listening to addresses from bro. Geo. A. Smith and Amasa Lyman my family engaged in the dance.

This afternoon, Capt. Tarlton Lewis and company returned. They had obtained information that the Sioux chief had sent his men on their spring hunt. The Indians had quarreled over the thirteen stolen horses and shot twelve of them.

Friday, February 19—I was considerably better today. The brethren of the Twelve called on me this evening; Bro. Hathaway came in, to whom I addressed myself emphatically on the necessity of saints being *honest* and upright in all their transactions.

Tuesday, February 23—I met with the brethren of the Twelve in the Historian's office. Conversation ensued relative to emigration westward. I related the following dream; While sick and asleep about noonday of the 17th inst., I dreamed that I went to (see) Joseph. He looked perfectly natural, sitting with his feet on the lower round of his chair. I took hold of his right hand and kissed him many times, and said to him: "Why is it that we cannot be together as we used to be, You have been from us a long time, and we want your society and I do not like to be separated from you."

Joseph rising from his chair and looking at me with his usual, earnest, expressive and pleasing countenance replied, "It is all right."

I said, "I do not like to be away from you."

Joseph said, "It is all right; we cannot be together yet; we shall be by and by; but you will have to do without me a while, and then we shall be together again."

I then discovered there was a hand rail between us, Joseph stood by a window and to the southwest of him it was very light. I was in the twilight and to the north of me it was very dark; I said, "Brother Joseph, the brethren you know well, better than I do; you raised them up, and brought the Priesthood to us. The brethren have a great anxiety to understand the law of adoption or sealing principles, and if you have a word of counsel for me I should be glad to receive it. "

Joseph stepped toward me, and looking, very earnestly, yet pleasantly said, "Tell the people to be humble and faithful, and be sure to keep the spirit of the Lord and it will lead them right. Be careful and not turn away the small still voice, it will teach you what to do and where to go; it will yield the fruits of the kingdom. Tell the brethren to keep their hearts open to conviction, so that when the Holy Ghost comes to them, their hearts will be ready to receive it. They can tell the Spirit of the Lord from all other spirits; it will whisper peace and joy to their souls; it will take malice, hatred, strife and all evil from their hearts; and their whole desire will be to do good, bring forth righteousness and build up the kingdom of God. Tell the brethren if they will follow the spirit of the Lord they will go right. Be sure to tell the people to keep he Spirit of the Lord; and if they will, they will find themselves just as they were organized by our Father in Heaven before they came into the world. Our Father in Heaven organized the human family, but they are all disorganized and in great confusion."

Joseph then showed me the pattern, how they were in the beginning. This I cannot describe, but I saw it, and saw where the Priesthood had been taken from the earth and how it must be joined together, so that there would be a perfect chain from Father Adam to his latest posterity. Joseph again said, "Tell the people to be sure to keep the Spirit of the Lord and follow it, and it will lead them just right."

With several of the Twelve I visited the Council House where the party gotten up by the Bishops for the benefit and entertainment of the poor was held. There were twenty-two baskets of provisions untouched and twelve baskets of fragment left. The total number feasted was about three hundred.

Wednesday, February 24—I met with the brethren of the Twelve. We investigated several orders purporting to be drawn by J. Allen, Lieut. Col., signed by James Pollick; which I requested should be burned. I swore by the Eternal Gods that if men in our midst would not stop this cursed work of stealing and counterfeiting their throats should be cut.

Friday, February 26—I Spent the afternoon and evening in Council with Elders H. C. Kimball, O. Pratt, E. T. Benson, W. Woodruff, Geo. A. Smith, A.

Lyman, N. K. Whitney, Wm. Clayton, and J. M. Grant. Conversation ensued relative to journey westward, the construction of boats, pioneer travelling, location, seeds, irrigation, science, etc.

A Mr. McCarey, professing to be a Spaniard, with Lucy, his wife, formerly Lucy Stanton, and a stranger came into the meeting; he was a natural musician and played on the flute, fife, saucepan, rattler, whistle, etc.

I made enquiry in the Council as to how many teams could be furnished for the Pioneer Company when, with mine, twelve were volunteered.

Saturday, February 27—I met with the officers of the first division in the Council House. Agreed to build two rawhide boats for the company and to fit out fifty wagons with horse and mule teams. Decided that three men go with each wagon and haul one bushel seed corn, one bushel potatoes, one and a half bushel of oats, and all the garden seeds that could be procured; also to take along twenty plows and ten sets of drag teeth for the division.

Wednesday, March 3—Accompanied by my bro. Joseph I went to the office. My brother thought one hundred pounds of provisions very little for each Pioneer. I did not want any to go who had not faith to start with that amount.

Bro. W. Richards and I attended the High Priests party; we retired at two on the morning of the 4th.

Friday, March 6—I preached at the funeral service of bro. John Neff's son, then proceeded to council with the brethren of the Twelve and others. The Captains of companies made their reports. Elders E. T. Benson, W. Richards and O. Pratt made remarks in relation to traveling, etc. I informed the brethren that in relation to our movements we should be dictated by the Spirit of God, and said if the brethren were humble and pliable all would be well; the best thing that could be done at present was to repair the mill dam so that the Pioneers could get their grain ground.

Dr. Richards and I walked up to the dam, found Elders Woodruff and Benson with about fifty others busy at work.

The Seventies held their weekly conference in the Council House at seven p.m., Elders Richards, Benson and I attended. The conduct of Jonathan Packer was canvassed and he was excommunicated. I remarked that any one had the privilege of coming to me to ask whether or not the counsel they had received was right, and I would tell them. I stated that I knew that bro. Packer had lied to the meeting in the name of the Lord; and as to bro. Packer's not wishing to reveal names because the guilty parties had been through the Temple I did not know of any law that required the brethren to hide the iniquity of others; and as to "mystic ties" I pronounced all ties, that would cloak a man's iniquity because he is a brother, devilish ties. The Devil has got up this plan to destroy the people. Do the ties of the Masonic lodge oblige bro. Packer to conceal the iniquity of a brother? No. There are no such ties.

Tuesday, March 9—Sharp frost; ground covered with snow.

I wrote to Sisters Allen and Rosecrantz, whose husbands are in the army, to prepare to emigrate.

I met with the brethren of the Twelve and Bishop Whitney. Bros. Alexander

McRae and Andrew L. Lamoreaux brought a mail of eighteen letters from Nauvoo, and confirmed the reports of the persecution of the saints near Farmington; the mob had hung bro. Wm. H. Folsom, whose friends had much difficulty to restore his sensation; Rodney Swazey was also hung by the mob by the heels for about five minutes; six other brethren were also hung on Sunday, Feb. 7th. Bros. McRae and Lamoreaux reported that they had left Nauvoo, Feb. 14th, were there were eight or nine stores on Main and Mulholland Streets; about one-third of the brick houses were occupied: the log houses and fences were burned up; the seventies hall was used for a school house; those living in Nauvoo were principally Methodists, very few saints; there were six taverns. Bro. McRae was put in jail, tried in Van Buren County, remanded to Lee County and discharged.

Thursday, March 11—Afternoon, I met with the Twelve and Bros. Levi Richards, Luke Johnson, and L. O. Littlefield. We all supped with Dr. Richards in his Octagon; then retired to the Historian's Office and heard read revelation purporting to be received by James J. Strang, but which was written by Charles Wesley Wandell, 6th March, 1846, to entrap John E. Page, who believed it and bore testimony that it was a revelation from the Almighty. This event afforded much merriment to Wandell and his friends, but in assuming to write a revelation in the name of the Lord, although he did it, as he supposed, with good intent to expose wickedness, he placed himself in the power of Satan and laid the foundation for much sorrow. Any man that presumes to write in the name of Jehovah is doing wrong and will see cause to repent in dust and ashes.

Saturday, March 13—Dr. Richards went with Elder Geo. A. Smith to his house, found three of his family sick in bed, his wife's mother dangerously ill, and others of his family unwell; a very unflattering prospect for his Pioneering journey: Father John Smith was also very feeble.

Sunday, March 14—I instructed the brethren to cease dancing and commence prayer meetings and administer the Sacrament. I called for men and teams to finish the mill dam tomorrow. I exhorted all who professed to have the priesthood to repent of their heart wanderings and dig about themselves and not be negligent in their duties to God. Asked them to pray for my brethren and me that we might be able to bear off the kingdom of God triumphantly.

Wednesday, March 17—I buried my wife, Mary H. Pierce, aged twenty-five years, daughter of Robt. and Hannah Pierce. She died of consumption.

Saturday, March 20—The grist mill commenced operating this afternoon. It ground 11 bushels of corn per hour; the machinery ran smoothly. The ferry-boat crossed the Missouri river two or three times.

Sunday, March 21—Dr. W. Richards remained up writing all last night; bros. T. Bullock and R. L. Campbell relieved him at seven a.m.

Evening, I attended a meeting of the Bishops and conversed about relieving the wants of the poor.

Tuesday, March 23—I held a family meeting at bro. Pierce's to organize for traveling the coming season.

Wednesday, March 24—John Barrows was stripped of his coat and had his dog shot by five Omaha Indians near Cutler's park. The Omahas have also killed several cattle.

Old Elk and Logan Fontanelle's brother, Interpreter, called on me for provisions. I gave them their dinner; they slept in the Council House.

I sold the grist mill to bro. John Neff who paid me Two thousand five hundred dollars for the same, which enabled me to pay the debts on it.

Thursday, March 25—Big Elk, Omaha Chief, visited me. I informed him that some of his men had stolen two of bro. Geo. A. Smith's horses last night, and that they were killing our cattle lately. Big Elk replied, that if the horses were among his people they should be returned, but that the Ponca and Pawnee Indians were in the neighborhood stealing horses and cattle.

I met with the brethren of the Twelve and the High Council in the evening. It was voted that John Neff might take one fifth of the grain for toll of the mill. I told the Council that if any of the brethren shot an Omaha Indian for stealing, they must deliver the murderer to Old Elk to be dealt with, as the Indians shall decide, as that was the only way to save the lives of the women and children.

Friday, March 26—I attended a special conference called to transact business, previous to the departure of the Twelve to seek out a location for a stake of Zion.

On motion of Elder Kimball the city of Winter Quarters was voted to be picketted or stockaded on the four sides according to the directions of the authorities left here.

I counselled those living in dug outs to get houses on the top of the ground to live in during the summer, or they would be sick. I advised the brethren to cover their houses with puncheon. I felt that it was wrong to indulge in feelings of hostility and bloodshed toward the Indian, the descendants of Israel, who might kill a cow, an ox or even a horse; to them the deer, the buffalo, the cherry and plum tree or strawberry bed were free. It was their mode of living to kill and eat. If the Omahas would persist in robbing and stealing, after being warned not to do so, whip them. I realized there were men among us who would steal, who knew better, whose traditions and earliest teachings were all against it. Yet such would find fellowship with those who would shoot an Indian for stealing. I suggested that should any persons be caught stealing who belonged here let them be dealt with according to law, should the thief belong to Missouri, let him be delivered to the officers of the law in Mo.

Elders Orson Pratt and Geo. A. Smith made some remarks.

I preached to the saints in the afternoon, and told them that it would be necessary for those who followed the Pioneers to take eighteen months provisions. A committee would be appointed and each wagon examined. The Pioneers would probably stay on the other side of the Mountains until the snow began to fill up the gaps in the mountains. If mob violence should render it necessary for all to remove, take your cows, put your loads on their backs and fasten your children on the top. Where the saints do all they can the Lord will do the rest.

Elder Orson Pratt read the revelation given at Winter Quarters in January last and commented on it. Elder Kimball preached.

At sundown, I met the brethren of the Twelve, and others, also William McCarey, the Indian negro, and his wife at the office. McCarey made a rambling statement, claiming to be Adam, the ancient of days, and exhibited himself in Indian costume; he also claimed to have an odd rib which he had discovered in his wife. He played on his thirty-six cent flute, being a natural musician and gave several illustrations of his ability as a mimic.

Saturday, March 27—Warm south wind. Great quantities of geese flying north. Missouri river free from ice.

Nancy Clement Smith, wife of George A. Smith, was buried in grave 118. Her parents names were James and Betsy Clement. She died of scurvy, aged 31 years, 4 months and 27 days.

Monday, March 29—The Presidents of the emigrating divisions, captains of companies, and the Pioneers met in the Council House. Twenty-five Pioneers reported themselves ready to start on their western journey; thirty-two more reported themselves ready to start within two days. I requested those who were ready to start, to assist in removing some families up to the farm (20 miles north), and notified those who desired to start on the Pioneer journey to do so in the morning.

Elizabeth McFate Richards, wife of Franklin D. Richards, died about eleven p.m.

Wednesday, March 31—Joseph A. Stratton brought a mail of 23 letters, mostly from St. Louis.

The Presidents of divisions and Captains of Companies met this evening at the Council House. I spoke against the selfish principles which actuated many. We deliberated on our contemplated movements. Letters from Elders O. Hyde and John Taylor who were in England were read. Elder W. W. Phelps was authorized to go east and procure a printing press and type. A recommendation to the saints in the east was subsequently given him. The saints were called upon to assist Elder Phelps on his mission.

Thursday, April 1—I met with the brethren of the Twelve Apostles; Joseph A. Stratton of St. Louis met with us. We heard read the minutes of the St. Louis conference. Bro. Stratton reported the names of three brethren who were living in St. Louis with two wives each.

Friday, April 2—The Missouri river has risen about two feet; the cotton-wood trees are budding and grass is springing. The brethren continue to move their houses into line. There was a meeting at the stand to divide the city into lots for planting this season and to accept bids for fencing the same.

I met with the brethren of the Twelve Apostles, Bishops Whitney and Miller and others. Bishop George Miller gave his views relative to the church removing to Texas, to the country lying between the Neuces and Rio Grande rivers. I informed Bishop Miller that his views were wild and visionary,—that when we moved hence it would be to the Great Basin, where the Saints would soon form a nucleus of strength and power sufficient to cope with mobs.

Sunday, April 4—Elders Orson Pratt and E. T. Benson preached this forenoon. My brother, Lorenzo, Elder Lyman and myself preached in the afternoon. John Y. Greene brought twenty-six letters from Nauvoo, Mount Pisgah, and other places. T. Bullock made a sketch of Cap. Fremont's topographical map of road to Oregon for the use of the Pioneers.

Elder Lyman Stoddard received a recommendation and certificate of authority to preach on the Pottawatomie lands.

The Twelve wrote a lengthy letter to Mrs. Lucy Smith, mother of the Prophet Joseph, inquiring after her whereabouts and circumstances, and offering to convey her westward if she desired to join the body of the Church

A letter was also written by the Council to Elder Nathaniel H. Felt, St. Louis, directing him to tarry and preside over the Church there. The Council advised the brethren there who were in the patriarchial order of marriage to emigrate westward this spring; and counselled the brethren to let dancing alone; else it would prove a snare and a trap in which the enemy would catch many souls. Dr. Darwin Richardson was invited to emigrate westward immediately bringing as good a stock of medicines as his circumstances would permit. The Church at St. Louis was directed to disfellowship all members who were disorderly, regardless of their professions or anointings.

Monday, April 5—Pres. H. C. Kimball moved out about four miles with six of his teams and formed an encampment.

A. W. Babbitt wrote from Nauvoo, Ill., that he had visited all the cities of the east, that $100,000, was the most he had been offered for the Temple and Church property, that forty suits had been commenced against the Church for Kirtland debts.

Tuesday, April 6—I attended General Conference, and was sustained as President of the Church and of the Twelve apostles. I preached.

Friday, April 9—I met with the Twelve early this morning; afterwards rode out to the Pioneer Camp and proceeded on our journey and encamped fourteen miles west of Winter Quarters.

Monday, April 12—I returned to Winter Quarters, the Twelve and Bishop Whitney also returned. A council was held; Elder Pratt attended. He reported that he had brought some means. I advised that Thomas Bullock go with the Pioneers and keep a journal of the Pioneer journey.

Wednesday, April 14—With the brethren of the Twelve I held a Council, then started on our journey to overtake the Pioneer company which we did near the Elk Horn river.

Thursday, April 15—We crossed the Elk Horn river and proceeded to the Platte river and encamped near a grove of cottonwood trees. I called the Pioneer camp together and addressed them on the necessity of being faithful, humble and prayerful on the journey. Exhorted the camp to vigilance in guarding and informed the brethren that I had intimations that the Pawnee Indians were advised to rob us. Said we should go to bed early, rest on Sabbath and go in such a manner as to claim the blessings of Heaven.

Friday, April 16—The company were called together in the morning, and numbered 143 men. Elder Geo. A. Smith, Pres. H. C. Kimball, and I preached. The company was organized in a military capacity, and on motion of Dr. W. Richards I nominated Col. Stephen Markham and A. P. Rockwood captains of Hundreds. Tarlton Lewis, James Case, Addison Everett, John Pack and Shadrach Roundy were elected Captains of Fifties. Captains were also elected over each ten. The Captains of Tens selected forty-eight men, who were divided into four watches to be on duty half the night at a time.

Saturday, April 17—The Pioneer company traveled eight miles and encamped. The Company was organized as a Regiment. I was elected commander of the Camp, Stephen Markham Colonel, Shadrach Roundy and John Pack majors, the captains of tens were re-elected under this organization. I instructed the brethren to be careful with their arms, and not to stray off from the camp.

Monday, April 19—The Pioneer Company rose at 5 a.m., at the sound of the bugle; started about seven and traveled till noon, dined and proceeded to encampment on the banks of the Platte river, having traveled about twenty miles.

Tuesday, April 20—Traveled twenty miles. Evening, Thomas Tanner set up his forge and set several wagon tires. Cottonwood trees cut down for the horses to browse on, which they eat readily. About 213 fish caught. Major Miller having called upon the Mormons to haul corn for the Omaha Indians, the Council wrote to bros. Daniel Spencer and Daniel Russell to use their influence to have the corn hauled for the Indians from Waldo's ferry on the Nishnebatona river to Bellevue, Council Bluffs. Jesse C. Little was appointed aid to Col. Markham.

Wednesday, April 21—The Pioneer Company traveled eighteen miles and camped on Looking Glass Creek where it runs into the Loup Fork. We encountered many Pawnee Indians. Elder Kimball and I stood guard the forepart of the night. Mules were stationed with the picket guard to help them notice the approach of Indians.

Thursday, April 22—Traveled about twenty miles, encamped at the Pawnee Mission House.

Elder Daniel Spencer met with the High Council at Winter Quarters, and reported that he had visited Major Miller, Indian Agent, and informed him that the Omahas were stealing and butchering the cattle of the saints. Old Elk and some of his braves met, who appeared to be full of complaints, alleging that the Mormons eat their grass, cut down their timber, etc.

Friday, April 23—The Pioneer company started about noon, crossed Plum Creek and passed a large corn field, the corn stalks still standing, left Pawnee town, soon crossed Ashcreek twelve feet wide, one foot deep, and proceeded two miles to the place designated for crossing the Loup Fork river. A few attempted to cross with their wagons but owing to the quicksand bed of the river experienced difficulty.

Dr. Richards reported that he had rode through the Pawnee town about half a mile west of us and had seen the ruins of about 175 houses or lodges averaging from twenty to sixty feet in diameter, all of which had been burnt to the ground by the Sioux Indians, at a time when the Pawnees were absent on their hunting expedition. The town had been partially fortified by an embankment of earth and sods about four feet high, having a ditch on the outside; this place has contained about six thousand souls who have been the terror of the Western tribes.

The Pioneer company met and after deliberation concluded to build two rafts about sixteen feet long each to carry over our goods on the morrow.

Saturday, April 24—The "Revenue Cutter" (a leather boat made for the expedition) was brought into requisition and some boated their loads over the river. The horses and cattle were driven back and forth loose across the river to pack the quicksand. Stakes were planted at intervals across the river as a guide for the Teamsters. The brethren continued rowing the boat over the river carrying goods, while the lightly loaded wagons continued crossing at the ford, which soon became packed and more solid. One of the rafts floated down the river just before the last team crossed. The Company proceeded four miles and encamped. Prof. O. Pratt took an observation.

Sunday, April 25—The Pioneer Camp rested. Afternoon, I preached.

Monday, April 26—About three this morning the guard encountered Indians crawling into Camp; an alarm being raised, all hands were found at their posts; the Indians ran off. Traveled about 17 miles; having nooned at Sloughs by the way side.

Tuesday, April 27—Traveled about eighteen miles in a southerly direction and encamped at Prairie Creek. Afternoon, thermometer 86 degrees Fah. in the shade. Thunder and lightning with very high wind and shower of rain.

Wednesday, April 28—Traveled twelve miles; roads exceedingly dusty. The hunters killed an antelope.

Thursday, April 29—Traveled 18 miles.

Friday, April 30—Traveled 16 miles. Weather cold. Very little grass for the animals.

Saturday, May 1—The Pioneer company traveled fourteen miles. The hunters killed four buffaloes and six buffalo calves. The company were somewhat excited at the vast herds of buffalo seen.

Sunday, May 2—Company rested most of the day. Traveled two miles for the purpose of getting feed for the animals.

Monday, May 3—The Camp did not travel. The blacksmiths repaired wagons and shod horses. The hunters killed three antelopes and two buffalo calves. About noon, a gentle shower of rain.

Tuesday, May 4—The company traveled eleven miles. Found the prairie on fire around the camp. A mail of 54 letters was made up and sent to Winter Quarters by W. Charles Beaumont, a trader who was going to Council Bluffs. Beaumont reported that there was a good road on the south side of the river, and that the feed was better.

Wednesday, May 5—Traveled thirteen miles.

Thursday, May 6—Traveled nineteen miles. The prairie appeared black being covered with immense herds of buffalo.

Friday, May 7—I preached in Camp and advised the brethren not to kill any more buffalo or other game until the meat was needed. Prof. O. Pratt took an observation. Traveled seven miles.

Saturday, May 8—Traveled 12 miles.

Sunday, May 9—Meeting in Camp. Elders W. Woodruff, O. Pratt, A. Lyman and E. T. Benson preached. Traveled four miles.

Monday, May 10—Traveled ten miles. Bro. Appleton M. Harmon made an odometer attached to the wheel of Wm. Clayton's wagon, enabling bro. Clayton to measure the distances of each days travel.

Tuesday, May 11—Traveled eight and a half miles.

Wednesday, May 12—Traveled twelve miles.

Thursday, May 13—Traveled ten and three quarter miles.

Friday, May 14—Traveled about nine miles. The Hunters killed a buffalo and three antelope.

Saturday, May 15—Traveled seven miles. Showers of rain this forenoon.

Sunday, May 16—The Pioneer company met. Elders Richards, Markham, and Rockwell preached. Also President Kimball. The laws and regulations of the Camp were read.

Monday, May 17—Traveled 12¾ miles. Hunters killed several buffalo.

Tuesday, May 18—Traveled 15¾ miles.

Wednesday, May 19—Traveled 8 miles. It rained last night and during the day.

Thursday, May 20—Traveled 15¾ miles.

Friday, May 21—Traveled 15½ miles.

Saturday, May 22—Traveled 15½ miles and camped at Ancient Bluff Ruins.

Sunday, May 23—The camp rested. Elder Erastus Snow and I preached.

Monday, May 24—Traveled 16½ miles. Horses failing, but the oxen are gaining. The Sioux chiefs, "O Wash te cha" and the "Brave Bear," visited us accompanied by thirty-three of their braves. They smoked the pipe of peace with us.

Tuesday, May 25—Traveled twelve miles.

Wednesday, May 26—Traveled 12¼ miles. When opposite Chimney Rock Prof. O. Pratt determined the height thereof to be 260 feet.

Thursday, May 27—Traveled 13¾ miles. Four antelopes were killed.

Friday, May 28—Traveled 11½ miles. Forenoon, a shower of rain.

Saturday, May 29—I called the camp together and remonstrated with those brethren who were giving way to trifling, dancing, and card playing. I warned them in the name of the Lord against the Spirit which many of the Camp possessed, and called upon them to cease their folly and turn to the Lord their God with full purpose of heart to serve him. The brethren of the Twelve, the High Priests, the Bishops, the Seventies, all covenanted to humble themselves, repent of their follies and remember their former covenants. I then told the few who did not belong to the Church that they were not at liberty to introduce cards, dancing, or iniquity of any description; but they should be protected in their rights and privileges while they conducted themselves well and did not seek to trample on the Priesthood nor blaspheme the name of God. Traveled eight and a half miles. Very heavy rain which commenced at five p.m. and continued during the evening, accompanied by thunder and lightning.

Sunday, May 30—The camp met for prayer, praise and confession of sins. In consequence of shower of rain, meeting soon closed. The Twelve and a few others went to an adjacent valley and prayed.

Monday, May 31—Traveled 16¾ miles.

Tuesday, June 1—The Pioneer company traveled twelve miles and encamped on the north side of the river from Fort Laramie Bros. Robert Crow and George W. Thirlkell of the Mississippi company who arrived at this point from Pueblo sixteen days ago visited us. They reported four deaths in the battalion, viz., Melcher Oyler, Scott, Arnold Stevens and _____.

Wednesday, June 2—Fort John or Laramie is occupied by Mr. James Bordeaux and about 18 French, half breeds, and a few Sioux Indians. Mr. Bordeaux trades solely with the Sioux who will not steal on their own lands. The Crows, lately, stole twenty-five horses, notwithstanding they were guarded and within 300 yards of the Fort. There had been no rain at the Fort for the last two years until within a few days.

Thursday, June 3—Elder Amasa Lyman was delegated by the Council to visit the detachments of the battalion at Pueblo and Santa Fe and give them such counsel as the Spirit of wisdom should dictate. Elders Woolsey, Tippets, and Stevens accompany Elder Lyman. These brethren were blessed and started this afternoon. The wagons were ferried over the river.

Friday, June 4—Elders Kimball, Richards and I visited Mr. Bordeaux at the Fort. We paid him $15.00 for the use of the ferryboat. Mr. Bordeaux said that this was the most civil and best behaved company that had ever passed the fort. Dr. Luke Johnson professionally attended several persons in the fort. Robert Crow's company, numbering 17 souls, joined the Pioneer Camp. Traveled 8¼ miles.

Saturday, June 5—Traveled 17 miles. Camped west side of Bitter Creek. Heavy rain with thunder and lightning.

Sunday, June 6—The brethren met in fasting and prayer. An emigrating company passed in the morning. After meeting another emigrating company passed of twenty-one wagons. A very heavy shower of rain fell. Traveled five miles.

Monday, June 7—Traveled thirteen miles.

Tuesday, June 8—Traveled 15½ miles and encamped. Camped on the "La Boute." Hunters killed two deer and one antelope. Met James H. Greeve, William Tucker, James Woodrie, James Bouvoir and six other Frenchmen from whom we learned the Mr. Bridger was located about 300 miles west, that the Mountaineers could ride to Salt Lake from Bridgers in two days and that the Utah country was beautiful.

Wednesday, June 9—Forty men and nineteen wagons started ahead of the main company for the north fork of the Platte to secure the boat left by Greeve's company and to build a raft. Main company traveled 19¼ miles and encamped on the La Prele. Three Antelope and two deer killed.

Thursday, June 10—Traveled 17¾ miles and encamped at Deer Creek. Two antelope killed. There is some cottonwood, ash, and box elder timber here, also some choke cherry and willow bushes. Some fish caught. George A. Smith brought into Camp a sample of bright black coal.

Friday, June 11—Traveled 17 miles. Seven antelope killed. Camped within half a mile of two emigrant companies from Missouri enroute to Oregon.

Saturday, June 12—Traveled to the upper Platte Ferry and Ford 11¼ miles. Found our advance company had obtained the boat left by Greeve and company and had ferried the Missouri immigrant companies, for which they had received $34.00 mostly in flour at $2.50 per 100 lbs. Several buffaloes, bears, and antelopes killed. Specimens of coal, mica, sandstone, limestone and quartz found. Judge Bowman, the leader of one of the Missouri companies of emigrants, was the father of "Bill Bowman" who had the custody of Joseph Smith at the time he escaped from Missouri. Bill was ridden to death on a bar of iron by a mob led on by Obadiah Jennings, for aiding Joseph Smith and his companions to escape. Obadiah Jennings was one of the murderers engaged in the Massacre of the Saints at Haun's Mill, Oct. 30, 1838. Judge Bowman said that Morgan, the Sheriff, who had the custody of the Prophet, Joseph, at the time of his escape from Mo., was in Oregon.

Sunday, June 13—Meeting in Camp. Elders H. C. Kimball, O. Pratt, and I preached.

Monday, June 14—Yesterday and today the brethren rafted their wagons over the river.

Wednesday, June 16—Two rafts were made in view of assisting the Summer emigrants.

Thursday, June 17—The rafting of the Pioneer company was concluded this afternoon. Some of the Pioneers continued ferrying the Missouri company all night. Prof. Pratt determined the latitude.

Friday, June 18—The brethren continued crossing the emigrants and received 1,295 lbs. flour at 2½¢ per lb., also meal, beans, soap and honey at corresponding prices, likewise two cows, total bill for ferrying $78.00.

Saturday, June 19—Captn. Thomas Grover and eight others of the Pioneers left at North Platte ferry and ford to ferry the companies that should arrive and specially to ferry the emigration from Winter Quarters. Traveled 21½ miles.

About 570 wagons of the emigration from Winter Quarters have crossed the Elk Horn river. While Jacob Weatherby, A. B. Lambson and two women were returning from the Elk Horn river to Winter Quarters the Indians shot Bro. Weatherby, who died soon after.

Sunday, June 20—The Pioneer company traveled 20 miles. Camped on Greasewood Creek.

Monday, June 21—Traveled 15¼ miles. Camped west of Devil's Gate.

Tuesday, June 22—Traveled 20¾ miles.

Wednesday, June 23—Traveled 17 miles.

Thursday, June 24—Traveled 17¾ miles.

Friday, June 25—Traveled 20¼ miles.

Saturday, June 26—Traveled 18¾ miles.

Sunday, June 27—Left the Sweetwater river and crossed the South pass of the Rocky Mountains and camped on the Dry Sandy after traveling 15¼ miles. Moses Harris, a mountaineer, camped with us; from whom we received some Oregon newspapers and a "California Star" published at Yerba Buena by bro. Sam Brannan. He said the country around Salt Lake was barren and sandy, destitute of timber and vegetation except wild sage.

Monday, June 28—Traveled 15¼ miles. Met Cap. James Bridger who said he was ashamed of Fremont's map of this country. Bridger considered it imprudent to bring a large population into the Great Basin until it was ascertained that grain could be raised; he said he would give one thousand dollars for a bushel of corn raised in the Basin.

Tuesday, June 29—Traveled 23¾ miles.

Wednesday, June 30—Traveled 11½ miles and camped on Green river. Samuel Brannan arrived from San Francisco bringing intelligence from the Saints who went around Cape Horn in the Ship Brooklyn, who were making farms and raising grain on the San Joaquin. He had a file of the California Star published by himself. He gave a very favorable account of the climate and soil of California. Brannan came by way of Fort Hall.

Saturday, July 3—The Pioneer Company concluded ferrying over the Green river. Some fine fish caught. Several brethren sick with mountain fever. Shower of rain fell accompanied by thunder, lightning and strong wind. Traveled three miles.

Sunday, July 4—I went back to the ferry with my brother, Phinehas H. Young and four others who had volunteered to return until they met the emigrants from Winter Quarters and pilot them on to this point. While at the ferry I had the pleasure of meeting thirteen battalion brethren who were in pursuit of stolen animals which they had mostly recovered. The Pioneers were so pleased to behold the battalion brethren that they gave three cheers, and I led out in exclaiming, "Hosannah! Hosannah! Give glory to God and the Lamb, Amen," in which all joined simultaneously.

Council decided that Thomas Williams and Sam. Brannan return and meet Captn. Brown and the battalion company from Pueblo, and inasmuch as they have neither received their discharge nor their full pay, Bro. Brannan should tender them his services as pilot to conduct them to California.

Wednesday, July 7—Arrived at, and encamped ½ mile west of Fort Bridger. Some succeeded in trading for buckskins; their clothing being worn out. A lengthy letter was written to the brethren at Winter Quarters.

Monday, July 12—Crossed Bear river. Afternoon, I was attacked with fever. Several sick in camp. My wagon with a few others encamped; the camp proceeded a few miles.

Tuesday, July 13—I continued very sick. The advance company voted that

Elder Orson Pratt take charge of an expedition to go on and make a road down the Weber river.

Thursday, July 15—I joined the main Camp. Elder Pratt's advance company crossed the Weber river.

Sunday, July 18—Spent the day (Sunday) in prayer for the recovery of the sick and partook of the Sacrament. Afternoon, I proposed that the Camp proceed to make their way over the mountains, and when a suitable location was found, plant potatoes and corn. The proposition was approved. Elders Kimball, Woodruff, Benson and a few others concluded to remain with me.

Tuesday, July 20—Elder Pratt's advance company passed the summit of the Big Mountain. Altitude 7,245 feet. The main company made their way through Canyon Creek. I crossed the Weber river. My health improving.

Wednesday, July 21—The advance company crossed the little mountain and camped in Emigration Kanyon. Elders Orson Pratt and Erastus Snow rode to the mouth of the kanyon, when they emerged from the same into an open valley apparently about 30 miles long by 20 broad at the northwest of which the extensive waters of Salt Lake glistened in the sun. They descended into the valley, made a circuit of about ten miles and returned to camp at 9 p.m.

Thursday, July 22—The advance and main body of the Pioneer company entered Salt Lake valley and encamped on the banks of Kanyon Creek (Emigration Kanyon). Elders O. Pratt and Geo. A. Smith who had been exploring northward reported that about three miles from the campground there were two beautiful streams of water with stony bottom (the forks of City Creek). They also described the warm and hot springs.

Friday, July 23—The advance company moved about three miles and encamped; (on what was subsequently known as the 8th Ward, Salt Lake City). Elder Orson Pratt called the camp together, dedicated the land to the Lord, entreated the blessings on the seeds about to be planted and on the labors of His saints in the valley. The camp was organized for work. Elders W. Richards and Geo. A. Smith exhorted the brethren to diligence.

11½ a.m., the committee appointed reported that 20 rods by 40 had been staked off by them on which to plant beans, corn, and buckwheat; soil friable, loam and gravel. About noon, the first furrow was turned over by Wm. Carter. Three plows and one harrow were at work most of the afternoon.

At two p.m., a company started to build a dam and cut trenches to convey the water on to the land. At three, Thermometer 96 degrees fah. A company commenced mowing the grass and preparing a turnip patch. At six, a thunder shower passed over the camp.

I ascended and crossed over the Big Mountain, when on its summit I directed Elder Woodruff, who had kindly tendered me the use of his carriage, to turn the same half way round so that I could have a view of a portion of Salt Lake valley. The spirit of light rested upon me and hovered over the valley, and I felt that there the Saints would find protection and safety. We descended and encamped at the foot of the Little Mountain.

Saturday, July 24—I started early this morning and after crossing

Emigration Kanyon Creek eighteen times emerged from the Kanyon. Encamped with the main body at 2 p.m. About noon, the five acre potato patch was plowed, when the brethren commenced planting their seed potatoes. At five, a light shower accompanied by thunder and stiff breeze.

Sunday, July 25—Meeting held. Elders Geo. A. Smith, H. C. Kimball, and E. T. Benson preached. The brethren noted the fact that no one had died on the journey, though many were sick when they started; neither had an animal died, though a few were lost through carelessness. Afternoon, Elders W. Woodruff, O. Pratt, W. Richards and I preached.

Monday, July 26—The Pioneer brethren busy plowing, planting corn, and irrigating. A company appointed to make a road into the kanyon, to facilitate the procuring of timber. Accompanied by several of the Twelve and others I ascended a hill north of the city site, which I named Ensign Peak.

We proceeded to the warm springs which are 109 degrees Fah. Dr. Willard Richards advised the sick brethren to bathe therein, because of the valuable medicinal properties of the waters. John Brown and Joseph Matthews returned from their tour westward; they reported the Mountains west to be about sixteen miles distant, most of the land west of the Jordan river covered with wild sage and destitute of fresh water.

Wednesday, July 28—Yesterday, accompanied by the brethren of the Twelve and a few others, I started westward. We crossed the river, Jordan, which is about six rods wide and three feet deep, proceeded hence about thirteen miles west to a brackish spring at the point of the mountain where we dined, after which we proceeded a few miles to a point on the Salt Lake shore within a few rods of Black Rock, where the party all bathed. Elders Orson Pratt, Willard Richards and Geo. A. Smith proceeded three miles further west and entered another valley (Tooele). Returned to the point of the Mountain and encamped for the night.

Today, proceeded in a south course about ten miles. Saw the course of several streams on the east side of the valley, but found no water on the west side; returned to the ford of the Jordan where we partook of refreshments and several bathed. Returned to encampment.

Some of the brethren talked about exploring the country further for a site for a settlement; I replied that I was willing that the country should be explored until all were satisfied, but every time a party went out and returned I believed firmly they would agree that this is the spot for us to locate.

Joseph Hancock and Lewis Barney returned from a two days' tour in the mountains East; they reported an abundance of good timber, principally pine, balsam fir and a little cottonwood; access to the same very difficult.

This afternoon, accompanied by Elders Heber C. Kimball, Willard Richards, Orson Pratt, Wilford Woodruff, Geo. A. Smith, Amasa Lyman, Ezra T. Benson and Thomas Bullock, I designated the site for the Temple block between the forks of City Creek, and on motion of Orson Pratt it was unanimously voted that the Temple be built on the site designated. It was also voted that the city lots be ten by twenty rods, 1¼ acres, and that the streets be eight rods wide.

Elder Geo. A. Smith proposed to lay out squares for markets and lots for school houses.

The brethren assembled this evening on the Temple Square site, and voted to build a Temple and lay out a city at this point. I addressed the brethren on the order of building the city and reviewed the persecutions of the Saints.

Thursday, July 29—The sick detachments of the battalion that were sent to winter at Pueblo on the Arkansas river, under Captns. James Brown and Nelson Higgins and Lieut. Wesley Willis arrived, accompanied by a small company of brethren who started from Mississippi in 1846.

Friday, July 30—The Twelve met with the officers of the battalion and held a lengthy council. All the brethren met at 8 p.m. when praise to God for the safe return of so many of the battalion was given by shouting Hosanna, Hosanna, Hosanna to God and the Lamb forever and ever, Amen. I preached till 10 p.m.

Saturday, July 31—A brush bowery of 40 by 28 feet made by the battalion brethren. Col. Markham reported that thirteen plows and three harrows had been stocked during the past week, three lots of ground broken up, one lot of 35 acres planted in corn, oats, buckwheat, potatoes, beans, and garden seed.